P9-AFA-664

Houghton Mifflin
Mathematics

HOUGHTON MIFFLIN

BOSTON • MORRIS PLAINS, NJ

California • Colorado • Georgia • Illinois • New Jersey • Texas

Copyright ©2002 by Houghton Mifflin Company. All rights reserved. No part of this work may be reproduced or transmitted in any form or by any means, electronic or mechanical, including photocopying or recording, or by any information storage or retrieval system without the prior written permission of Houghton Mifflin Company unless such copying is expressly permitted by federal copyright law. Address inquiries to School Permissions, 222 Berkeley Street, Boston, MA 02116.

ISBN-13: 978-0-618-08176-9
ISBN-10: 0-618-08176-3

15 16 17 18 19 20 -WC- 11 10 09 08 07 06

Authors

Senior Authors

Dr. Carole Greenes
Professor of Mathematics Education
Boston University
Boston, MA

Dr. Miriam A. Leiva
Distinguished Professor of
Mathematics, Emerita
University of North Carolina
Charlotte, NC

Dr. Bruce R. Vogeli
Clifford Brewster Upton Professor
of Mathematics
Teachers College, Columbia University
New York, NY

Program Authors

Dr. Matt Larson
Curriculum Specialist for Mathematics
Lincoln Public Schools
Lincoln, NE

Dr. Jean M. Shaw
Professor of Elementary Education
University of Mississippi
Oxford, MS

Dr. Lee Stiff
Professor of Mathematics Education
North Carolina State University
Raleigh, NC

Content Reviewers

Lawrence Braden (Grades 5–6)
Mathematics Teacher
St. Paul's School
Concord, NH

Dr. Don Chakerian (Grades 3–4)
Emeritus Professor of Mathematics
University of California
Davis, CA

Dr. Kurt Kreith (Grades 3–4)
Emeritus Professor of Mathematics
University of California
Davis, CA

Dr. Liping Ma (Grades K–2)
Visiting Scholar
Carnegie Foundation for the
Advancement of Teaching
Menlo Park, CA

Dr. David Wright (Grades 5–6)
Professor of Mathematics
Brigham Young University
Provo, UT

Reviewers

California Math Teacher Advisory Board

Grade K

Lee Arsenian
Hoover Street Elementary
  School
Los Angeles, CA

Kathy Dyer
Alice Birney Elementary
  School
Fresno, CA

Paula Ferrett
Hyatt Elementary School
Riverside, CA

Linda Hill
Crestline Elementary
  School
Barstow, CA

Rene Jimenez
Ralph J. Bunche
  Elementary School
Compton, CA

Christina Kruse-Pennes
Cesar Chavez Elementary
  School
Richmond, CA

Mary L. Paredes
Cahuenga Elementary
  School
Los Angeles, CA

Grade 1

Michelle Enriquez
Crestline Elementary
  School
Barstow, CA

Terri Ortiz
Sunny Brae Ave.
  Elementary School
Winnetka, CA

Shelia Patterson
Cypress School
Tulare, CA

Maria Tarabotto
Hazeltine Elementary
  School
Van Nuys, CA

Grade 2

Nancy Burgei
Blossom Hill School
Los Gatos, CA

Tracy Green
Figarden School
Fresno, CA

Barbara Page
Elihu Beard Elementary
  School
Modesto, CA

Barbara Park
Sunny Brae Ave.
  Elementary School
Winnetka, CA

Kim Seto
Sierra Madre School
Sierra Madre, CA

Judy Trette
Gregory Gardens
  Elementary School
Pleasant Hill, CA

Grade 3

Rita Bennett
Santa Susana Elementary
  School
Simi Valley, CA

Karen Choi
Pasadena Unified
  Education Center
Pasadena, CA

Karen Ciraulo
Kingwood Elementary
  School
Citrus Heights, CA

Cheryl Dultz
Kingswood Elementary
  School
Los Gatos, CA

Doug Hedin
Park Oaks Elementary
   School
Thousand Oaks, CA

Vicky Holman
Mount Pleasant Elementary
   School
San Jose, CA

Jennifer Rader
Desert Trails Elementary
   School
Adelanto, CA

Fran Range-Long
Alice Birney Elementary
   School
Fresno, CA

Sylvia Kyle
Chester Nimitz Elementary
   School
Cupertino, CA

Karlene Seitz
Citrus Glen Elementary
   School
Ventura, CA

Grade 4

Beth Holguin
Graystone Elementary
   School
San Jose, CA

Marilyn Higbie
Jane Addams Elementary
   School
Long Beach, CA

Tarie Lewis
Melrose Elementary School
Oakland, CA

Sandra Jo McIntee
Haynes Street School
West Hills, CA

Mike Tokmakoff
Hoover Street Elementary
   School
Los Angeles, CA

Nancy Yee
Valhalla Elementary School
Pleasant Hill, CA

Grade 5

Patty Jernigan
Santa Susana
Simi Valley, CA

Joe Koski
Nu-View Elementary
   School
Nuevo, CA

Bill Laraway
Silver Oak Elementary
San Jose, CA

Steve Monson
Castro Elementary School
El Cerrito, CA

Sherri Qualls
Weibel Elementary School
Fremont, CA

Arlene Sackman
Earlimart Middle School
Earlimart, CA

Robyn Suskin
Sierra Madre School
Sierra Madre, CA

Grade 6

Herb Brown
Lake Gregory Elementary
   School
Crestline, CA

German Palabyab
Harding Elementary School
El Cerrito, CA

Carole Patty
West Riverside Elementary
   School
Riverside, CA

Maureen Smith
Patterson Elementary
   School
Fremont, CA

Jeff Varn
Sierra Madre Elementary
   School
Sierra Madre, CA

Family Letter

Dear Family,

Every parent hopes his or her child will be confident and successful in school. *Houghton Mifflin Mathematics* is designed to provide children with a solid foundation in mathematics that will help lead to such success.

This program is based on the Mathematics Content Standards for California. The goals of this program are

- Providing a curriculum that balances skills, conceptual understanding, and problem solving

- Providing instruction and practice to help children become proficient in computational skills

- Helping children become good mathematical problem solvers

- Enabling children to use correct mathematical terms to communicate their understanding of math concepts

Look for the standards box in each lesson.

Standards
NS **1.1**

The notation in this box represents the following standard.

Number Sense 1.1   **Count, read, and write whole numbers to 1,000 and identify the place value for each digit.**

On pages viii–x you will find a full listing of all the Mathematics Content Standards for California for Grade 2.

As you work with your child throughout the year, the listing of these standards will help you understand what he or she is learning in each lesson.

We trust your child will have a successful year!

Sincerely,
Houghton Mifflin Company

California
MATH STANDARDS

By the end of grade two, students understand place value and number relationships in addition and subtraction, and they use simple concepts of multiplication. They measure quantities with appropriate units. They classify shapes and see relationships among them by paying attention to their geometric attributes. They collect and analyze data and verify the answers.

Number Sense (NS)

1.0 Students understand the relationship between numbers, quantities, and place value in whole numbers up to 1,000:

1.1 Count, read, and write whole numbers to 1,000 and identify the place value for each digit.

1.2 Use words, models, and expanded forms (e.g., 45 = 4 tens + 5) to represent numbers (to 1,000).

1.3 Order and compare whole numbers to 1,000 by using the symbols <, =, >.

2.0 Students estimate, calculate, and solve problems involving addition and subtraction of two- and three-digit numbers:

2.1 Understand and use the inverse relationship between addition and subtraction (e.g., an opposite number sentence for 8 + 6 = 14 is 14 − 6 = 8) to solve problems and check solutions.

2.2 Find the sum or difference of two whole numbers up to three digits long.

2.3 Use mental arithmetic to find the sum or difference of two two-digit numbers.

3.0 Students model and solve simple problems involving multiplication and division:

3.1 Use repeated addition, arrays, and counting by multiples to do multiplication.

3.2 Use repeated subtraction, equal sharing, and forming equal groups with remainders to do division.

3.3 Know the multiplication tables of 2s, 5s, and 10s (to "times 10") and commit them to memory.

4.0 Students understand that fractions and decimals may refer to parts of a set and parts of a whole:

4.1 Recognize, name, and compare unit fractions from $\frac{1}{12}$ to $\frac{1}{2}$.

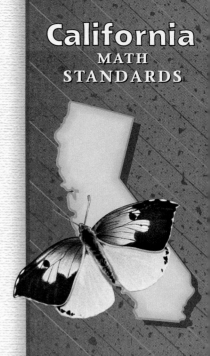

4.2 Recognize fractions of a whole and parts of a group (e.g., one-fourth of a pie, two-thirds of 15 balls).

4.3 Know that when all fractional parts are included, such as four-fourths, the result is equal to the whole and to one.

5.0 Students model and solve problems by representing, adding, and subtracting amounts of money:

5.1 Solve problems using combinations of coins and bills.

5.2 Know and use the decimal notation and the dollar and cent symbols for money.

6.0 Students use estimation strategies in computation and problem solving that involve numbers that use the ones, tens, hundreds, and thousands places:

6.1 Recognize when an estimate is reasonable in measurements (e.g., closest inch).

Algebra and Functions (AF)

1.0 Students model, represent, and interpret number relationships to create and solve problems involving addition and subtraction:

1.1 Use the commutative and associative rules to simplify mental calculations and to check results.

1.2 Relate problem situations to number sentences involving addition and subtraction.

1.3 Solve addition and subtraction problems by using data from simple charts, picture graphs, and number sentences.

Measurement and Geometry (MG)

1.0 Students understand that measurement is accomplished by identifying a unit of measure, iterating (repeating) that unit, and comparing it to the item to be measured:

1.1 Measure the length of objects by iterating (repeating) a nonstandard or standard unit.

1.2 Use different units to measure the same object and predict whether the measure will be greater or smaller when a different unit is used.

1.3 Measure the length of an object to the nearest inch and/or centimeter.

1.4 Tell time to the nearest quarter hour and know relationships of time (e.g., minutes in an hour, days in a month, weeks in a year).

1.5 Determine the duration of intervals of time in hours (e.g., 11:00 a.m. to 4:00 p.m.).

California
MATH
STANDARDS

2.0 Students identify and describe the attributes of common figures in the plane and of common objects in space:

   2.1 Describe and classify plane and solid geometric shapes (e.g. circle, triangle, square, rectangle, sphere, pyramid, cube, rectangular prism) according to the number and shape of faces, edges, and vertices.

   2.2 Put shapes together and take them apart to form other shapes (e.g., two congruent right triangles can be arranged to form a rectangle).

Statistics, Data Analysis, and Probability (SDP)

1.0 Students collect numerical data and record, organize, display, and interpret the data on bar graphs and other representations:

   1.1 Record numerical data in systematic ways, keeping track of what has been counted.

   1.2 Represent the same data set in more than one way (e.g., bar graphs and charts with tallies).

   1.3 Identify features of data sets (range and mode).

   1.4 Ask and answer simple questions related to data representations.

2.0 Students demonstrate an understanding of patterns and how patterns grow and describe them in general ways:

   2.1 Recognize, describe, and extend patterns and determine a next term in linear patterns (e.g., 4, 8, 12 . . . ; the number of ears on one horse, two horses, three horses, four horses).

   2.2 Solve problems involving simple number patterns.

Mathematical Reasoning (MR)

1.0 Students make decisions about how to set up a problem:

   1.1 Determine the approach, materials, and strategies to be used.

   1.2 Use tools, such as manipulatives or sketches, to model problems.

2.0 Students solve problems and justify their reasoning:

   2.1 Defend the reasoning used and justify the procedures selected.

   2.2 Make precise calculations and check the validity of the results in the context of the problem.

3.0 Students note connections between one problem and another.

Contents

CHAPTER 1 Addition and Subtraction Facts

$3 + 3 = 6$

Numbers and Patterns to 100

CHAPTER 3

Data and Graphing

Favorite Sports	
Sport	**Number of Children**
Soccer	★ ★ ★ ★
Baseball	★ ★ ★
Football	★ ★
Kickball	★ ★ ★ ★

Each ★ stands for 2 votes.

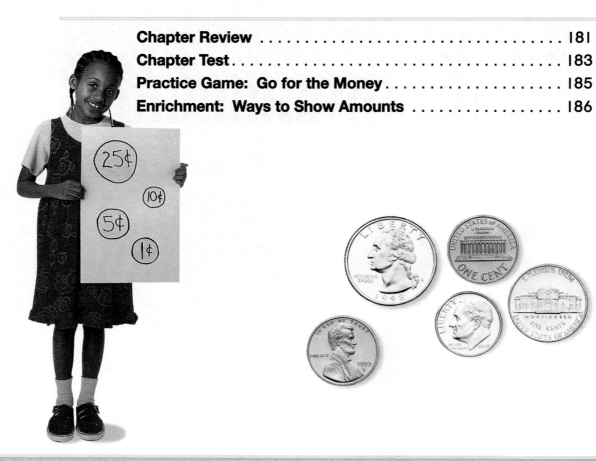

Adding Two-Digit Numbers

Subtracting Two-Digit Numbers

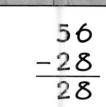

$$
\begin{array}{r}
5\,6 \\
-\,2\,8 \\
\hline
2\,8
\end{array}
$$

Geometry, Fractions, and Probability

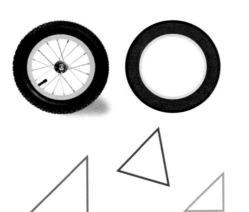
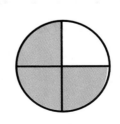

CHAPTER 8

Multiplication and Division

Measurement

I pound

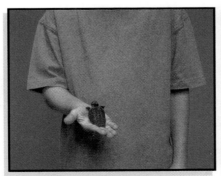

less than I pound

more than I pound

CHAPTER 10

Time and Calendar

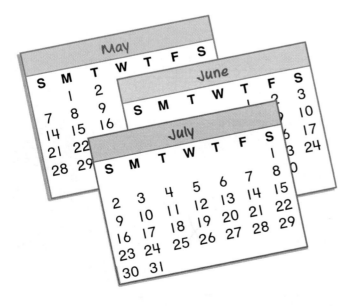

Time

24 hours = 1 day

7 days = 1 week

52 weeks = 1 year

12 months = 1 year

Numbers and Patterns to 1,000

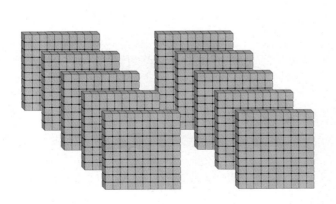

Adding and Subtracting Three-Digit Numbers

Book Resources

Name _____

Addition Facts to 10

Write the missing numbers in order.

September						
Sunday	**Monday**	**Tuesday**	**Wednesday**	**Thursday**	**Friday**	**Saturday**
1	2					7
		10				
15					20	
			25			
	30					

Write each sum. Memorize each fact.

1. 2 +1	2. 3 +1	3. 4 +1	4. 5 +1	5. 6 +1	6. 7 +1
7. 8 +1	8. 9 +1	9. 2 +2	10. 3 +2	11. 4 +2	12. 5 +2
13. 6 +2	14. 7 +2 9	15. 8 +2 10	16. 3 +3	17. 4 +3	18. 5 +3
19. 6 +3 9	20. 7 +3 10	21. 4 +4 8	22. 5 +4	23. 6 +4	24. 5 +5

A

Write each sum.

1. 2 + 3 = 5
2. 1 + 5 = 6
3. 2 + 7 = 9

4. 9 + 1 = 16
5. 5 + 5 = 10
6. 3 + 5 = 7

7. 2 + 5 = 7
8. 1 + 8 = 9
9. 1 + 2 = 3

10. 4 + 4 = 8
11. 1 + 7 = 8
12. 2 + 4 = 6

13. 3 + 6 = 9
14. 3 + 3 = 6
15. 4 + 6 = 10

16. 1 + 4 = 5
17. 4 + 5 = 9
18. 2 + 8 = 10

19. 2 + 6 = 8
20. 1 + 3 = 4
21. 2 + 2 = 4

22. 3 + 4 = 7
23. 1 + 6 = 7
24. 3 + 7 = 10

Write the word name for the sum.

25. 1 + 2 = three
26. 3 + 4 = seven

27. 2 + 4 = six
28. 1 + 1 = two

29. 2 + 2 = four
30. 5 + 5 = ten

B

Copyright © Houghton Mifflin Company. All rights reserved.

Name _____

Subtraction Facts to 10

Write the missing numbers in order.

| 1 | 2 | 3 | 4 | 5 | 6 | 7 | 8 | 9 | 10 |

Write each difference. Memorize each fact.

1. 2
  − 1
  1

2. 3
  − 1
  2

3. 4
  − 1
  3

4. 5
  − 1
  4

5. 6
  − 1
  5

6. 7
  − 1
  f

7. 8
  − 1
  1

8. 9
  − 1
  8

9. 10
  − 1
  9

10. 3
  − 2
  1

11. 4
  − 2
  2

12. 5
  − 2
  3

13. 6
  − 2
  4

14. 7
  − 2
  5

15. 8
  − 2
  6

16. 9
  − 2
  7

17. 10
  − 2
  8

18. 4
  − 3
  1

19. 5
  − 3
  2

20. 6
  − 3
  3

21. 7
  − 3
  4

22. 8
  − 3
  5

23. 9
  − 3
  6

24. 10
  − 3
  7

25. 5
  − 4
  1

26. 6
  − 4
  2

27. 7
  − 4
  3

28. 8
  − 4
  4

29. 9
  − 4
  5

30. 10
  − 4
  6

31. 6
  − 5
  1

32. 7
  − 5
  2

33. 8
  − 5
  3

34. 9
  − 5
  4

35. 10
  − 5
  5

c

Write each difference.

1. $8 - 2 = 6$

2. $5 - 1 = 4$

3. $4 - 2 = 2$

4. $7 - 5 = 2$

5. $9 - 3 = 6$

6. $5 - 4 = 1$

7. $6 - 4 = 2$

8. $8 - 5 = 3$

9. $10 - 3 = 7$

10. $5 - 3 = 2$

11. $9 - 1 = 8$

12. $6 - 5 = 1$

13. $3 - 2 = 1$

14. $7 - 1 = 6$

15. $8 - 7 = 1$

16. $10 - 1 = 9$

17. $4 - 3 = 1$

18. $7 - 2 = 5$

19. $9 - 5 = 4$

20. $10 - 8 = 2$

21. $9 - 7 = 2$

22. $8 - 4 = 4$

23. $10 - 5 = 5$

24. $4 - 1 = 3$

25. $7 - 6 = 1$

26. $6 - 1 = 5$

27. $8 - 1 = 7$

28. $10 - 9 = 1$

29. $9 - 8 = 1$

30. $6 - 3 = 3$

31. $9 - 4 = 5$

32. $10 - 6 = 4$

33. $7 - 4 = 3$

34. $10 - 4 = 6$

35. $6 - 2 = 4$

36. $9 - 6 = 3$

Copyright © Houghton Mifflin Company. All rights reserved.

D

Name _____

Adding and Subtracting Zero

$$5 + 0 = \underline{5} \qquad\qquad 0 + 5 = \underline{5}$$

Write each sum. Memorize each fact.

1. $1 + 0 = \underline{1}$
   $0 + 1 = \underline{1}$

2. $2 + 0 = \underline{2}$
   $0 + 2 = \underline{2}$

3. $3 + 0 = \underline{3}$
   $0 + 3 = \underline{3}$

4. $4 + 0 = \underline{4}$
   $0 + 4 = \underline{4}$

5. $5 + 0 = \underline{5}$
   $0 + 5 = \underline{5}$

6. $6 + 0 = \underline{6}$
   $0 + 6 = \underline{0}$

7. $7 + 0 = \underline{7}$
   $0 + 7 = \underline{7}$

8. $8 + 0 = \underline{8}$
   $0 + 8 = \underline{8}$

9. $9 + 0 = \underline{9}$
   $0 + 9 = \underline{9}$

10. $\begin{array}{r} 6 \\ +0 \\ \hline 6 \end{array}$

11. $\begin{array}{r} 10 \\ +\ 0 \\ \hline 10 \end{array}$

12. $\begin{array}{r} 0 \\ +5 \\ \hline 5 \end{array}$

13. $\begin{array}{r} 0 \\ +0 \\ \hline 0 \end{array}$

14. $\begin{array}{r} 0 \\ +3 \\ \hline 3 \end{array}$

15. $\begin{array}{r} 0 \\ +10 \\ \hline 10 \end{array}$

16. $\begin{array}{r} 10 \\ +\ 0 \\ \hline 10 \end{array}$

17. $\begin{array}{r} 2 \\ +0 \\ \hline 20 \end{array}$

18. $\begin{array}{r} 0 \\ +9 \\ \hline 9 \end{array}$

19. $\begin{array}{r} 0 \\ +8 \\ \hline 8 \end{array}$

20. $\begin{array}{r} 7 \\ +0 \\ \hline 7 \end{array}$

21. $\begin{array}{r} 0 \\ +4 \\ \hline 4 \end{array}$

E

5 – 0 = _5_   5 – 5 = _0_

Write each difference.

1. 1 – 0 = _1_   2. 2 – 0 = _2_   3. 3 – 0 = _3_

   1 – 1 = _0_   2 – 2 = _0_   3 – 3 = _0_

4. 4 – 0 = _4_   5. 5 – 0 = _5_   6. 6 – 0 = _6_

   4 – 4 = _0_   5 – 5 = _0_   6 – 6 = _0_

7. 7 – 0 = _7_   8. 8 – 0 = _8_   9. 9 – 0 = _9_

   7 – 7 = _0_   8 – 8 = _0_   9 – 9 = _0_

10. 3   11. 1 0   12. 4   13. 6   14. 3   15. 8
    – 3   –   0   – 0   – 0   – 3   – 0
    ___   ___   ___   ___   ___   ___
     0   1 0   4   6   0   8

16. 9   17. 0   18. 5   19. 9   20. 1 0   21. 7
    – 9   – 0   – 5   – 0   – 1 0   – 7
    ___   ___   ___   ___   ___   ___
     0   0   0   9   0   0

Copyright © Houghton Mifflin Company. All rights reserved.

F

**Accessing Prior
Knowledge**

This story will help
you review
• Counting
• Counting
back 1, 2, or 3

Good Homes Wanted

A Read-Aloud Story

written by Rob Arego
illustrated by Deborah Melmon

A Math Storybook for

Railyn celiz

1

Jim has 10 little kittens
that need a nice family.
Kate takes 1 with a black-and-white coat,
and so does Mr. Lee.
How many kittens are left?

___8___ kittens

Now Jim has 8 little kittens
that need a nice family.
Mrs. Salas takes 1 with a bushy tail.
It is as cute as cute can be.
How many kittens are left?

____ kittens

Now Jim has 7 little kittens
that need a nice family.
Jamal takes 1 with a spotted coat.
It makes him so happy.
How many kittens are left?

 kittens

Now Jim has 6 little kittens
that need a nice family.
Layla takes 1 with very long whiskers.
And the Johnson cousins take 3.
How many kittens are left?

___2___ kittens

Now Jim has 2 little kittens
that need a nice family.
The Greens can't choose which kitten to take.
But finally they do agree.
How many kittens are left?

____ kitten

Now Jim has 1 little kitten
that sits upon his knee.
And whenever anyone asks him, he says,
"This one is coming home with me!"

Family Letter

Dear Family,

During the next few weeks, our math class will be learning and practicing addition facts through 20.

You can expect to see work that provides practice with addition and subtraction facts.

As we learn about counting on, counting back, and fact families, you may wish to keep the following samples as a guide.

Counting on

$3 + 8$ Think: **8**, 9, 10, 11

Counting back

$12 - 3$ Think: **12**, 11, 10, 9

Fact Family

$$\begin{array}{cccc} 4 & 2 & 6 & 6 \\ +\,2 & +\,4 & -\,2 & -\,4 \end{array}$$

All the facts use the same numbers.

Knowing addition facts can help children learn the related subtraction facts.

Sincerely,

Your child's teacher

Vocabulary

addend One of the numbers added in an addition problem.

count back In subtraction, begin with the greater number and count backward.

count on In addition, begin with the greater number and count forward.

difference The answer to a subtraction problem.

double fact A fact where both addends are the same.

related facts Addition and subtraction facts that use the same numbers.

sum The answer to an addition problem.

Standards
NS **2.2**, AF **1.1**
MR **3.0**

 LESSON 1

Add in Any Order

New Vocabulary

add
sum

Learn About It

You can **add** two numbers in any order and get the same **sum.**

$5 + 3 =$ _8_ ←sum $3 + 5 =$ _8_ ←sum

These number sentences have the same sum.

Guided Practice

Add. Then change the order and add again to check your answer.

1.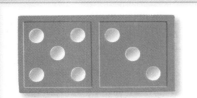

$4 + 6 =$ _10_

$6 + 4 =$ _10_

2.

$5 + 4 =$ _9_

$4 + 5 =$ _9_

3.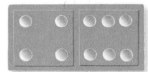

$$\begin{array}{r} 3 \\ +4 \\ \hline 7 \end{array} \qquad \begin{array}{r} 4 \\ +3 \\ \hline 7 \end{array}$$

4.

$$\begin{array}{r} 6 \\ +2 \\ \hline 8 \end{array} \qquad \begin{array}{r} 2 \\ +6 \\ \hline 8 \end{array}$$

5.
$$\begin{array}{r} 2 \\ +1 \\ \hline 3 \end{array} \qquad \begin{array}{r} 1 \\ +2 \\ \hline 3 \end{array}$$

6.
$$\begin{array}{r} 9 \\ +0 \\ \hline 9 \end{array} \qquad \begin{array}{r} 0 \\ +9 \\ \hline 9 \end{array}$$

7.
$$\begin{array}{r} 2 \\ +7 \\ \hline 9 \end{array} \qquad \begin{array}{r} 7 \\ +2 \\ \hline 9 \end{array}$$

Explain Your Thinking Why do 7 + 3 and 3 + 7 have the same sum?

because your Just switching the numbers

nine **9**

Independent Practice

Add. Then change the order and add
again to check your answer.

1.

$\begin{array}{r} 2 \\ +5 \\ \hline 7 \end{array}$ $\begin{array}{r} 5 \\ +2 \\ \hline 7 \end{array}$

2.

$\begin{array}{r} 3 \\ +6 \\ \hline 9 \end{array}$ $\begin{array}{r} 6 \\ +3 \\ \hline 9 \end{array}$

3. $\begin{array}{r} 9 \\ +0 \\ \hline 9 \end{array}$ $\begin{array}{r} 0 \\ +9 \\ \hline 9 \end{array}$

4. $\begin{array}{r} 8 \\ +2 \\ \hline 10 \end{array}$ $\begin{array}{r} 2 \\ +8 \\ \hline 10 \end{array}$

5. $\begin{array}{r} 7 \\ +1 \\ \hline 8 \end{array}$ $\begin{array}{r} 1 \\ +7 \\ \hline 8 \end{array}$

6. $\begin{array}{r} 8 \\ +1 \\ \hline 9 \end{array}$ $\begin{array}{r} 1 \\ +8 \\ \hline 9 \end{array}$

7. $\begin{array}{r} 2 \\ +7 \\ \hline 9 \end{array}$ $\begin{array}{r} 7 \\ +2 \\ \hline 9 \end{array}$

8. $\begin{array}{r} 1 \\ +9 \\ \hline 10 \end{array}$ $\begin{array}{r} 9 \\ +1 \\ \hline 10 \end{array}$

9. $10 + 0 = \underline{10}$

   $0 + 10 = \underline{10}$

10. $8 + 0 = \underline{8}$

    $0 + 8 = \underline{8}$

11. $7 + 3 = \underline{10}$

    $3 + 7 = \underline{10}$

Problem Solving • Reasoning

Algebra Readiness • Number Sentences

Use what you know about adding in any
order to find the missing numbers.

12. $3 + 2 = 2 + \underline{3}$

13. $6 + 0 = 0 + \underline{6}$

14. $4 + 1 = \underline{1} + 4$

15. $6 + 2 = \underline{2} + 6$

16. $5 + \underline{3} = 3 + \underline{5}$

17. $2 + \underline{4} = 4 + \underline{2}$

10 ten

At Home Ask your child to explain why the two addition problems
in each exercise have the same answer.

Copyright © Houghton Mifflin Company. All rights reserved.

Count On to Add

Learn About It

You can add by using a **number line** to count on.

New
Vocabulary
number line

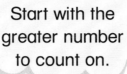

Think:
Start with the greater number to count on.

Find 3 + 8.

Start at 8. Count on 3.

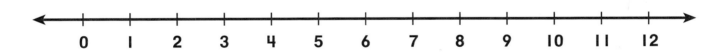

3 + 8 = ___   ___ = 3 + 8

These are the same.

3 + 8 = ___
___ = 3 + 8

Guided Practice

Count on to add.
Use the number line to help you.

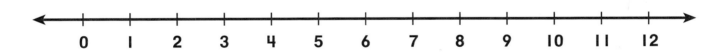

1. 4 + 1 = _5_

2. 3 + 7 = _10_

3. 6 + 2 = _8_

4. 8 + 1 = _9_

5. 1 + 5 = ___

6. 2 + 9 = _11_

7. _9_ = 7 + 2

8. _7_ = 5 + 2

9. _9_ = 6 + 3

10. 2
   + 3
   ———
   5

11. 4
   + 3
   ———
   7

12. 2
   + 8
   ———
   10

13. 3
   + 5
   ———
   8

14. 1
   + 6
   ———
   7

15. 3
   + 9
   ———
   12

Explain Your Thinking Why is it easier to count on from the greater number?

Independent Practice

Count on to add.
Use the number line to help you.

Remember:
Start with the greater number.

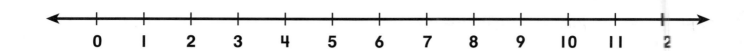

0 1 2 3 4 5 6 7 8 9 10 11 12

1. $5 + 2 = \underline{7}$

2. $7 + 1 = \underline{8}$

3. $3 + 4 = \underline{7}$

4. $1 + 3 = \underline{4}$

5. $2 + 2 = \underline{4}$

6. $6 + 1 = \underline{7}$

7. $\underline{11} = 9 + 2$

8. $\underline{6} = 3 + 3$

9. $\underline{3} = 2 + 1$

10. $\underline{10} = 8 + 2$

11. $\underline{6} = 4 + 2$

12. $\underline{11} = 8 + 3$

13. $\begin{array}{r} 9 \\ + 1 \\ \hline 10 \end{array}$

14. $\begin{array}{r} 6 \\ + 3 \\ \hline 9 \end{array}$

15. $\begin{array}{r} 3 \\ + 5 \\ \hline 8 \end{array}$

16. $\begin{array}{r} 10 \\ + 1 \\ \hline 11 \end{array}$

17. $\begin{array}{r} 9 \\ + 3 \\ \hline 12 \end{array}$

18. $\begin{array}{r} 10 \\ + 2 \\ \hline 12 \end{array}$

19. $\begin{array}{r} 2 \\ + 4 \\ \hline 6 \end{array}$

20. $\begin{array}{r} 3 \\ + 1 \\ \hline 4 \end{array}$

21. $\begin{array}{r} 2 \\ + 7 \\ \hline 9 \end{array}$

22. $\begin{array}{r} 8 \\ + 3 \\ \hline 11 \end{array}$

23. $\begin{array}{r} 1 \\ + 7 \\ \hline 9 \end{array}$

24. $\begin{array}{r} 3 \\ + 4 \\ \hline 7 \end{array}$

Problem Solving • Reasoning

25. Fred's dad is cooking 6 hot dogs.
He cooks 2 more hot dogs. How many
hot dogs is he cooking altogether?

$\underline{8}$ hot dogs

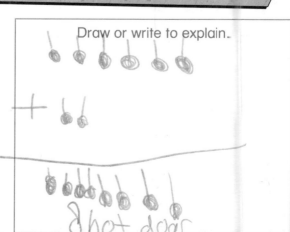

Draw or write to explain.

8 hot dogs

26. **Write Your Own** Write another addition
problem about hot dogs. Use the
number line to help. Then solve.

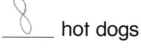

At Home Have your child explain how he or she used the number line to
solve the addition problems.

Copyright © Houghton Mifflin Company. All rights reserved

Use Double Facts to Add

Learn About It

Double facts can help you find other sums.

Double fact.

$6 + 6 = \underline{12}$

Double-plus-one facts.

6 + 6 and 1 more.

$6 + 7 = \underline{13}$ $7 + 6 = \underline{13}$

Guided Practice

Write the sum.
Then write two addition facts that are one more.

1.
$7 + 7 = \underline{14}$ $\underline{7} + \underline{8} = \underline{15}$ $\underline{8} + \underline{7} = \underline{15}$

2.
$8 + 8 = \underline{16}$ $\underline{8} + \underline{9} = \underline{17}$ $\underline{9} + \underline{8} = \underline{17}$

3. $9 + 9 = \underline{18}$ $\underline{9} + \underline{8} = \underline{17}$ $\underline{10} + \underline{7} = \underline{17}$

Explain Your Thinking How does using 6 + 6 = 12
help you solve 6 + 7?

Independent Practice

1. Complete the addition table. Then circle the
   sums for the double facts. Memorize each fact.

+	0	1	2	3	4	5	6	7	8	9
0										
1		1 + 1 = 2								
2									10	
3										
4				4 + 3 = 7						
5								12		
6										
7										
8	8									
9										

Problem Solving•Reasoning

Using Vocabulary

Draw or write to explain.

2. The **sum** of two numbers is 12.
   Write a number sentence to show
   what the two numbers could be.

   _____ + _____ = _____

16 sixteen

	Standards
	NS **2.1, 2.2,**
	MR **2.1**

LESSON 11 Subtract From Numbers to 20

Learn About It

The same numbers are used in related
addition and subtraction facts.

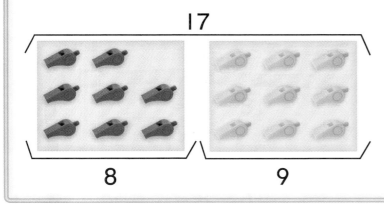

The numbers 8, 9, and 17 are in these related facts.

17

8 · 8
+ 9
―――
17

17
− 9
―――
8

17
− 8
―――
9

8   9

Guided Practice

Add or subtract. Memorize each fact.

1. 9   19   19
   +10   −10   − 9
   ―――   ―――   ―――
    19   9   10

2. 7   16   16
   +9   − 9   − 7
   ―――   ―――   ―――

3. 10   17   17
   + 7   −10   − 7
   ―――   ―――   ―――

4. 10   16   16
   + 6   − 6   −10
   ―――   ―――   ―――

5. 9   18
   +9   − 9
   ―――   ―――

6. 10   20
   +10   −10
   ―――   ―――

7. 8   16
   +8   − 8
   ―――   ―――

Explain Your Thinking Why is there only one related subtraction
fact for each addition fact in Exercises 5, 6, and 7?

Independent Practice

Add or subtract. Then match related facts.

1.
$8 + 10 = \underline{18}$

$9 + 8 = \underline{\hphantom{00}}$

$9 + 10 = \underline{\hphantom{00}}$

$7 + 9 = \underline{\hphantom{00}}$

$17 - 8 = \underline{\hphantom{00}}$

$16 - 9 = \underline{\hphantom{00}}$

$19 - 10 = \underline{\hphantom{00}}$

$18 - \underline{10} = 8$

2.
$8 + 8 = \underline{\hphantom{00}}$

$8 + 10 = \underline{\hphantom{00}}$

$10 + 6 = \underline{\hphantom{00}}$

$10 + 7 = \underline{\hphantom{00}}$

$10 + \underline{\hphantom{00}} = 20$

$18 - 8 = \underline{\hphantom{00}}$

$20 - 10 = \underline{\hphantom{00}}$

$16 - 8 = \underline{\hphantom{00}}$

$16 - 10 = \underline{\hphantom{00}}$

$17 - 7 = \underline{\hphantom{00}}$

Problem Solving • Reasoning

Write About It

3. Myra's score is 19. She tosses a beanbag three times and subtracts each number from her score. Now her score is 4.

   On which three numbers did the beanbag land?

   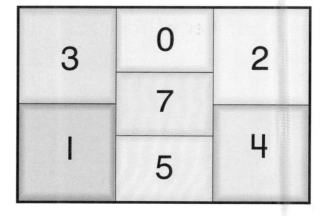

   _____, _____, and _____

4. Explain how you know you are right.

At Home Ask your child to choose a pair of matching facts on this page and explain why they match.

Name _____

LESSON 12

Problem Solving: Write a Number Sentence

Standards
AF **1.0, 1.2,**
MR **1.0, 1.1**

You can write a number sentence to solve a problem.

There are 9 girls and 7 boys in the talent show. How many children are in the talent show?

Understand

Circle what you need to find out.

How many children are in the show?

How many more girls than boys are there?

Plan

What information in the problem do you need?

_____ boys in the show

_____ girls in the show

Solve

Use the information to write a number sentence.

_____ + _____ = _____ children

Look Back

Does your answer solve the problem?

There are _____ children in the talent show, 9 girls and 7 boys.

Guided Practice

Solve. Write each number sentence.

Remember:
► Understand
► Plan
► Solve
► Look Back

Remember to use these 4 steps.

1 14 people are watching the talent show. 9 people leave. How many people are still watching the show?

Think:
What number do I start with?

Draw or write to explain.

__14__ − __9__ = __5__ people

2 6 people dance in the show. 3 people sing. How many people dance and sing?

Think:
What do I want to find out?

_____ + _____ = _____ people

3 Avi sells 7 bags of popcorn at the show. He sells 5 more after the show. How many bags of popcorn does Avi sell?

Think:
How can I find the total?

_____ + _____ = _____ bags of popcorn

4 Beth needs 12 prizes for the talent show. She makes 9 prizes. How many more should she make?

Think:
What do I want to find out?

_____ − _____ = _____ prizes

At Home Choose one problem on this page and ask your child to explain how he or she solved the problem.

Choose a Strategy

Solve.

1. There are 3 boy singers and 4 girl singers. How many singers are in the talent show?

   Draw or write to explain.

   singer

   _____ + _____ = _____ singers

2. There are 6 tap dancers on stage. 3 dancers leave. How many dancers are still on stage?

   tap dancer

   _____ − _____ = _____ dancers

3. A juggler throws 5 scarves in the air. She drops 2 scarves. How many scarves are still in the air?

   juggler

   _____ − _____ = _____ scarves

4. There are 2 drummers in the show. 3 more enter. How many drummers are in the show?

   drummer

   _____ + _____ = _____ drummers

Name _____

Mixed Practice

Memorize Your Facts

Add or subtract.

1. $4 - 1 =$ _____
2. $6 + 5 =$ _____
3. $8 - 8 =$ _____

4. $6 - 5 =$ _____
5. $4 + 9 =$ _____
6. $7 + 10 =$ _____

7. _____ $= 5 + 7$
8. _____ $= 9 + 6$
9. _____ $= 10 + 4$

10. $8 + 3 =$ _____ $+ 8$
11. $9 + 4 = 4 +$ _____
12. $6 + 8 = 8 +$ _____

13. $\begin{array}{r} 4 \\ -4 \\ \hline \end{array}$
14. $\begin{array}{r} 6 \\ +4 \\ \hline \end{array}$
15. $\begin{array}{r} 7 \\ +8 \\ \hline \end{array}$
16. $\begin{array}{r} 1 \\ -1 \\ \hline \end{array}$
17. $\begin{array}{r} 4 \\ +5 \\ \hline \end{array}$
18. $\begin{array}{r} 14 \\ -10 \\ \hline \end{array}$

19. $\begin{array}{r} 13 \\ -\ 9 \\ \hline \end{array}$
20. $\begin{array}{r} 7 \\ -7 \\ \hline \end{array}$
21. $\begin{array}{r} 2 \\ +5 \\ \hline \end{array}$
22. $\begin{array}{r} 6 \\ +8 \\ \hline \end{array}$
23. $\begin{array}{r} 11 \\ -\ 7 \\ \hline \end{array}$
24. $\begin{array}{r} 10 \\ -\ 5 \\ \hline \end{array}$

25. $\begin{array}{r} 3 \\ +1 \\ \hline \end{array}$
26. $\begin{array}{r} 12 \\ -\ 3 \\ \hline \end{array}$
27. $\begin{array}{r} 4 \\ +7 \\ \hline \end{array}$
28. $\begin{array}{r} 6 \\ -0 \\ \hline \end{array}$
29. $\begin{array}{r} 13 \\ -\ 4 \\ \hline \end{array}$
30. $\begin{array}{r} 8 \\ -3 \\ \hline \end{array}$

 Brain Teaser Letter Points

The letters A, E, I, O, and U are worth 4 points each. All other letters are worth 2 points. Write a word worth more than 10 points.

D   **O**   **G**
↓   ↓   ↓
2   +   4   +   2

This word is worth 8 points.

Draw or write to explain

 Safe Site

Internet Brain Teaser
Visit **www.eduplace.com/kids/mhm**
for more *Brain Teasers*.

Copyright © Houghton Mifflin Company. All rights reserved.

Name _____

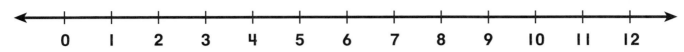

Check Your Understanding of Lessons 8–12

Count back to subtract.

$$\longleftarrow \quad 0 \quad 1 \quad 2 \quad 3 \quad 4 \quad 5 \quad 6 \quad 7 \quad 8 \quad 9 \quad 10 \quad 11 \quad 12 \longrightarrow$$

1. $9 - 3 =$ _____   2. $11 - 1 =$ _____   3. $12 - 3 =$ _____

Add or subtract.

4.
$$4 + 7 =$$ _____

$$11 - 7 =$$ _____

5.
$$5 + 7 =$$ _____

$$12 - 7 =$$ _____

6.
$$\begin{array}{r} 6 \\ +7 \\ \hline \end{array} \qquad \begin{array}{r} 13 \\ - 6 \\ \hline \end{array} \qquad \begin{array}{r} 13 \\ - 7 \\ \hline \end{array}$$

7.
$$\begin{array}{r} 9 \\ +8 \\ \hline \end{array} \qquad \begin{array}{r} 17 \\ - 8 \\ \hline \end{array} \qquad \begin{array}{r} 17 \\ - 9 \\ \hline \end{array}$$

8.
$$\begin{array}{r} 8 \\ +10 \\ \hline \end{array} \qquad \begin{array}{r} 18 \\ - 8 \\ \hline \end{array} \qquad \begin{array}{r} 18 \\ -10 \\ \hline \end{array}$$

9.
$$\begin{array}{r} 7 \\ +8 \\ \hline \end{array} \qquad \begin{array}{r} 15 \\ - 8 \\ \hline \end{array} \qquad \begin{array}{r} 15 \\ - 7 \\ \hline \end{array}$$

10.
$$\begin{array}{r} 6 \\ +8 \\ \hline \end{array} \qquad \begin{array}{r} 14 \\ - 8 \\ \hline \end{array} \qquad \begin{array}{r} 14 \\ - 6 \\ \hline \end{array}$$

11.
$$\begin{array}{r} 9 \\ +7 \\ \hline \end{array} \qquad \begin{array}{r} 16 \\ - 7 \\ \hline \end{array} \qquad \begin{array}{r} 16 \\ - 9 \\ \hline \end{array}$$

Solve. Write the number sentence.

12. Sandy finds 12 leaves.
She gives 5 leaves to Todd.
How many leaves does she have?

_____ $\bigcirc$ _____ = _____

Draw or write to explain.

Name _____

Test Prep • Cumulative Review

Maintaining the Standards

Fill in the ○ for the correct answer. NH means Not Here.

1 Subtract.

$$10 - 3 = \blacksquare$$

7	8	9	NH
◉	○	○	○

2 Add.

$$6 + 7 = \blacksquare$$

14	13	12	NH
○	◉	○	○

3 Mark the related number sentence for 8 + 7 = 15.

○ 8 + 8 = 16

○ 15 − 9 = 6

◉ 7 + 7 = 14

○ 15 − 7 = 8

4 Mark the number that belongs in the box.

$$8 + \blacksquare = 12$$

4	5	6	7
○	○	○	○

5 Subtract.

4	6	8	NH
◉	○	○	○

6 Subtract.

$$17 - 8 = \blacksquare$$

11	10	9	NH
○	○	◉	○

7

Jan sees 11 flowers. She picks 3. Write a number sentence to show how many flowers are left.

_____

Explain how you know your answer is correct.

_____

Safe Site

Internet Test Prep
Visit **www.eduplace.com/kids/mhm**
for more *Test Prep Practice.*

Copyright © Houghton Mifflin Company. All rights reserved.

Subtract to Compare

LESSON 13

Learn About It

Subtracting helps you answer the questions
"How many more?" and "How many fewer?"

There are 5 more blue cubes than yellow cubes.

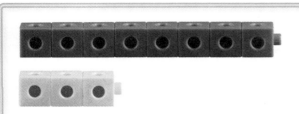

How many fewer 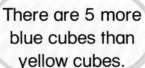 are there?

$\underline{8} - \underline{3} = \underline{5}$

Guided Practice

Use cubes. Write each number sentence.

1. 4 ▪ 7 ▪

   How many fewer ▪ are there?

   $\underline{7} - \underline{4} = \underline{3}$

2. 9 ▪ 8 ▪

   How many more ▪ are there?

   _____ – _____ = _____

3. 14 ▪ 6 ▪

   How many more ▪ are there?

   _____ – _____ = _____

4. 7 ▪ 16 ▪

   How many fewer ▪ are there?

   _____ – _____ = _____

5. 6 ▪ 9 ▪

   How many fewer ▪ are there?

   _____ – _____ = _____

6. 13 ▪ 8 ▪

   How many more ▪ are there?

   _____ – _____ = _____

Explain Your Thinking How can you find how many
more without subtracting?

Independent Practice

Write each number sentence. Use cubes if you want.

1. Jon sees 9 birds. Anna sees 4 birds. How many more birds does Jon see than Anna?

   _9_ – _4_ = _5_

2. Ellen finds 8 nests. Pat finds 10 nests. How many fewer nests does Ellen find than Pat?

   _____ – _____ = _____

3. Lin trains 5 birds. Carolyn trains 12 birds. How many fewer birds does Lin train than Carolyn?

   _____ – _____ = _____

4. Dana sees 7 cats. Al sees 5 cats. How many more cats does Dana see than Al?

   _____ – _____ = _____

5. Bill catches 8 fish. Pete catches 11 fish. How many more fish does Pete catch than Bill?

   _____ – _____ = _____

6. Amy hears 7 birds. Will hears 10 birds. How many more birds does Will hear than Amy?

   _____ – _____ = _____

Problem Solving • Reasoning

Using Data

Use the picture graph to solve the problem.

7. How many more red birds than green birds are there?

   _____ more red birds

8. **Write Your Own** Use the graph to write your own subtraction problem. Then solve.

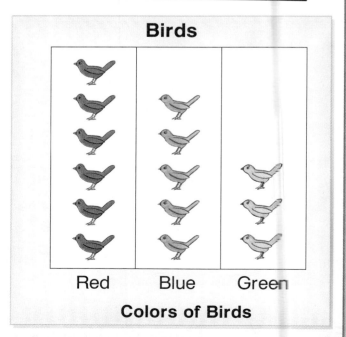

Birds

Red   Blue   Green

Colors of Birds

At Home Have your child tell you how to use subtraction to find how many more of one object than another.

Standards
NS **2.2**, AF **1.0**

LESSON 14
Algebra Readiness:
Names for Numbers

Learn About It

You can use addition or subtraction to name a number.

Here are names for 7.

Think: $5 + 2 = 7$

Think: $11 - 4 = 7$

Think: $12 - 5 = 7$

$5 + 2$ $11 - 4$ $12 - 5$

Guided Practice

Circle the names for each number.

1.	**6**	(12 − 6)	14 − 4	(5 + 1)	(10 − 4)
2.	**3**	10 − 7	3 − 0	13 − 3	12 − 9
3.	**9**	6 + 3	12 − 3	11 − 6	10 − 1
4.	**4**	9 + 6	10 − 6	8 − 4	15 − 9
5.	**12**	8 + 4	12 − 10	7 + 5	12 − 0

Explain Your Thinking Why are 7 + 1 and 14 − 6 both names for 8?

Independent Practice

Write an addition and subtraction
name for each number.

1. **5** $\underline{5} - \underline{0}$ $\underline{4} + \underline{1}$ $\underline{10} - \underline{5}$

2. **2** $\underline{2} + \underline{0}$ $\underline{} + \underline{}$ $\underline{} - \underline{}$

3. **8** $\underline{13} - \underline{5}$ $\underline{} + \underline{}$ $\underline{} - \underline{}$

4. **10** $\underline{14} - \underline{4}$ $\underline{} + \underline{}$ $\underline{} - \underline{}$

5. **11** $\underline{5} + \underline{6}$ $\underline{} + \underline{}$ $\underline{} - \underline{}$

6. **1** $\underline{9} - \underline{8}$ $\underline{} + \underline{}$ $\underline{} - \underline{}$

Problem Solving • Reasoning

Algebra Readiness · Number Sentences

You can name numbers in different ways.
Use what you know to write each missing number.

7. $4 + 1 = \underline{\ ?\ } + 3$
   $\underline{5} = \underline{\ \ } + 3$

8. $4 + 3 = \underline{\ ?\ } + 4$
   $\underline{\ \ } = \underline{\ \ } + 4$

9. $11 - 7 = 8 - \underline{\ ?\ }$
   $\underline{\ \ } = 8 - \underline{\ \ }$

10. $14 - \underline{\ ?\ } = 6 + 2$
    $14 - \underline{\ \ } = \underline{\ \ }$

At Home Ask your child for two different addition facts that name 9 and two
different subtraction facts that name 9.

Name _____

Standards
AF **1.0, 1.2**
MR **1.0, 1.1, 3.0**

LESSON 16

Problem Solving: Choose the Operation

You may need to add or subtract to solve a problem.

There are races at the picnic.
8 children are in the relay race.
5 children are in the egg race.

You can add to solve a problem.

How many children are in the relay race and the egg race?

_____ ◯ _____ = _____ children

Think:
What am I trying to find? Am I comparing or finding a total?

You can subtract to compare.

How many more children are in the relay race than the egg race?

_____ ◯ _____ = _____ children

Think:
Which number comes first when I subtract?

You can subtract to find how many are left.

If 2 children drop their eggs, how many children are still in the egg race?

_____ ◯ _____ = _____ children

Think:
Which numbers do I use?

Guided Practice

Write the number sentence.

1 9 children play softball. 7 children join them. How many children are playing softball?

Think: Do I need to add or subtract?

$\underline{9}$ (+) $\underline{7}$ = $\underline{16}$ children

Draw or write to explain.

2 Tina made 14 prizes. Ben made 9 prizes. How many more prizes did Tina make?

Think: What do I want to find out?

_____ ◯ _____ = _____ prizes

3 Kyla made 12 muffins. She sold 6 muffins. How many muffins does she have?

Think: Do I add or subtract?

_____ ◯ _____ = _____ muffins

4 8 children enter the sack race. 5 more want to join them. How many children are in the sack race?

Think: How do I find the total?

_____ ◯ _____ = _____ children

At Home Ask your child to explain how he or she solved each problem.

Name_____

Choose a Strategy

Solve.

① There are 7 people on the roller coaster. 4 more join them. How many people are on the roller coaster?

_____ people

Draw or write to explain.

Roller Coaster

② There are 3 lines for the giant slide. There are 3 children in each line. How many children are in line for the giant slide?

_____ children

Slide

③ 16 are waiting for the Boat Ride. 9 get on the first boat. How many people get on the second boat?

_____ people

Boat

④ 12 people ride go-carts. 7 people ride bumper cars. How many fewer people ride the bumper cars?

_____ people

Bumper Cars

Mixed Practice

Add or subtract.

1. $6 - 4 = $ _____

2. $17 - 8 = $ _____

3. $3 + 6 = $ _____

4. _____ $= 9 + 8$

5. $5 - 4 = $ _____

6. $5 + $ _____ $= 15$

7. _____ $+ 9 = 18$

8. _____ $- 7 = 8$

9. $7 - $ _____ $= 5$

10. $6 + 6 = $ _____ $+ 4$

11. $13 - 6 = 9 - $ _____

12. $\begin{array}{r} 8 \\ -7 \\ \hline \end{array}$

13. $\begin{array}{r} 11 \\ -5 \\ \hline \end{array}$

14. $\begin{array}{r} 3 \\ +7 \\ \hline \end{array}$

15. $\begin{array}{r} 6 \\ +9 \\ \hline \end{array}$

16. $\begin{array}{r} 13 \\ -8 \\ \hline \end{array}$

17. $\begin{array}{r} 10 \\ +3 \\ \hline \end{array}$

18. $\begin{array}{r} 0 \\ +4 \\ \hline \end{array}$

19. $\begin{array}{r} 9 \\ +4 \\ \hline \end{array}$

20. $\begin{array}{r} 11 \\ -4 \\ \hline \end{array}$

21. $\begin{array}{r} 4 \\ -3 \\ \hline \end{array}$

22. $\begin{array}{r} 5 \\ +1 \\ \hline \end{array}$

23. $\begin{array}{r} 12 \\ -2 \\ \hline \end{array}$

24. $\begin{array}{r} 11 \\ -10 \\ \hline \end{array}$

25. $\begin{array}{r} 16 \\ -8 \\ \hline \end{array}$

26. $\begin{array}{r} 4 \\ +10 \\ \hline \end{array}$

27. $\begin{array}{r} 6 \\ +7 \\ \hline \end{array}$

28. $\begin{array}{r} 20 \\ -10 \\ \hline \end{array}$

29. $\begin{array}{r} 0 \\ -1 \\ \hline \end{array}$

 Brain Teaser Mixed Up Cats

Which cat belongs to each child?

- Joe's cat is not black.
- Kim's cat is next to the black cat.
- Ala's cat is all one color.

Write each child's name under their cat.

_____   _____   _____

Internet Brain Teasers
Visit www.eduplace.com/kids/mhm
for more *Brain Teasers.*

Safe Site

Quick ✔ Check

Check Your Understanding of Lessons 13–16

Write each number sentence. Use cubes if you want.

1. May finds 12 shells. Jen finds 9 shells. How many more shells does May find?

   _____ – _____ = _____

2. Tony reads 6 books. Mike reads 8 books. How many more books does Mike read?

   _____ – _____ = _____

Circle the names for each number.

3. | 9 | $5 + 4$ $11 - 7$ $12 - 3$ $7 + 5$

4. | 7 | $13 - 8$ $10 - 3$ $6 + 3$ $5 + 2$

5. | 4 | $6 - 3$ $2 + 2$ $10 - 6$ $3 + 2$

6. | 10 | $16 - 6$ $10 - 8$ $7 + 4$ $9 + 1$

Complete each number sentence.

7. $9 + 4 =$ _____

   $13 -$ _____ $= 9$

   $13 - 9 =$ _____

   $4 +$ _____ $= 13$

8. $12 - 7 =$ _____

   _____ $+ 7 = 12$

   $7 + 5 =$ _____

   $12 -$ _____ $= 7$

9. $6 + 8 =$ _____

   _____ $- 6 = 8$

   _____ $+ 6 = 14$

   $14 -$ _____ $= 6$

Write the number sentence.

10. There are 6 children playing tag. 5 more join them. How many children are playing tag?

    _____ ◯ _____ = _____ children

11. 14 children want ice cream. 9 want dishes. The rest want cones. How many want cones?

    _____ ◯ _____ = _____ cones

Test Prep • Cumulative Review

Maintaining the Standards

Fill in the ○ for the correct answer. NH means Not Here.

1 Add.   9
        + 3

9   10   11   NH
○   ○   ○   ○

2 There are 8 birds on a branch. 3 more join them. How many birds are on the branch? Mark the number sentence that solves this problem.

○ 8 − 3 = 5
○ 11 − 3 = 8
○ 8 + 3 = 11
○ 11 − 8 = 3

3 Subtract.

13 − 7 = ■

6   7   8   NH
○   ○   ○   ○

4 Mark the one that is **not** a name for five.

○ 7 − 2   ○ 2 + 2
○ 5 + 0   ○ 3 + 2

5 Mark the number sentence that belongs in this fact family.

9 + 3 = 12   12 − 3 = 9
3 + 9 = 12

○ 9 − 3 = 6
○ 9 + 6 = 15
○ 12 − 8 = 4
○ 12 − 9 = 3

6 Will has 9 stamps. Jane has 16 stamps. How many more stamps does Jane have?

_____ stamps

Explain how you find the answer.

_____

Copyright © Houghton Mifflin Company. All rights reserved.

Safe Site

Internet Test Prep
Visit **www.eduplace.com/kids/mhm**
for more *Test Prep Practice.*

Chapter Review

Use these problems to answer Exercises 1–5.

$$\begin{array}{r} 6 \\ +\ 4 \\ \hline 1\ 0 \end{array} \qquad \begin{array}{r} 5 \\ -\ 3 \\ \hline 2 \end{array}$$

1. Write the sign that means to **add**. _____

2. Write the number that is the **sum**. _____

3. Write the numbers that are **addends**. _____, _____

4. Write the number that is the **difference**. _____

5. Write the sign that means to **subtract**. _____

Add.

6. $\begin{array}{r} 3 \\ +4 \\ \hline \end{array}$ $\begin{array}{r} 4 \\ +3 \\ \hline \end{array}$

7. $\begin{array}{r} 5 \\ +2 \\ \hline \end{array}$ $\begin{array}{r} 2 \\ +5 \\ \hline \end{array}$

8. $\begin{array}{r} 9 \\ +1 \\ \hline \end{array}$ $\begin{array}{r} 1 \\ +9 \\ \hline \end{array}$

9. $5 + 5 =$ _____ $5 + 6 =$ _____ $6 + 5 =$ _____

10. $8 + 8 =$ _____ $8 + 9 =$ _____ $9 + 8 =$ _____

11. $\begin{array}{r} 2 \\ +1\ 0 \\ \hline \end{array}$

12. $\begin{array}{r} 7 \\ +8 \\ \hline \end{array}$

13. $\begin{array}{r} 8 \\ +3 \\ \hline \end{array}$

14. $\begin{array}{r} 1\ 0 \\ +\ 6 \\ \hline \end{array}$

15. $\begin{array}{r} 4 \\ +8 \\ \hline \end{array}$

16. $\begin{array}{r} 6 \\ +7 \\ \hline \end{array}$

17. $7 + 4 =$ _____

18. $10 + 9 =$ _____

19. $5 + 8 =$ _____

20. $6 + 4 + 7 =$ _____

21. $3 + 4 + 3 =$ _____

Subtract.

22. $7 - 2 =$ ___   23. $4 - 1 =$ ___   24. $5 - 2 =$ ___

25. $12 - 3 =$ ___   26. $10 - 2 =$ ___   27. $11 - 3 =$ ___

Add or subtract.

28.
$$\begin{array}{r} 6 \\ +7 \\ \hline \end{array} \quad \begin{array}{r} 13 \\ -6 \\ \hline \end{array} \quad \begin{array}{r} 13 \\ -7 \\ \hline \end{array}$$

29.
$$\begin{array}{r} 10 \\ +9 \\ \hline \end{array} \quad \begin{array}{r} 19 \\ -10 \\ \hline \end{array} \quad \begin{array}{r} 19 \\ -9 \\ \hline \end{array}$$

30. $9 + 8 =$ ___

$8 +$ ___ $= 17$

$17 - 9 =$ ___

$17 -$ ___ $= 9$

31. $12 - 7 =$ ___

___ $+ 7 = 12$

$7 +$ ___ $= 12$

$12 -$ ___ $= 7$

32. $6 + 5 =$ ___

___ $+ 6 = 11$

$11 - 6 =$ ___

$11 -$ ___ $= 6$

Circle the names for each number.

33. **9** $11 - 2$ $19 - 10$ $5 + 5$ $8 + 2$

34. **6** $3 + 3$ $12 - 7$ $4 - 2$ $1 + 5$

Write the number sentence. Then solve.

35. Marta won 12 ribbons.
Kevin won 8 ribbons.
How many more ribbons
did Marta win?

___ ◯ ___ = ___

Draw or write to explain.

Name _____

Chapter Test

Add.

1. $8 \atop +2$ $\;\;$ $2 \atop +8$
   $\underline{10}$ $\;\;$ $\underline{10}$

2. $1 \atop +6$ $\;\;$ $6 \atop +1$
   $\underline{7}$ $\;\;$ $\underline{7}$

3. $7 \atop +3$ $\;\;$ $3 \atop +7$
   $\underline{10}$ $\;\;$ $\underline{10}$

4. $3 + 3 = \underline{6}$ $\quad$ $3 + 4 = \underline{7}$ $\quad$ $4 + 3 = \underline{7}$

5. $7 + 7 = \underline{14}$ $\quad$ $7 + 8 = \underline{15}$ $\quad$ $8 + 7 = \underline{15}$

6. $10 \atop +\;\;6$
   $\underline{16}$

7. $9 \atop +5$
   $\underline{14}$

8. $4 \atop +8$
   $\underline{12}$

9. $5 \atop 3 \atop +5$
   $\underline{13}$

10. $3 \atop 2 \atop +1$
    $\underline{6}$

11. $3 \atop 7 \atop +9$
    $\underline{19}$

Subtract.

12. $12 \atop -\;\;2$
    $\underline{10}$

13. $9 \atop -3$
    $\underline{6}$

14. $6 \atop -2$
    $\underline{4}$

15. $7 \atop -1$
    $\underline{6}$

16. $11 \atop -\;\;4$
    $\underline{07}$

17. $10 \atop -\;\;3$
    $\underline{07}$

Add or subtract.

18. $8 \atop +6$ $\;\;$ $14 \atop -\;\;8$ $\;\;$ $14 \atop -\;\;6$
    $\underline{14}$ $\;\;$ $\underline{14}$ $\;\;$ $\underline{08}$

19. $7 \atop +10$ $\;\;$ $17 \atop -\;\;7$ $\;\;$ $17 \atop -10$
    $\underline{17}$ $\;\;$ $\underline{10}$ $\;\;$ $\underline{07}$

Circle the names for each number.

20. **5**   5 + 5   10 − 5   8 − 3   2 + 3

21. **11**   9 − 2   7 + 4   6 − 5   8 + 3

Add or subtract.

22. 6 + 3 = _____

3 + _____ = 9

9 − 6 = _____

9 − _____ = 6

23. 15 − 8 = _____

_____ + 8 = 15

8 + _____ = 15

15 − _____ = 8

24. 7 + 3 = _____

_____ + 7 = 10

10 − 7 = _____

10 − _____ = 7

Write the number sentence. Then solve.

25. There are 18 children playing soccer. There are 10 children playing tag. How many fewer children are playing tag?

_____ ◯ _____ = _____

Draw or write to explain.

Write About It

Suni has 9 red apples and 6 yellow apples. Circle the number sentence that shows how many apples she has.

9 + 6 = 15

9 − 6 = 3

Explain why the number sentence shows how many apples Suni has in all.

_____

_____

_____

Name _____

Spin A Fact

What You Need

spinner
9 counters for each player

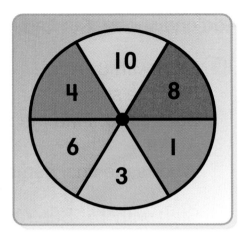

How to Play

① Choose red or yellow counters.

② Take turns spinning the spinner two times each.

③ Decide whether to add or subtract the two numbers.

④ If the sum or difference is on the game board, put a counter on it.

⑤ The first player to have three counters on the game board wins.

12	14	7
4	9	11
6	5	3

Enrichment

Number Riddles

Read each riddle.
Add and subtract to find the final number.

1. Start with 8. Add 1.
   Find the sum.
   Subtract 6. Find the difference.
   Add 4.
   What's the final number? _____

   Draw or write to explain.

2. Start with 16. Subtract 8.
   Find the difference.
   Subtract 3. Find the difference.
   Double the number.
   What's the final number? _____

3. Start with 19. Subtract 9.
   Find the difference.
   Add 5. Find the sum.
   Subtract 10.
   What's the final number? _____

4. Start with 6.
   Add 2. Find the sum.
   Double the number.
   Subtract 10. Find the difference.
   Add 4.
   What's the final number? _____

Write Your Own

Write your own riddle. Share it with a friend.

_____

_____

_____

Copyright © Houghton Mifflin Company. All rights reserved.

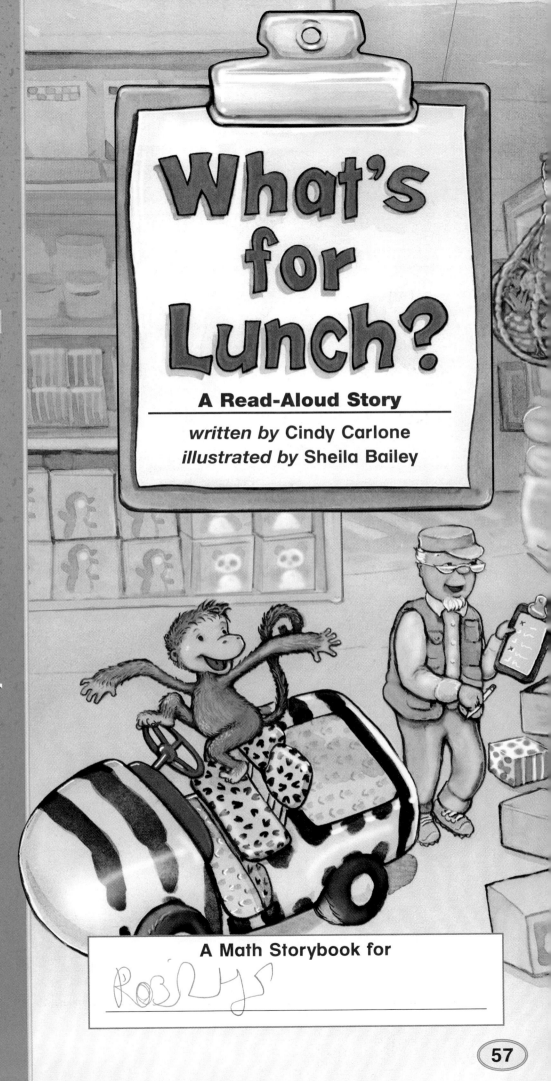

CHAPTER
2

Numbers and Patterns to 100

Accessing Prior Knowledge

This story will help you review

- Counting
- Counting by 2s
- Counting by 5s

What's for Lunch?

A Read-Aloud Story

written by Cindy Carlone
illustrated by Sheila Bailey

A Math Storybook for

RObRLYS

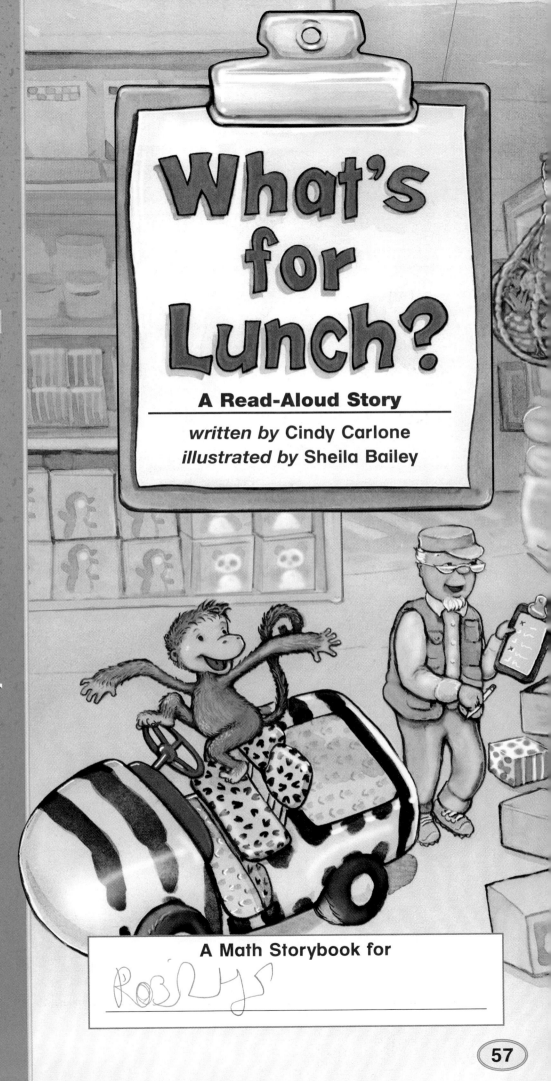

Charlie the Monkey helps Mr. Lou
feed the animals at the zoo.
Bananas, peanuts, cabbage, meat,
and fish are what animals like to eat.

How many boxes are on the cart?

1, 2, __3__, __4__, __5__

Copyright © Houghton Mifflin Company. All rights reserved.

Momma Seal is the first to get lunch.
"Would you like a banana from this bunch?"
"Oh no, Charlie, that is not my wish.
What I want are some great-big fish."

Count the fish that Momma Seal gets.

1, 2 , 3 , 4 , 5 , 6

Charlie tosses bananas through the door
to Rory the Lion, who starts to roar.
"Bananas are fine, but lions don't eat them.
We'd rather have steaks—you just can't beat them!"

Count the number of steaks that Rory gets.

1, 2, 3, 4, 5, 6, _7_, _8_, _9_, _10_

Copyright © Houghton Mifflin Company. All rights reserved.

Tommy the Tortoise is next to be fed.
He sees the bananas, then shakes his head.
"When I'm hungry, Charlie, what I like to eat
are cabbages and greens—but nothing sweet."

Count the number of cabbages that Tommy eats.

2, 4, 6, __8__, __10__, __12__

Hanna the Elephant also says no
to bananas—they just don't help elephants grow!
"Hay and carrots are fun to munch,
but peanuts are better, especially for lunch."

Count the number of peanuts Hanna gets.

5, 10, 15, 20, _25_, _30_, _35_

62

Copyright © Houghton Mifflin Company. All rights reserved.

"Mr. Lou," Charlie started to say,
"Why did we have bananas today?
Momma Seal, Rory, Tommy, and Hanna—
not one of them wanted to eat a banana!"

Mr. Lou smiled and held up the bunch.
"I wonder what monkeys are having for lunch."
Then Charlie smiled. "Oh, now I see!
Hooray! These bananas are meant for me!"

Count the number of bananas that Charlie gets.

1, 2, 3, 4, 5, 6 , 7 , 8 , 9 , 10

Family Letter

Vocabulary

digit Any of the symbols 0, 1, 2, 3,…9

even number A number that when divided by 2 has none left over.

greater than The symbol > is used to show greater than.

less than The symbol < is used to show less than.

odd number A number that when divided by 2 has one left over.

regroup To rename a number by trading 10 ones for 1 ten.

Dear Family,

During the next few weeks, our math class will be learning about place value through 100.

You can expect to see work that provides practice with reading, writing, comparing, and ordering numbers through 100.

Understanding place value can help children read, write, count, and compare numbers and quantities.

As we learn about place value, you may wish to use the following samples as a guide.

Place Value

Tens	Ones
1	4

10 + 4
14

25 > 21   25 is greater than 21
21 < 25   21 is less than 25

Sincerely,

Your child's teacher

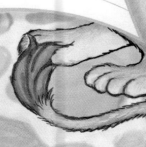

Standards
NS **1.1, 1.2, 5.0**
MR **1.2**

LESSON 1 — Tens to 100

New **Vocabulary**
tens

Learn About It

You can count by **tens** to 100.

I can count by tens: 10, 20...

10 ones = 1 ten	20 ones = 2 tens
10 ten	20 twenty

Guided Practice

Count tens. Write the numbers.

1. 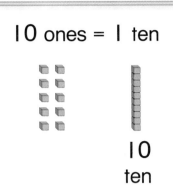 thirty — _3_ tens _30_

2. forty — ____ tens ____

3. fifty — ____ tens ____

4. sixty — ____ tens ____

5. seventy — ____ tens ____

6. eighty — ____ tens ____

7. ninety — ____ tens ____

8. one hundred — ____ tens ____

Explain Your Thinking Why is 5 tens the same as 50 ones?

Independent Practice

Write the tens and ones.
Write the number.

1.

5 tens

Tens	Ones
5	0

50

2.

2 tens

Tens	Ones

____

3.

7 tens

Tens	Ones

____

4.

1 ten

Tens	Ones

____

5.

8 tens

Tens	Ones

____

6.

9 tens

Tens	Ones

____

7.

3 tens

Tens	Ones

____

8.

4 tens

Tens	Ones

____

9.

6 tens

Tens	Ones

____

10.

5 tens

Tens	Ones

____

11. Write the missing numbers.

100, 90, 80, ____, 60, 50, ____, ____, 20, 10

Problem Solving • Reasoning

12. How many are there in all?

Draw or write to explain.

10   10   10   ____ in all

 At Home Say a multiple of 10 that is less than 100, such as 40.
Ask your child how many tens are in the number.

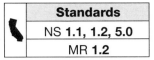

Hands-On Activity LESSON 2

Tens and Ones to 100

Review Vocabulary

tens

ones

Learn About It

You can show a number as **tens** and **ones**.

This is 1 one.

This is 1 ten.
10 ones = 1 ten.

Workmat

Tens	Ones

Tens	Ones
2	3

23

twenty-three

Guided Practice

Use Workmat 3 with ▭▭ and ▫.

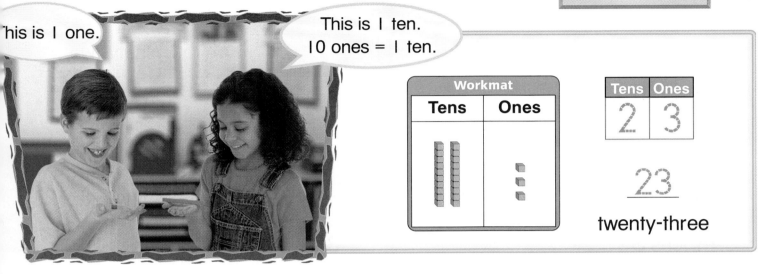

	Show this many.	Write the tens and ones.	Write the number.
1.		Tens: 5 Ones: 2	52 fifty-two
2.		Tens: ___ Ones: ___	___ seventy-six
3.		Tens: ___ Ones: ___	___ sixty-seven
4.		Tens: ___ Ones: ___	___ forty-five

Explain Your Thinking How is 76 different from 67? Explain.

Independent Practice

Use Workmat 3 with and 🔲 if you want.
Write the tens and ones. Write the number.

1. 6 tens 8 ones

Tens	Ones
6	8

_68_

sixty-eight

2. 9 tens 2 ones

Tens	Ones

_____

ninety-two

3. 8 tens 7 ones

Tens	Ones

_____

eighty-seven

4. 5 tens 6 ones

Tens	Ones

_____

fifty-six

5. 4 tens 3 ones

Tens	Ones

_____

forty-three

6. 3 tens 7 ones

Tens	Ones

_____

thirty-seven

7. 6 tens 1 one

Tens	Ones

_____

sixty-one

8. 7 tens 4 ones

Tens	Ones

_____

seventy-four

Problem Solving • Reasoning

9. Each dime is worth 10¢.
Each penny is worth 1¢.
Count the coins. Write how much.

Draw or write to explain.

____¢ ____¢ ____¢ ____¢ ____¢

At Home Say a number between 10 and 100 and have your child write it. Repeat several times.

Standards
NS **1.1, 1.2,** MR **2.1**

LESSON 3 Identify Place Value

Learn About It

New Vocabulary
digit

To find the value of a **digit,** find the value of the place it is in.

What is the value of the digits in 58?

58

Tens	Ones
5	8

50 + **8**

The value of 5 tens is 50.

The value of 8 ones is 8.

Guided Practice

Circle the value of each red digit.

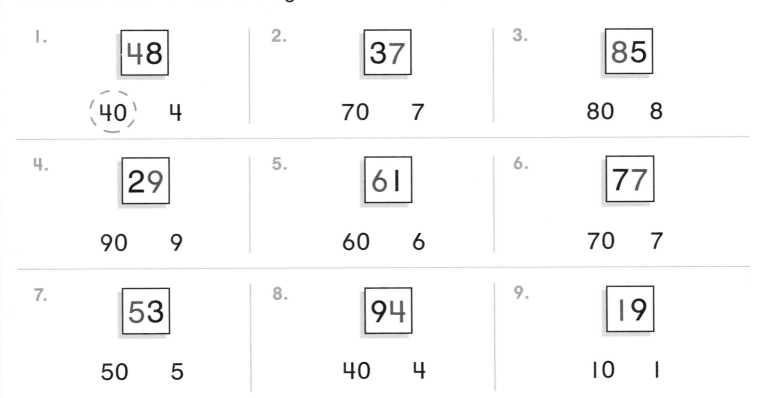

1. 48
    (40)   4

2. 37
    70   7

3. 85
    80   8

4. 29
    90   9

5. 61
    60   6

6. 77
    70   7

7. 53
    50   5

8. 94
    40   4

9. 19
    10   1

Explain Your Thinking Why does the digit 7 have a value of 70 in the number 79?

Independent Practice

Write the numbers.

	How many tens and ones?	What is the value of each digit?	What is the number?
1.	__7__ tens __4__ ones	__70__ + __4__	__74__
2.	_____ tens _____ ones	_____ + _____	_____
3.	_____ tens _____ one	_____ + _____	_____
4.	_____ tens _____ ones	_____ + _____	_____
5.	_____ tens _____ ones	_____ + _____	_____
6.	_____ tens _____ ones	_____ + _____	_____

Problem Solving · Reasoning

Logical Thinking

7. I have more ones than tens.
   The value of my tens digit is 70.
   What numbers could I be?

   _____ or _____

Draw or write to explain.

8. **Write About It** Explain how you decided
   what numbers fit the clues.

At Home Ask your child how many tens and ones there are in two-digit numbers such as 39 and 52.

Copyright © Houghton Mifflin Company. All rights reserved.

Name _____

Regroup Tens as Ones

New Vocabulary
regroup

Learn About It

You can **regroup** 1 ten as 10 ones.

Here is one way to show 25.

Workmat

Tens	Ones

2 tens 5 ones = 25

Regroup 1 ten as 10 ones.

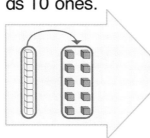

Here is another way to show 25.

Workmat

Tens	Ones

1 ten 15 ones = 25

Guided Practice

Use Workmat 3 with ▭▭▭▭▭ and ▯.

	Show the number with ▭▭▭▭▭ and ▯.	Regroup 1 ten as 10 ones. Record.	Regroup another ten as 10 ones. Record.
1.	36	__2__ tens __16__ ones	__1__ ten __26__ ones
2.	43	____ tens ____ ones	____ tens ____ ones
3.	28	____ ten ____ ones	____ tens ____ ones
4.	90	____ tens ____ ones	____ tens ____ ones
5.	65	____ tens ____ ones	____ tens ____ ones

Explain Your Thinking Why is 3 tens 6 ones the same as 2 tens 16 ones?

Independent Practice

Use Workmat 3 with ▭▭ and ▫ .

Show the number with ▭▭ and ▫ .	Regroup 1 ten as 10 ones. Record.	Regroup another ten as 10 ones. Record.
1. 25	__1__ ten __15__ ones	__0__ tens __25__ ones
2. 34	_____ tens _____ ones	_____ ten _____ ones
3. 56	_____ tens _____ ones	_____ tens _____ ones
4. 70	_____ tens _____ ones	_____ tens _____ ones
5. 23	_____ ten _____ ones	_____ tens _____ ones
6. 52	_____ tens _____ ones	_____ tens _____ ones
7. 48	_____ tens _____ ones	_____ tens _____ ones
8. 67	_____ tens _____ ones	_____ tens _____ ones

Problem Solving•Reasoning

Write About It

9. Write the number of tens and ones blocks.

Explain how you could regroup the tens and ones blocks to show the number in another way. Write how many tens and ones you would have.

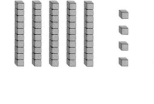

_____

At Home Ask your child to tell you what number equals 7 tens 15 ones.

Copyright © Houghton Mifflin Company. All rights reserved.

LESSON 5 — Different Ways to Show Numbers

Learn About It

You can show a number in different ways.

These are ways to show 23.

| | 2 tens 3 ones | 20 + 3 |

Guided Practice

Circle ways to show each number.

| 1. | | | 31 | | | 3 tens 1 one |

| 1. | **31** | | *(3 tens 1 one)* |

| 2. | **54** | 50 + 4 |  |

| 3. | **60** | 60 + 10 | 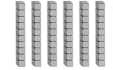 |

| 4. | **29** |  | 9 tens 2 ones |

| 5. | **57** |  | 5 tens 2 ones |

Explain Your Thinking Why is 3 tens 15 ones another way to show 45?

Independent Practice

1. Write each number. Then draw lines to match the same numbers.

70 + 2 = _72_

3 tens 3 ones = ____

 = ____

60 + 7 = ____

 = ____

5 tens 6 ones = ____

 = ____

 = _72_

30 + 3 = ____

4 tens 3 ones = ____

50 + 6 = ____

____ = ____

Problem Solving • Reasoning

Number Sense

2. You have these tens and ones blocks. How many tens and ones blocks would you use to show 36?

____ tens blocks   ____ ones blocks

At Home Ask your child to draw pictures to show 35 in two ways.

Copyright © Houghton Mifflin Company. All rights reserved.

Name _____

LESSON 6

Problem Solving:
Too Much Information

Standards
AF **1.0**, MR **1.1, 3.0**

A problem may have information
that you do not need.

**Sometimes a problem has more
information than you need.**

A tiger can live 20 years.
A bear can live 30 years.
A monkey can live 15 years.
Does the tiger or the bear live longer?

Cross out any information you do not need.

Think:
What am I trying
to find? What
information do
I need?

_____ lives longer

Sometimes you need all the information.

A tiger is 15 years old.
A bear is 12 years old.
A bobcat is 8 years old.
Write the three animals in order from
youngest to oldest.

Cross out any information you do not need.

Think:
Is there any
information that I
can cross out?

_____ , _____ , _____

Guided Practice

Cross out any information
you do not need. Then solve.

Remember:
► Understand
► Plan
► Solve
► Look Back

Remember to
use the 4 steps.

1 A bear ran 30 miles per hour.
A zebra ran 40 miles per hour.
~~An elephant ran 25 miles~~
~~per hour.~~ Who ran faster,
the bear or the zebra?

Think:
Can I cross out
any information?

Draw or write to explain.

zebra
_____ ran faster

2 A bear slept for 7 months
in the winter. A frog slept for
6 months. A bat slept for
5 months. Which animal
slept the longest?

Think:
What information
do I need?

_____ slept the longest

3 Rosa saw 8 hippos and
9 zebras. Brett saw
13 hippos. Did Rosa or
Brett see more hippos?

Think:
Can I cross out
any information?

_____ saw more hippos

4 The zoo has 6 zebras and
3 camels. They get 4 more
zebras. How many zebras
does the zoo have?

Think:
Do I add
or subtract to
find how many
there are?

_____ ◯ _____ = _____ zebras

At Home Have your child explain what the extra
information is in each problem.

Name ______________________________

Choose a Strategy

Strategies

Draw a Picture
Use Models to Act It Out
Write a Number Sentence

Solve.

1. There are 6 whales in one tank. There are 2 tanks. There are 7 whales in the other tank. How many whales are there?

   _____ whales

Draw or write to explain.

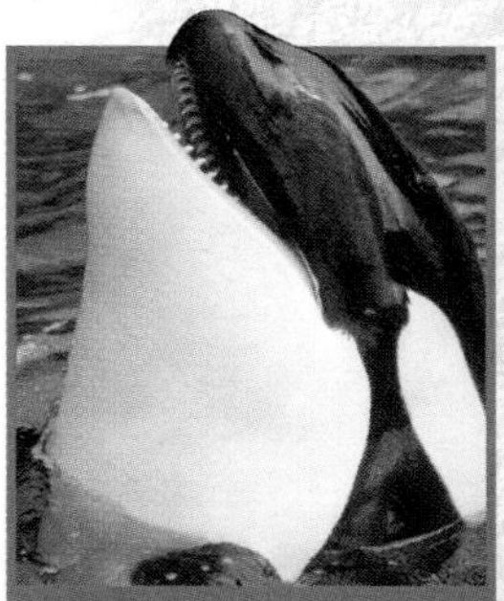

Whale

2. 11 sea otters are in the water. 2 get out. How many are still in the water?

   _____ sea otters

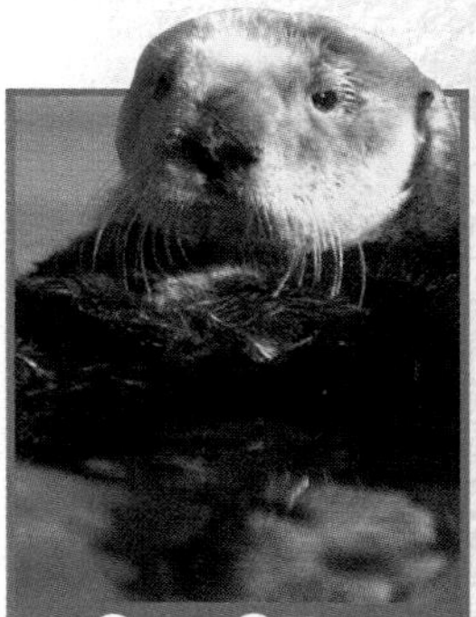

Sea Otter

3. There are 2 dolphins. Each dolphin eats 9 fish during the show. 4 people get wet at the show. How many fish are needed?

   _____ fish

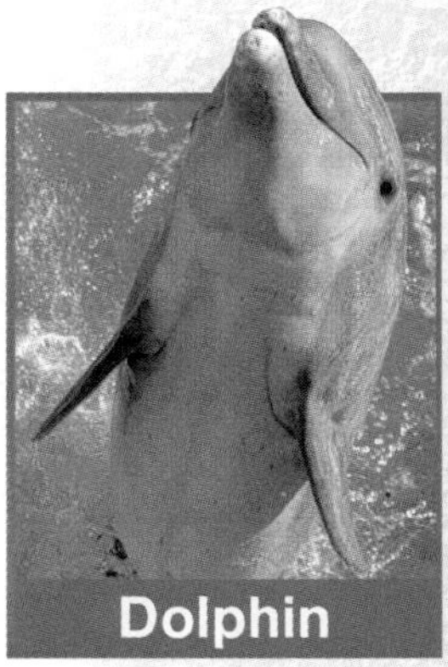

Dolphin

4. There are 6 seals in the seal show. Each seal uses 2 balls. How many balls are needed for the show?

   _____ balls

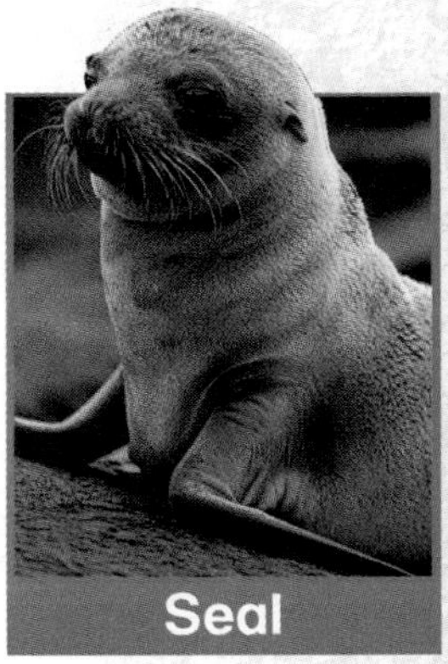

Seal

Name_____

Mixed Practice

Memorize Your Facts

Add or subtract.

1. 7 − 6 = _____

2. 8 + 9 = _____

3. 14 − 5 = _____

4. _____ = 7 + 4

5. _____ = 1 + 8

6. _____ = 5 + 5

7. 13
  − 10

8. 3
  + 2

9. 8
  + 6

10. 3
  − 1

11. 4
  + 8

12. 11
  − 0

13. 0
  + 5

14. 17
  − 7

15. 13
  − 5

16. 9
  + 6

17. 7
  + 5

18. 2
  − 1

19. 2
  − 2

20. 11
  − 6

21. 1
  + 5

22. 10
  + 9

23. 10
  − 4

24. 2
  + 6

25. 9
  + 5

26. 1
  − 0

27. 10
  − 9

28. 4
  + 6

29. 6
  − 2

30. 7
  + 7

Brain Teaser Guess the Score

Use the clues. Write the score for each team.

Hawks   • score between 80 and 90
         • tens and ones digits are the same

Lions   • score between 85 and 95
         • tens digit is one less than the ones digit.

LIONS   HAWKS

Internet Brain Teasers
Visit **www.eduplace.com/kids/mhm**
for more *BrainTeasers*.

Copyright © Houghton Mifflin Company. All rights reserved.

Quick ✓ Check

Check Your Understanding of Lessons 1–6

Write the tens and ones. Write the number.

1. 6 tens

Tens	Ones

_____

2. 5 tens 3 ones

Tens	Ones

_____

Circle the value of each red digit.

3. | 94 |

90   9

4. | 18 |

80   8

5. | 31 |

30   3

	Show the number with ▭▭▭ and ▫.	Regroup 1 ten as 10 ones. Record.	Regroup another ten as 10 ones. Record.
6.	67	_____ tens _____ ones	_____ tens _____ ones
7.	84	_____ tens _____ ones	_____ tens _____ ones

Circle another way to show the number.

8. | 71 |    7 tens 1 one

Cross out any information you do not need. Solve.

9. The zookeeper fed 8 lions. Then he fed 7 tigers. The monkeys were waiting for lunch. How many lions and tigers did he feed?

_____ lions and tigers

Draw or write to explain.

Test Prep • Cumulative Review

Maintaining the Standards

Fill in the ○ for the correct answer. NH means Not Here.

1 Mark the number shown here.

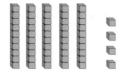

45	54	55	64
○	○	○	○

2 Add.   6
    + 9

13	14	15	NH
○	○	○	○

3 Mark the value of the red digit.

37

3	30	7	70
○	○	○	○

4 Subtract.   16 − 8 = ▨

9	7	5	NH
○	○	○	○

5 Mark another way to show 39.

○ 3 tens 9 ones
○ 3 ones 9 tens
○ 30 + 90
○ 3 + 90

6 12 seals are swimming in a tank. 5 seals get out. How many seals are still in the tank?

16	12	7	4
○	○	○	○

7 Lisa had 2 tens and 7 ones blocks. These are Lisa's blocks now.

Explain how she regrouped her blocks.

_____

_____

_____

Copyright © Houghton Mifflin Company. All rights reserved.

Safe Site

Internet Test Prep
Visit **www.eduplace.com/kids-mhm**
for more *Test Prep Practice.*

Name_____

Standards
NS **1.0, 1.1**
SDP **2.0, 2.1,** MR **1.2**

Even and Odd Numbers

Learn About It

You can make groups of two to decide if
a number is **even** or **odd.**

A number is **even** when you
make groups of two and there
are none left over.

A number is **odd** when you make
groups of two and there is one left
over.

Guided Practice

Show each number with cubes.
Then circle **even** or **odd**.

There is one left over.
15 is an odd number.

1. 15   even   (odd)

2. 26   even   odd

3. 13   even   odd

4. 12   even   odd

5. 21   even   odd

6. 7   even   odd

7. 18   even   odd

Explain Your Thinking When you make groups of two, can you
ever have more than one left over? Tell why or why not.

Independent Practice

Show each number with cubes.
Then circle even or odd.

1. **11** even   (odd)

2. **12** even   odd

3. **13** even   odd

4. **14** even   odd

5. **15** even   odd

6. **16** even   odd

7. **17** even   odd

8. **18** even   odd

9. **19** even   odd

10. **20** even   odd

Problem Solving•Reasoning

Patterns

11. Color the even numbers .
    Color the odd numbers .

1	2	3	4	5	6	7	8	9	10
11	12	13	14	15	16	17	18	19	20

12. Write the next even number _____.

    Write the next odd number _____.

13. **Write About It** Is 68 even or odd?
    Write how you know.

At Home Toss a handful of small items, such as buttons, on a table. Ask your child to tell you if there are an odd or an even number of items.

LESSON 8

Number Patterns

Learn About It

You can find number patterns in a **hundred** chart.

New
Vocabulary
hundred

Counting by 2s
makes this pattern.

Counting by 5s
makes this pattern.

Guided Practice

Use the hundred chart.

1. Count by 2s. Color
   the numbers ▨ .

2. Count by 5s. Circle
   the numbers.

3. Count by 3s. Put an
   ✕ on the numbers.

1	2	3	4	5	6	7	8	9	10
11	12	13	14	15	16	17	18	19	20
21	22	23	24	25	26	27	28	29	30
31	32	33	34	35	36	37	38	39	40
41	42	43	44	45	46	47	48	49	50
51	52	53	54	55	56	57	58	59	60
61	62	63	64	65	66	67	68	69	70
71	72	73	74	75	76	77	78	79	80
81	82	83	84	85	86	87	88	89	90
91	92	93	94	95	96	97	98	99	100

Explain Your Thinking Which number is likely to
come next in this pattern: 10, 20, 30, 40, 50?

Independent Practice

1. Write the missing numbers in the hundred chart.

1	2	3	4					9	10
11	12			15			18		
21		23	24		26				
	32			35		37		39	
41			44				48		50
	53		55					59	
		64							70
	72			75		77		79	
81			84		86				
91	92				96		98	99	100

Use the hundred chart to complete the pattern.

2. 5, 10, 15, _____, 25, _____, _____, _____, 45

3. 20, 22, 24, _____, 28, _____, _____, _____, 36, 38

Problem Solving•Reasoning

Visual Thinking

4. Describe the pattern Sue made. How should the last three boxes be colored to extend the pattern? Circle the answer.

At Home   Ask your child to use the hundred chart to count by 3s to 30.

LESSON 9 Compare Two-Digit Numbers

New
Vocabulary
greater than
less than

Learn About It

You can show that numbers are **greater than** using **>** or **less than** using **<**.

First compare tens.

34   25

3 tens is greater than 2 tens.

3**4 is greater than** 2**5**.

34 > 25

If tens are the same, compare ones.

45   46

5 ones is less than 6 ones.

45 is less than **46**.

45 < 46

If tens and ones are the same, the numbers are equal.
21 = 21

Guided Practice

Write each number.
Write **>** or **<**.

1.

__38__   is less than   __42__

__38__ ⊘ __42__

2.

____   is greater than   ____

____ ◯ ____

3. 87 ◯ 78

4. 31 ◯ 37

5. 19 ◯ 91

Explain Your Thinking Did you need to compare the ones in Exercise 1 to compare the two numbers? Tell why or why not.

Independent Practice

Spin the spinner.
Write the number on a line. Compare.
Write >, <, or = in the ◯.

Remember:
- = equals
- > is greater than
- < is less than

47 ◯< 53

85 ◯ 68

58 ◯ 91

49 ◯ 85

85 ◯ 68

32 ◯ 32

51 ◯ 85

98 ◯ 91

61 ◯ 49

68 ◯ 68

74 ◯ 32

91 ◯ 91

37 ◯ 85

At Home Have your child choose two numbers between 10 and 100. Ask your child to tell which number is greater. Repeat this with other numbers.

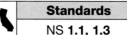

Order Two-Digit Numbers

New Vocabulary

before
between
after

Learn About It

A number line can help you find a number that comes just **before**, **between**, or just **after**.

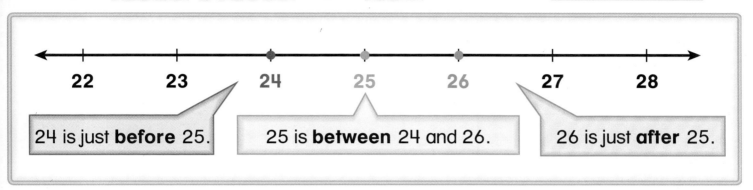

24 is just **before** 25.   25 is **between** 24 and 26.   26 is just **after** 25.

Guided Practice

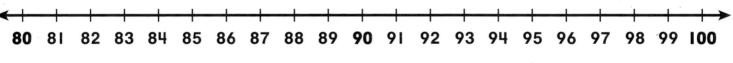

80 81 82 83 84 85 86 87 88 89 **90** 91 92 93 94 95 96 97 98 99 **100**

Use the number line.
Write the number that comes just after.

1. 83, __84__   2. 99, ____   3. 89, ____   4. 93, ____

5. 90, ____   6. 86, ____   7. 95, ____   8. 81, ____

Write the number that comes just before.

9. ____, 94   10. ____, 81   11. ____, 97   12. ____, 83

13. ____, 85   14. ____, 100   15. ____, 90   16. ____, 88

Write the number that comes between.

17. 88, ____, 90   18. 92, ____, 94   19. 81, ____, 83

20. 85, ____, 87   21. 96, ____, 98   22. 89, ____, 91

Explain Your Thinking Explain how a number line can help you when you want to find the number that comes just before.

Independent Practice

Use the number line. Write the numbers.

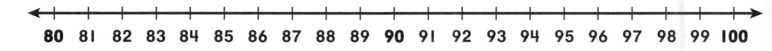

30 31 32 33 34 35 36 37 38 39 **40** 41 42 43 44 45 46 47 48 49 **50**

	Just Before	Between	Just After
1.	_30_, 31	32, ____, 34	35, ____
2.	____, 44	45, ____, 47	48, ____
3.	____, 32	39, ____, 41	42, ____

80 81 82 83 84 85 86 87 88 89 **90** 91 92 93 94 95 96 97 98 99 **100**

4. What number is just before 100? _____

5. What number is between 81 and 83? _____

6. What number is just after 89? _____

7. 84, 85, 86, ____, ____, ____, ____, 91, ____, ____, 94

8. 100, 99, 98, ____, ____, 95, ____, ____, ____, ____, ____

Problem Solving·Reasoning

Logical Thinking

9. I am a number between 43 and 46. I have more ones than tens. What number am I?

_____

Draw or write to explain.

10. **Write Your Own** Write a riddle using the numbers 89, 90, 91, or 92.

At Home Say a number between 10 and 99. Ask your child to tell you the numbers that come just before and just after your number.

Standards
NS 6.0

LESSON 11 Round to the Nearest Ten

Learn About It

You can use a number line to **round** a number to the nearest ten.

New Vocabulary
round

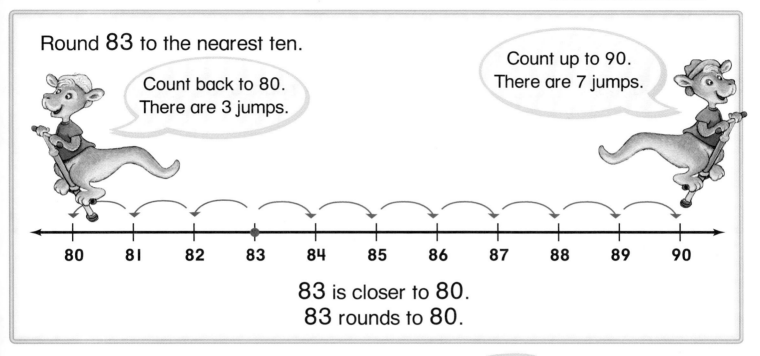

Round **83** to the nearest ten.

Count back to 80.
There are 3 jumps.

Count up to 90.
There are 7 jumps.

80 81 82 83 84 85 86 87 88 89 90

83 is closer to **80**.
83 rounds to **80**.

Guided Practice

Use the number line.
Round each number to the nearest ten.

Think:
Is 14 closer to 10 or 20?

1. 14 rounds to __10__.

10 11 12 13 14 15 16 17 18 19 20

2. 36 rounds to _____.

30 31 32 33 34 35 36 37 38 39 40

3. 58 rounds to _____.

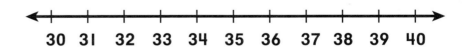

50 51 52 53 54 55 56 57 58 59 60

Explain Your Thinking How can you round a number to the nearest ten?

Independent Practice

Use the number line.
Round each number to the nearest ten.

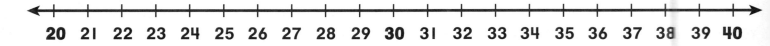

20 21 22 23 24 25 26 27 28 29 **30** 31 32 33 34 35 36 37 38 39 **40**

1. 22 rounds to _20_ .

2. 37 rounds to ____ .

3. 34 rounds to ____ .

4. 24 rounds to ____ .

5. 36 rounds to____ .

6. 28 rounds to ____ .

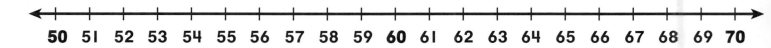

50 51 52 53 54 55 56 57 58 59 **60** 61 62 63 64 65 66 67 68 69 **70**

7. 67 rounds to ____ .

8. 51 rounds to ____ .

9. 59 rounds to ____ .

10. 68 rounds to ____ .

11. 63 rounds to ____ .

12. 54 rounds to ____ .

Problem Solving·Reasoning

Logical Thinking

13. I am a number between 40 and 50.
I am closer to 50.
One of my digits is 2 greater than
the other. What number am I?

Draw or write to explain

40 ?? 50

 At Home Ask your child to use the number line above Exercise 1 and to round 23 to the nearest ten.

Name_____

Problem Solving: Find a Pattern

LESSON 12

Standards
AF **1.3**, SDP **2.1, 2.2**
MR **1.1, 2.2**

Animal cards are sold in packs.
There are 3 cards in one pack.
There are 6 cards in two packs.
How many cards are in five packs?

ELEPHANT
LION
GIRAFFE

Number of Packs	1	2	3	4	5
Number of Cards	3	6	9	?	?

Understand

Circle what you need to find out.

How many cards in 1 pack?

How many cards in 5 packs?

Plan

Making a table can help you find a pattern.

1 pack has _____ cards.

2 packs have _____ cards.

Solve

Use the table. Extend the pattern.

Number of Packs	1	2	3	4	5
Number of Cards	3	6			

Look Back

How many cards are in 5 packs? _____ cards

What is the pattern?

_____

Guided Practice

Look for the pattern. Then solve.

1 There are 2 animals in each box.
How many toy animals are in 6 boxes?

Boxes	1	2	3	4	5	6
Animals	2	4	6	8	10	12

_12_ toy animals

> **Think:** What numbers do I already know?

2 Each sticker costs 5¢.
How much do 5 stickers cost?

Stickers	1	2	3	4	5
Cost	5¢	10¢	15¢		

_____ ¢

> **Think:** What is the pattern?

3 Each bunch has 3 bananas.
How many bananas are in 7 bunches?

Bunches	1	2	3	4	5	6	7
Bananas	3	6	9				

_____ bananas

> **Think:** How many bananas are in each bunch?

4 There are 10 people in each van.
How many people are in 5 vans?

Vans	1	2	3	4	5
People	10	20	30		

_____ people

> **Think:** How many people are in each van?

At Home Make a pattern using coins or cups. Ask your child to identify the pattern.

Choose a Strategy

Solve.

1 There are 2 sharks in each tank.
How many sharks are in 5 tanks?

Tanks	1	2	3	4	5
Sharks	2	4			

_____ sharks

Shark

2 There are 5 llamas in each pen. There
are 6 pens. How many llamas are there?

Pens	1	2	3	4	5	6
Llamas	5	10				

_____ llamas

Llama

3 Stan saw 5 elk on Monday.
On Tuesday he saw 8 more elk.
How many elk did Stan see?

_____ elk

Draw or write to explain.

Elk

4 16 people are waiting to see the
giant panda. 7 people leave. How
many people are still waiting to
see the giant panda?

_____ people

Giant Panda

Name _____

Mixed Practice

Memorize Your Facts

Add or subtract.

1. 17 − 10 = _____   2. 12 − 6 = _____   3. 2 − 0 = _____

4. _____ = 1 + 3   5. _____ = 5 + 6   6. _____ = 8 + 10

7. 1 0   8. 1 4   9.   4   10.   5   11.   7   12.   8
   − 7   − 9   + 3   + 8   − 2   + 8

13.   6   14. 1 2   15.   0   16. 1 4   17.   5   18.   3
    + 1   − 5   + 6   − 7   − 5   − 9

19.   8   20. 1 5   21.   8   22.   5   23. 1 3   24. 1 0
    − 0   − 6   + 4   + 9   − 3   + 8

25.   5   26.   7   27. 1 2   28.   8   29.   4   30. 1 5
    + 3   + 9   − 9   − 5   + 0   − 5

Brain Teaser Favorite Number

My number is between 17 and 25.
You say it when you start at zero and
count by 2s. You say it when you start
at zero and count by 5s.
What is my number? _____

Internet Brain Teasers
Visit **www.eduplace.com/kids/mhm**
for more *Brain Teasers.*

Quick ✓ Check

Check Your Understanding of Lessons 7–12

Show each number with 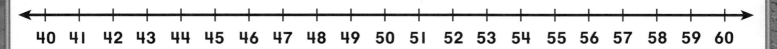 .
Then circle even or odd.

1. | 25 | even

  odd

2. | 18 | even

  odd

3. | 11 | even

  odd

4. Write the missing numbers in the chart.

11	12		14	15		17	18		20
21	22	23		25	26	27		29	30

Write **>** or **<** in the ◯.

5. 56 ◯ 49

6. 28 ◯ 35

7. 68 ◯ 65

Use the number line.

40 41 42 43 44 45 46 47 48 49 50 51 52 53 54 55 56 57 58 59 60

Just Before	Between	Just After
8. _____ ,48	53, _____ ,55	41, _____

Use the number line. Round to the nearest 10.

9. 48 rounds to _____.

10. 53 rounds to _____.

Look for the pattern. Then solve.

11. Each basket has 5 apples.
How many apples in 4 baskets?

Baskets	1	2	3	4
Apples	5	10		

_____ apples

Name _____

Test Prep • Cumulative Review

Maintaining the Standards

Fill in the ○ for the correct answer. NH means Not Here.

1 Mark the number that comes just before 35.

30	34	36	38
○	○	○	○

2 Add.   9
       + 8

16	15	14	NH
○	○	○	○

3 Mark the missing numbers from the chart.

35	36	37		
	46	47	48	49

○ 38, 40, 41

○ 43, 44, 45

○ 38, 39, 45

○ 38, 39, 40

4 Subtract.

$$16 - 7 = \blacksquare$$

9	10	11	NH
○	○	○	○

5 One sticker costs 5¢. How much do 4 stickers cost?

Stickers	1	2		
Cost	5¢	10¢		

5¢	10¢	15¢	20¢
○	○	○	○

6 Choose a sign to make the sentence true.

43 ○ 34

>	<	=	¢
○	○	○	○

7 Eli has 9 pencils. He finds 2 more. How many pencils does he have?

_____ pencils

Explain how you solved this problem.

_____

_____

Copyright © Houghton Mifflin Company. All rights reserved.

Safe Site

Internet Test Prep
Visit **www.eduplace.com/kids/mhm**
for more *Test Prep Practice.*

Name _____

Chapter Review

Use these numbers to answer each question. **16** **27**

1.	Which number is **even**?	_____
2.	Which number is **odd**?	_____
3.	Which number is **greater than** 19?	_____
4.	Which number is **less than** 25?	_____
5.	Which number can be **regrouped** as 1 ten 17 ones?	_____

Write each number.

	How many tens and ones?	What is the value?	What is the number?
6.	____ tens ____ ones	____ + ____	_____
7.	____ tens ____ ones	____ + ____	_____

Circle another way to show the number.

8. **45**   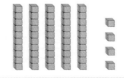   3 tens 15 ones

Circle even or odd. Use cubes if you want.

9. **9**   even   odd

10. **14**   even   odd

Use the chart to complete each pattern.

21	22	23	24	25	26	27	28	29	30
31	32	33	34	35	36	37	38	39	40
41	42	43	44	45	46	47	48	49	50

11. 22, 24 ,26, _____, _____, _____, 34

12. 50, 45, 40, _____, _____, _____

Write >, <, or = in the ◯.

13. 86 ◯ 89   14. 34 ◯ 34   15. 56 ◯ 23

Use the number line for Exercises 16–20.

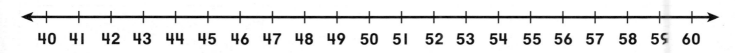

40 41 42 43 44 45 46 47 48 49 50 51 52 53 54 55 56 57 58 59 60

Just Before	Between	Just After
16. _____, 44	45,_____, 47	48, _____

Round each number to the nearest ten.

17. 42 rounds to _____.   18. 56 rounds to _____.

19. 49 rounds to _____.   20. 54 rounds to _____.

Look for a pattern. Then solve.
Cross out any information you do not need.

21. There are 5 seals. There are
6 lions. Each seal eats 3 fish.
How many fish do the seals
eat altogether?

_____ fish

Seals	1	2	3	4	5
Fish	3				

Name _____

Chapter Test

Write each number.

	How many tens and ones?	What is the value?	What is the number?
1.	_____ tens _____ ones	_____ + _____	_____
2.	_____ tens _____ ones	_____ + _____	_____
3.	_____ ten _____ ones	_____ + _____	_____

Circle another way to show the number.

4. | 36 | 2 tens 16 ones

5. | 71 | 70 + 1

Circle even or odd. Use cubes if you want.

6. | 20 | even   odd   **7.** | 17 | even   odd

Write >, <, or = in the ◯.

8. 31 ◯ 36   **9.** 45 ◯ 19   **10.** 30 ◯ 50

11. 77 ◯ 71   **12.** 58 ◯ 58   **13.** 21 ◯ 41

Use the chart to complete each pattern.

41	42	43	44	45	46	47	48	49	50
51	52	53	54	55	56	57	58	59	60
61	62	63	64	65	66	67	68	69	70

14. 45, 50, 55, _____, _____, _____

15. 68, 66, 64, _____, _____, _____, _____, 54

Use the number line for Exercises 16–19.

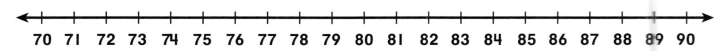

70 71 72 73 74 75 76 77 78 79 80 81 82 83 84 85 86 87 88 89 90

	Just Before	Between	Just After
16.	_____, 73	74, _____, 76	77, _____
17.	_____, 80	81, _____, 83	84, _____

Round each number to the nearest ten.

18. 77 rounds to _____.   19. 82 rounds to _____.

Look for a pattern. Then solve.
Cross out any information you do not need.

20. There are 6 fish tanks and 3 zookeepers. There are 5 fish in each tank. How many fish are there in all?

Tanks	1	2	3	4	5	6
Fish	5					

_____ fish

Write About It

76

Is the value of the red digit 7 or 70? **Explain** why.

_____

_____

_____

Name _____

Race to 100

Players
2–3

What You Need

- 2 yellow, 2 blue, 2 red, and 2 green cubes
- Workmat 2
- tens and ones blocks
- paper bag

How to Play

1. Put all the cubes in the bag.

2. Take turns picking a cube from the bag.

3. Use the chart to find the value of the cube picked. Take that number of tens and ones blocks.

4. Regroup 10 ones as 1 ten when you can.

5. Return the cube to the bag.

6. The first player to get 10 tens wins.

Cube Value	
Color	**Value**
blue	5 ones
yellow	7 ones
red	1 ten
green	2 tens

Standards
NS 1.0

Enrichment

Number Patterns With 4s and 6s

Green Frog and Blue Frog each hop up 100 steps.
Green Frog hops by 4s.
Blue Frog hops by 6s.
Which steps do they land on together?

I hop by 4s.

I hop by 6s.

1. Use a hundred chart to find out.
   Count by 4s. Color the numbers green.
   Count by 6s. Color the numbers blue.

1	2	3	4	5	6	7	8	9	10
11	12	13	14	15	16	17	18	19	20
21	22	23	24	25	26	27	28	29	30
31	32	33	34	35	36	37	38	39	40
41	42	43	44	45	46	47	48	49	50
51	52	53	54	55	56	57	58	59	60
61	62	63	64	65	66	67	68	69	70
71	72	73	74	75	76	77	78	79	80
81	82	83	84	85	86	87	88	89	90
91	92	93	94	95	96	97	98	99	100

2. Which steps do Green Frog and Blue Frog both land on?

_____, _____, _____, _____, _____, _____, _____, _____

3. **Write About It**   What do you notice about the numbers that both Green Frog and Blue Frog land on?

Copyright © Houghton Mifflin Company. All rights reserved.

Accessing Prior Knowledge

This story will help you review
- Counting
- Comparing

Where Are My Soccer Shoes?

A Read-Aloud Story

written by Janet Ann Burgess

illustrated by Susan Swan

A Math Storybook for

_____

"It's the first day of soccer practice.
I'll hurry to get dressed.
I think my shoes are in this closet,
underneath all the mess!"

Copyright © Houghton Mifflin Company. All rights reserved.

"So far I haven't found my shoes.
But I see some puzzles and games.
I think I'll put them on a shelf
so I can read their names."

How many more puzzles than games
are there?

2 ___ more puzzles

"Just look at all the caps we have!
I don't know where we got them.
My favorites are the baseball caps
with blue stripes—can you spot them?"

Circle the type of cap that there is
more of.

Copyright © Houghton Mifflin Company. All rights reserved.

"I think I'll count the sweatshirts,"
says Maria as she smiles.
"Those with zippers and those without
are now in two neat piles."

How many sweatshirts are there in all?

____ sweatshirts

"You see, the shoes and sneakers
are in neat rows on the floor.
But my soccer shoes aren't with them,
and they're not in any drawer!"

Circle the type of shoe that there is
more of.

Copyright © Houghton Mifflin Company. All rights reserved.

"Mom, my soccer shoes aren't here,
and practice begins at four."
"Maria, they've been here all along—
just close the closet door."

Family Letter

Vocabulary

bar graph Uses bars of different lengths to show data.

mode The number that occurs most often in a data set.

pictograph Uses pictures to show data.

range The difference between the greatest number and the least number in a data set.

tally A way to keep track of what has been counted.

Dear Family,

During the next few weeks, our math class will be learning about data and graphing.

You can expect to see work that provides practice collecting and recording data and reading tables and graphs. There will also be work that provides practice with making tables and graphs.

As we learn about data and graphing, you may wish to use the following as a guide.

A tally mark is written for each one that is counted.

I = | 2 = || 3 = ||| 4 = |||| 5 = ||||

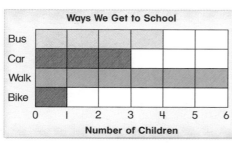

This bar graph shows that there are 6 children who walk to school.

Sincerely,

Your child's teacher

Copyright © Houghton Mifflin Company. All rights reserved.

Problem Solving: Use Logical Thinking

Standa...
MR 1.0, 1.1, 2.2, 3.

Sometimes you can use clues to solve problems.

Kim's favorite drink got more than 12 votes but less than 16 votes. Which drink is Kim's favorite?

Favorite Drinks	
Drink	Number of Votes
Apple juice	17
Orange juice	14
Grape juice	11
Milk	9

Understand

Circle what you need to find out.

Which drink got the most votes?

Which drink is Kim's favorite?

Plan

Use the clues to solve the problem.

Kim's favorite drink
got more than _____ votes.

It got less than _____ votes.

Solve

Read each clue. Cross out each drink that does not match the clue. Circle the drink that is left.

Apple juice   Orange juice

Grape juice   Milk

ok Back

Does your answer make sense? How do you know?

Which drink is Kim's favorite?

_____

number of
snack got.

Practice

the clues to find each person's
favorite snack. Cross out each snack
that does not match the clues.

Favorite Snacks	
Snacks	**Number of Votes**
Raisins	6
Pretzels	17
Cheese	14
Crackers	1

1. Kate's favorite snack got
more than 7 votes but
less than 13 votes. Which
snack is Kate's favorite?

Think:
Which snacks
do not match
the clues?

~~Raisins~~
~~Pretzels~~
~~Cheese~~
Crackers

crackers

2. Ali likes the snack that got
more than 12 votes. It got
an odd number of votes.
Which snack does Ali like?

Think:
Which snacks
can I cross out?

Raisins
Pretzels
Cheese
Crackers

3. Kara's snack got less than
13 votes. It got an even
number of votes. Which
snack does Kara like?

Think:
Which snacks did
not get an even
number of votes?

Raisins
Pretzels
Cheese
Crackers

4. Chen's favorite snack got
more than 12 votes. It
did not get the most votes.
Which is Chen's favorite
snack?

Think:
Which snack got
the most votes?

Raisins
Pretzels
Cheese
Crackers

118 one hundred eighteen

At Home Ask your child to show you how he or she used the information in the table to solve these problems.

Name_____

Favorite Fruit	
Fruit	**Number of Votes**
Plum	9
Apple	12
Watermelon	8
Banana	11

watermelon

Choose a Strategy

Use the table. Solve.

① Mr. Lopez likes the fruit that got more votes than watermelon. It got an even number of votes. Which fruit does he like?

_____

Draw or write to explain.

banana

② How many votes did watermelon and banana get altogether?

_____ votes

③ How many more votes did plum get than watermelon?

_____ more vote

plum

④ How many more votes did apple get than plum?

_____ more votes

apple

Mixed Practice

subtract.

1. $8 + 4 =$ _____

2. $11 - 9 =$ _____

3. $10 + 7 =$ _____

4. $9 - 0 =$ _____

5. $12 - 7 =$ _____

6. $16 - 8 =$ _____

7. _____ $= 9 + 3$

8. _____ $= 5 + 8$

9. _____ $= 7 + 8$

10.
$$\begin{array}{r} 1\,0 \\ +\ 9 \\ \hline \end{array}$$

11.
$$\begin{array}{r} 1\,2 \\ -\ 8 \\ \hline \end{array}$$

12.
$$\begin{array}{r} 8 \\ -\,6 \\ \hline \end{array}$$

13.
$$\begin{array}{r} 9 \\ +\,2 \\ \hline \end{array}$$

14.
$$\begin{array}{r} 5 \\ +\,5 \\ \hline \end{array}$$

15.
$$\begin{array}{r} 1\,3 \\ -\ 3 \\ \hline \end{array}$$

16.
$$\begin{array}{r} 1\,0 \\ -\ 8 \\ \hline \end{array}$$

17.
$$\begin{array}{r} 8 \\ +\,3 \\ \hline \end{array}$$

18.
$$\begin{array}{r} 7 \\ +\,3 \\ \hline \end{array}$$

19.
$$\begin{array}{r} 6 \\ -\,3 \\ \hline \end{array}$$

20.
$$\begin{array}{r} 1\,8 \\ -\ 9 \\ \hline \end{array}$$

21.
$$\begin{array}{r} 4 \\ +\,7 \\ \hline \end{array}$$

22.
$$\begin{array}{r} 1\,0 \\ -\ 4 \\ \hline \end{array}$$

23.
$$\begin{array}{r} 1\,1 \\ -\ 7 \\ \hline \end{array}$$

24.
$$\begin{array}{r} 8 \\ +\,9 \\ \hline \end{array}$$

25.
$$\begin{array}{r} 5 \\ -\,3 \\ \hline \end{array}$$

26.
$$\begin{array}{r} 8 \\ +\,5 \\ \hline \end{array}$$

27.
$$\begin{array}{r} 1\,6 \\ -\ 8 \\ \hline \end{array}$$

Brain Teaser Race to the Finish

In what order did the children finish the race?

Anna ran faster than Tom.
Tom and Anna ran slower
than Joe. Pam ran faster
than Joe.

_____ _____ _____ _____
first   second   third   fourth

Safe Site

Internet Brain Teasers
Visit **www.eduplace.com/kids/mhm**
for more *Brain Teasers*.

Name _____

Check Your Understanding of Lessons 1–4

1. Make a tally mark for each flower. Write the numbers. Then use the table to answer the questions.

2. How many red and yellow flowers are there altogether?

_____ red and yellow flowers

Flowers for Sale		
Color	**Tally Mark**	**Number**
Red	_____	_____
Yellow	_____	_____

Use the pictographs to answer Questions 3–6.

Books Sold in March	
Joke Books	📖📖📖📖📖📖📖
Picture Books	📖📖📖📖📖

Books Sold in April	
Joke Books	📖📖📖📖📖📖
Picture Books	📖📖📖📖

Each 📖 stands for 2 books.

3. How many joke books were sold in March? _____ joke books

4. How many picture books were sold in April? _____ picture books

5. How many more joke books were sold in March than in April?

_____ more joke books

6. In which month were more picture books sold? _____

7. The number of sports books sold was less than 21. It was greater than 18. It was an even number. How many sports books were sold? _____ sports books

Name _____

Maintaining the Standards

Fill in the ○ for the correct answer. NH means Not Here.

Use the tally chart to answer Questions 1 and 2.

Favorite Season	
Spring	|||
Summer	||||| |||||
Fall	|||||	
Winter	||||| ||

1 How many children chose summer?

3 9 10 15
○ ○ ○ ○

2 Mark the season that was chosen the least.

○ spring   ○ summer
○ fall   ○ winter

3 Find the difference.

$$15 - 8 = \blacksquare$$

7   8   9   NH
○   ○   ○   ○

4 Mark how many balls are in 6 boxes.

Boxes	1	2			
Balls	3	6			

17   18   9   21
○   ○   ○   ○

5 Choose a sign to make the sentence true.

32 ○ 45

>   <   =   ¢
○   ○   ○   ○

6 There are 4 fish in one bowl. There are 6 fish in another bowl.

$$4 + 6 = 10$$

Explain why this number sentence shows how many fish are in both bowls.

_____

_____

Safe Site

Internet Test Prep
Visit **www.eduplace.com/kids/mhm**
for more *Test Prep Practice.*

Copyright © Houghton Mifflin Company. All rights reserved.

Range and Mode

LESSON 7

Learn About It

You can compare data to find how often something happens.

These are the ages of children at after-school activities.

Ages	Number of Children
5	||
6	||||
7	||||
8	|||

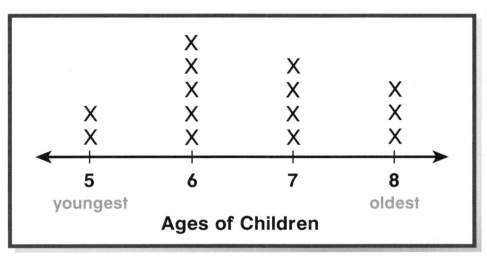

Ages of Children

The **mode** is the age of the greatest number of children.

The **range** is the difference between the oldest and the youngest age.

Guided Practice

Use the information above to answer each question.

1. How many children are 7 years old? ___4___ children

2. Which age has the greatest number of X's? _____
   mode

3. What is the difference between the oldest and the youngest age?

   ___8___ – _____ = _____
   oldest   youngest   range

Explain Your Thinking Show the data above in a bar graph. How is it the same? How is it different?

Independent Practice

Use the information to answer each question.

Points Scored	Number of Children
1	|
2	||||
3	||||
4	|||
5	||

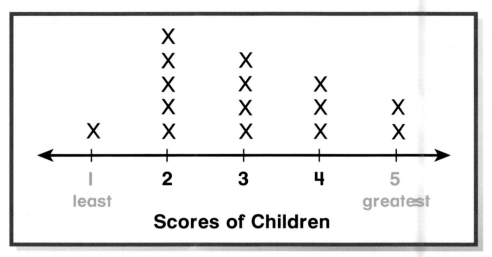

Scores of Children

1. How many children scored 2 points?   _5_ children

2. How many children scored 4 points?   ____ children

3. Which score has the greatest number of X's?   ____
   mode

4. What is the difference between the
   greatest score and the least score?   ____ − ____ = ____
   greatest   least   range

Problem Solving • Reasoning

Using Vocabulary

5. Make a **pictograph** and a **bar graph**
   to show the same data as the table.

Books Read	
Alice	15 books
Josh	5 books

Books Read

Alice	
Josh	

Each ▮ stands for 5 books.

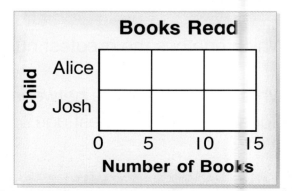

Books Read

At Home Ask your child to tell you how the bar graph and pictograph in Exercise 5 show the same information.

Name_____

LESSON
8

Problem Solving:
Use a Graph

Standards
MR **1.0, 1.1**
SDP **1.0, 1.4**

You can use data in a bar graph
to solve a problem. This graph shows
what's found in a bookcase.

**You can use a graph and
add to solve a problem.**

How many games and books
are there altogether?

☐ games

⊕ ☐ books
_____
☐ altogether

Think:
How many games
are there? How many
books are there?

You can use a graph to compare.

How many more books than pictures
are there?

☐ books

⊖ ☐ pictures
_____
☐ more books

Think:
Do I add or subtract
to compare?

Jenny's Books

Number

	Story	Sports	Puzzles	Mystery
10				
8				
6				
4				
2				
0				

Book

Guided Practice

Use the graph to solve each problem.

1. How many sports books and storybooks does Jenny have?

   Think: How do I use the graph to answer the question?

   Draw or write to explain.

   __18__ books

2. How many more storybooks than puzzle books does Jenny have?

   Think: Which numbers do I use?

   _____ storybooks

3. How many puzzle books and mystery books does Jenny have?

   Think: How do I find the total number of books?

   _____ books

4. How many more sports books does Jenny have than mystery books?

   Think: Which numbers do I use?

   _____ sports books

At Home Have your child explain how he or she used the bar graph to answer each question.

Copyright © Houghton Mifflin Company. All rights reserved.

Name_____

Dan's Sports Card Collection

Choose a Strategy

Use the graph to solve each problem.

① How many hockey cards
does Dan have?

_____ hockey cards

hockey

---

② How many hockey cards and
basketball cards does Dan
have altogether?

_____ hockey and basketball cards

Draw or write to explain.

basketball

---

③ How many more basketball cards
than football cards are there?

_____ basketball cards

football

---

④ Dan loses one baseball card. He
gives one to his sister. How many
baseball cards does he have now?

_____ baseball cards

baseball

Name _____

Mixed Practice

Memorize Your Facts

1. $7 + 9 =$ __17__

2. $13 - 4 =$ __9__

3. $3 + 9 =$ __12__

4. $14 - 5 =$ __9__

5. $11 - 7 =$ __4__

6. $2 + 8 =$ __5__

7. __14__ $= 4 + 10$

8. __15__ $= 9 + 6$

9. __12__ $= 6 + 6$

10.
$$\begin{array}{r} 8 \\ + 6 \\ \hline \end{array}$$

11.
$$\begin{array}{r} 12 \\ - 4 \\ \hline \end{array}$$

12.
$$\begin{array}{r} 14 \\ - 9 \\ \hline \end{array}$$

13.
$$\begin{array}{r} 8 \\ + 9 \\ \hline \end{array}$$

14.
$$\begin{array}{r} 5 \\ + 9 \\ \hline \end{array}$$

15.
$$\begin{array}{r} 11 \\ - 6 \\ \hline \end{array}$$

16.
$$\begin{array}{r} 10 \\ - 4 \\ \hline \end{array}$$

17.
$$\begin{array}{r} 9 \\ + 7 \\ \hline \end{array}$$

18.
$$\begin{array}{r} 10 \\ + 3 \\ \hline \end{array}$$

19.
$$\begin{array}{r} 9 \\ - 9 \\ \hline \end{array}$$

20.
$$\begin{array}{r} 9 \\ - 4 \\ \hline \end{array}$$

21.
$$\begin{array}{r} 10 \\ - 8 \\ \hline \end{array}$$

Brain Teaser A Fruity Graph

Use the clues to complete the graph. Write: **oranges**, **apples**, **pears**.

- 4 people chose apples.

- More people chose pears than apples.

- More people chose oranges than pears.

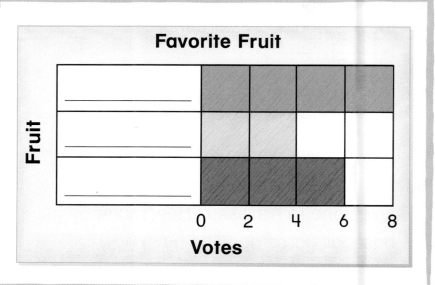

Favorite Fruit

Fruit

0   2   4   6   8

Votes

Copyright © Houghton Mifflin Company. All rights reserved.

Safe Site

Internet Brain Teaser
Visit **www.eduplace.com/kids-mhm**
for more *Brain Teasers*.

Name_____

Check Your Understanding of Lessons 5–8

Use the bar graph to answer each question.

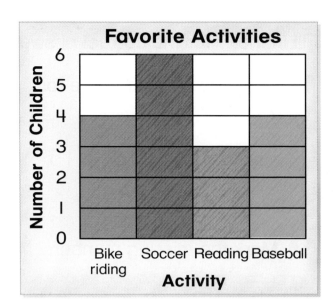

Favorite Activities

1. How many children chose reading?

   _____ children

2. How many more children chose soccer than baseball?

   _____ more children

3. Which activity got 3 votes?

   _____

4. Which activity was chosen most often? _____

5. Which activity was chosen least often? _____

6. Use the table to complete the bar graph.

Favorite Color	
Color	Number of Children
Red	8
Blue	2
Yellow	4
Green	6

Favorite Color

7. How many children chose red? _____ children

8. How many children chose yellow? _____ children

9. Which color was chosen most often? _____

10. Which color was chosen least often? _____

Test Prep • Cumulative Review

Maintaining the Standards

Fill in the ○ for the correct answer. NH means Not Here.

1 Mark the number name for 7 + 9.

18	17	16	15
○	○	○	○

2 Mark the missing number.

48, 49, __?__, 51, 52

49	50	51	52
○	○	○	○

3 Add.   8
        + 5

14	15	16	NH
○	○	○	○

4 Mark the number shown here.

○ 90 + 4

○ 4 tens 7 ones

○ 40 + 90

○ 4 tens 9 ones

Use the table to answer Questions 5 and 6.

Points Scored	Number of Children
10	10
20	16
30	9
40	8

5 How many children scored 20 points?

16	10	9	8
○	○	○	○

6 How many more children scored 30 points than 40 points?

8	7	2	1
○	○	○	○

Explain how you found the answer.

_____

_____

Copyright © Houghton Mifflin Company. All rights reserved.

Safe Site

Internet Test Prep
Visit www.eduplace.com/kids/mhm
for more *Test Prep Practice.*

Chapter Review

Name_____

Write the letter that tells about each one.

1. **bar graph** _____

2. **pictograph** _____

   A. A graph that uses pictures to show information.

   B. A graph that uses bars of different lengths to show information.

Show each number with tally marks.

3. four _____   4. ten _____   5. thirteen _____

Write the total numbers in each table.
Then answer each question.

Favorite Snacks

6.

Lyn's Class		
Snack	**Tally Marks**	**Number**
Cheese	||||	
Pretzels	|||||	
Fruit	||||| |||	

Adam's Class		
Snack	**Tally Marks**	**Number**
Cheese	||||| ||	
Pretzels	||	
Fruit	||||| |	

7. In whose class did more children choose cheese?

_____

8. In whose class did more children choose pretzels?

_____

9. How many more children chose fruit in Lyn's class than in Adam's class?

_____ more children

10. How many children voted in Adam's class?

_____ children

Use the pictograph to answer each question.

11. How many children chose soccer?

_____ children

12. How many children chose baseball?

_____ children

13. How many more children chose baseball than football?

_____ more children

Favorite Sports	
Sport	Number of Children
Soccer	⭐ ⭐ ⭐ ⭐
Baseball	⭐ ⭐ ⭐
Football	⭐ ⭐
Kickball	⭐ ⭐ ⭐ ⭐

Each ⭐ stands for 2 children.

Use the pictograph above to fill in the bar graph.

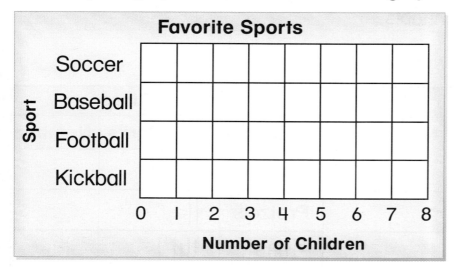

Use the bar graph to answer each question.

14. How many children voted altogether? _____ children

15. Which two sports did the same number of children choose?

_____ and _____

16. Maria's favorite sport got more than 4 votes. It got less than 7 votes. Which sport is Maria's favorite? _____

Name_____

Chapter Test

Write the total number in each table.
Then answer each question.

Favorite Lunch Food

1.

Tim's Class		
Lunch	**Tally Marks**	**Number**
Sandwich	ЖІІ	
Salad	ІІІ	
Tacos	ЖІІІ	

Mandy's Class		
Lunch	**Tally Marks**	**Number**
Sandwich	ІІІІ	
Salad	ЖІ	
Tacos	ЖІІІ	

2. In whose class did more children
   choose sandwiches?   _____

3. In Tim's class, which lunch food got
   the greatest number of votes?   _____

Use the pictograph to answer each question.

4. Which drink got the greatest
   number of votes?

   _____

5. How many people voted for
   apple juice?

   _____ people

6. What is the total number
   of votes for all drinks?

   _____ votes

Favorite Drinks	
Drink	**Number of Votes**
Apple Juice	🥤 🥤 🥤
Milk	🥤 🥤 🥤 🥤
Lemonade	🥤 🥤 🥤

Each 🥤 stands for 5 votes.

Use the table to fill in the bar graph.
Then answer each question.

7.

Cards Collected	
Name	Number of Cards
Bob	|||| ||||
Su	||||	
Ronald	||||
Erica	||||	

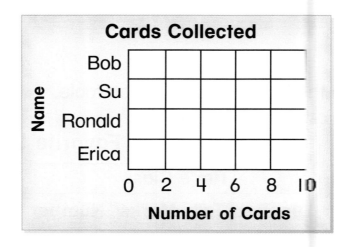

Cards Collected

Name

Number of Cards

8. How many cards did Su collect?   _____ cards

9. How many more cards did Bob
   collect than Ronald?   _____ more cards

10. Ben has more cards than Su.
    He has fewer cards than Bob.
    He has an even number of cards.
    How many cards does Ben have?   _____ cards

Write About It

Eli wants to find how many votes
there are for biking and hiking
altogether. How can Eli use the
bar graph to find this information?

_____

_____

_____

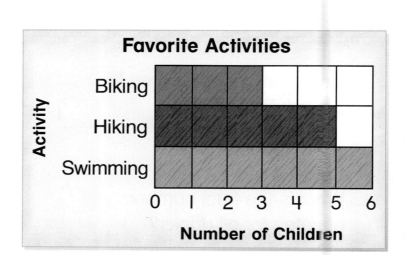

Favorite Activities

Activity

Number of Children

Race to the Finish

What You Need

- red crayon
- blue crayon

How to Play

1. Choose a red or blue crayon.

2. Take turns spinning the spinner. Follow the directions on the spinner.

3. The first player to color 8 boxes wins.

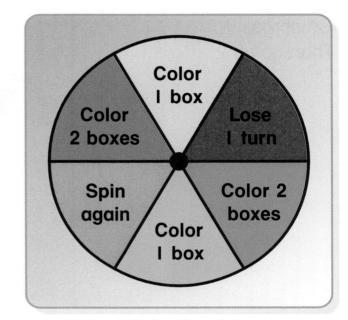

Race to the Finish

Players

Red

Blue

0   1   2   3   4   5   6   7   8

Number of Players

Enrichment

Number Pairs

You can use number pairs to find a place on a map.

Find .

Start at 0.

Go across 4.
Then go up 2.

Use the number pairs. First go across.
Then go up. Circle the place you find.

1. 2 1

2. 6 4

3. 4 2

4. 6 6

5. 2 6

6. 4 5

Copyright © Houghton Mifflin Company. All rights reserved.

CHAPTER 4

Money

The Big Hit

A Read-Aloud Story

written by Sarah Curran
illustrated by Shari Warren

Accessing Prior Knowledge

This story will help you review
- Counting dimes
- Counting nickels
- Counting pennies

A Math Storybook for

_____

It's out of here! It's gone!
A long, long home run.
But without another ball,
our game is over and done.

I have 6 dimes to buy a ball.
Now let me count.

10,   20,   30,   40 ,   50 , 60

Do I have the right amount?

How much money does Sara have? 60 ¢

Copyright © Houghton Mifflin Company. All rights reserved.

I have 8 nickels to buy a ball.
Now let me count.

5,   10,   15,   20,   _25_,   _30_,   _35_,   _40_

Do I have the right amount?

How much money does Pedro have? _40_ ¢

I have 10 pennies to buy a ball.
Now let me count.

1,   2,   3,   9,   5,   6,   7,   8,   9,   10

Do I have the right amount?

How much money does Jared have? 10 ¢

Copyright © Houghton Mifflin Company. All rights reserved.

I have 3 dimes to buy a ball.

Now let me count.

10, 20, 30

Do I have the right amount?

How much money does Lauren have? 30 ¢

Let's count the money.

Count it all.

Is it enough to buy a ball?

Count the dimes.

10,   20,   30,   _40_ , _50_ , _60_ , _70_ , _80_ , _90_

Count the nickels.

5,   10,   15,   20,   _25_ , _30_ , _35_ , _40_

Count the pennies.

1,   2,   3,   _4_ , _5_ , _6_ , _7_ , _8_ , _9_ , _10_

146

Copyright © Houghton Mifflin Company. All rights reserved.

Family Letter

Vocabulary

decimal point The dot used to separate dollars and cents.

dollar sign The sign used to indicate dollars ($).

cent sign The sign used to indicate cents (¢).

equal amounts Coins that have the same value such as one dime and two nickels.

Dear Family,

During the next few weeks, our math class will be learning about money, up to and including one dollar.

You can expect to see work that provides practice with counting money, using money, and equivalent amounts. There will also be work that provides practice with making change.

Use the following as a guide to help your child learn about counting money.

Using money in the real world will help your child become familiar with the coins and their value.

Start counting with the coin of the greatest value.

half-dollar	quarter	dime	nickel	penny
50¢	75¢	85¢	90¢	91¢

Sincerely,

Your child's teacher

LESSON 2

Quarter, Dimes, and Nickels

Standards
Review Grade 1 Standards

Learn About It

When a group of coins has a **quarter**, start counting with 25¢.

New **Vocabulary**
quarter

A quarter = 25¢.

<u>25</u> ¢   <u>35</u> ¢   <u>40</u> ¢

<u>40</u> ¢

total

Guided Practice

Write the total value of the coins.

1.

<u>25</u> ¢ <u>35</u> ¢ <u>45</u> ¢ <u>50</u> ¢ <u>55</u> ¢ <u>60</u> ¢

<u>60</u> ¢

total

2.

_____ ¢ _____ ¢ _____ ¢ _____ ¢ _____ ¢ _____ ¢

_____ ¢

total

Explain Your Thinking What other coins could you use to show 25¢?

Independent Practice

Write the total value of the coins.

1.     50 ¢

2.      60 ¢

3.      35 ¢

4.    40 ¢

5.       55 ¢

Problem Solving·Reasoning

6. Each child has 25¢. Write the number of
coins each child has.

Robert has 3 coins.	Margo has 5 coins.
2 dimes 1 nickel	2 dimes 1 nickels

7. **Write About It** Explain how you found your answer.

152 one hundred fifty-two

 **At Home** Have your child show you how he or she counts a small group of coins that include one quarter and some dimes and nickels.

LESSON 3

Count Coins

Learn About It

When counting coins, start with the coin of the greatest value.

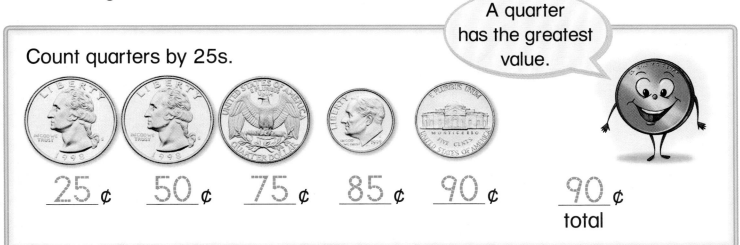

Count quarters by 25s.

A quarter has the greatest value.

<u>25</u> ¢   <u>50</u> ¢   <u>75</u> ¢   <u>85</u> ¢   <u>90</u> ¢   <u>90</u> ¢
                                                                      total

Guided Practice

Write the total value of the coins.

1.

<u>25</u> ¢   <u>50</u> ¢   <u>55</u> ¢   <u>56</u> ¢   <u>57</u> ¢   <u>57</u> ¢
                                                                      total

2.

<u>25</u> ¢   <u>50</u> ¢   <u>75</u> ¢   <u>85</u> ¢   <u>90</u> ¢   <u>95</u> ¢   <u>95</u> ¢
                                                                                    total

Explain Your Thinking Why does it help to have coins in order from the greatest to the least value when you count?

Independent Practice

Write the total value of the coins.

1.  __53__ ¢

2.  __100__ ¢

3. 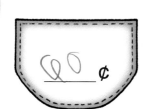 __80__ ¢

4.  _____ ¢

5.  __65__ ¢

6.  __56__ ¢

Problem Solving • Reasoning

7. Rachel has 3 quarters. Brian has 7 dimes. Write how much each child has.

Rachel _____ ¢   Brian _____ ¢

Circle the greater amount.

Draw or write to explain.

At Home Ask your child to explain how he or she would count to find the total value of 3 quarters. (25¢, 50¢, 75¢)

Copyright © Houghton Mifflin Company. All rights reserved.

Standards
NS **5.1, 5.2;** MR **1.2**

Equal Amounts

Learn About It

Different groups of coins can **equal** the same amount.

Review Vocabulary
equal

Here are some ways to show 25¢.

Count the coins with the greatest value first.

Guided Practice

Use coins. Show two ways to make 50¢.
Draw the coins.

Draw coins like this.

1.

50¢

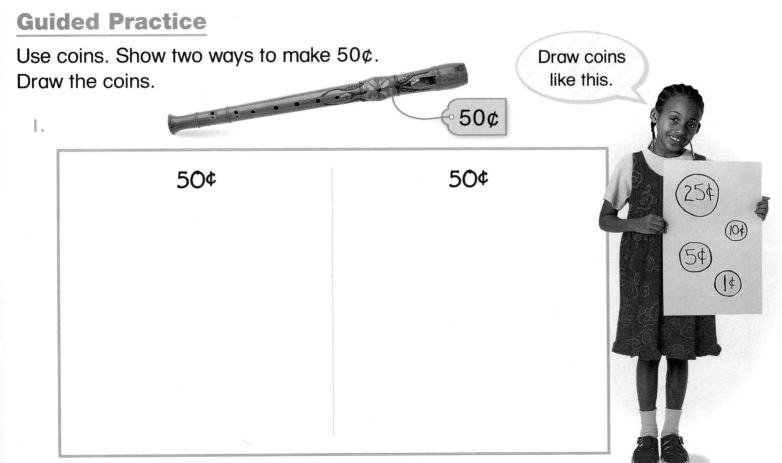

| 50¢ | 50¢ |

25¢ 10¢
5¢ 1¢

Explain Your Thinking How many ways can you find to show 10¢? Name the ways.

Independent Practice

Use coins. Show two ways to make each amount. Draw the coins.

1¢	5¢	10¢	25¢

1.

26¢

26¢	26¢

2.

35¢

35¢	35¢

Problem Solving • Reasoning

Number Sense

3. Dana has 22¢. She has no nickels. Draw the coins she could have.

4. **Write About It** Explain how Bill can have 41¢ with no dimes.

Draw or write to explain.

At Home Give your child several quarters, dimes, and nickels. Ask him or her to show 45¢ in two ways.

LESSON 5 Compare Money Amounts

Review
Vocabulary

**greater than
less than**

Learn About It

You can count groups of coins to compare their values.

25 ¢ $>$ 15 ¢ 30 ¢ $<$ 35 ¢

25¢ is **greater than** 15¢.   30¢ is **less than** 35¢.

Guided Practice

Write the total value of each group of coins.
Compare. Write **>**, **<**, or **=** in the ◯.

Remember:
> is greater than
< is less than
= equals

1.

56 ¢ $=$ 56 ¢

2.

85 ¢ $>$ 55 ¢

85¢

Explain Your Thinking Does a group of 4 coins always have
a greater value than a group of 2 coins? Tell why.

Independent Practice

Write the total value of each group of coins.
Compare. Write >, <, or = in the ◯.

Remember:
> is greater than
< is less than
= equals

1.

$$\underline{45}¢ \quad \bigcirc\!> \quad \underline{42}¢$$

2.

$$\underline{}¢ \quad \bigcirc \quad \underline{}¢$$

3.

$$\underline{}¢ \quad \bigcirc \quad \underline{}¢$$

Problem Solving • Reasoning

Use coins to solve the problem.

4. Maria has two quarters, a dime, and a nickel. How much more does she need to buy the drum?

   $\underline{}¢$

83¢

85¢

5. **Write Your Own** Write a subtraction problem about buying the toys. Then solve.

At Home Arrange several coins into two groups. Ask your child to count the coins and tell which group has the greater amount.

Check Your Understanding of Lessons 1-6

Count the coins. Write the total amount.

1.

25 ¢   05 ¢   10 ¢   1 ¢   1 ¢   62 ¢
total

2.    95 ¢

3.  42 ¢

4. Show 35¢ two ways. Draw the coins.

| 35¢ | 10+10+10+5¢ |
| 35¢ | 0+35 |

5. Write each amount. Compare. Write >, <, or = in the ◯.

36 ¢   ◯   _____ ¢

Solve each problem.

6. Maria has 2 quarters, a nickel and a penny. How much more does she need to buy a game for 60¢? _____ ¢ more

7. Carla has a quarter and a dime. She buys juice for 30¢. How much does she have left? _____ ¢

Name _____

Test Prep • Cumulative Review

Maintaining the Standards

Fill in the ○ for the correct answer. NH means Not Here.

Use the bar graph to answer Questions 1 and 2.

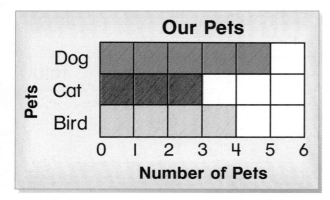

Our Pets

Pets							
Dog							
Cat							
Bird							

0 1 2 3 4 5 6

Number of Pets

1 How many more dogs than cats are there?

1	2	3	4
○	○	○	○

2 Which tally marks show the number of dogs?

○	○	○	○

3 Which number is most likely to come next?

23, 22, 21, _____

31	24	21	20
○	○	○	○

4 Mark the amount of money shown.

46¢	36¢	31¢	28¢
○	○	○	○

5 Add.

9 + 6 =

12	15	18	NH
○	○	○	○

6 Write the total amount.

_____ ¢

Explain how you counted the coins.

_____

_____

Safe Site

Internet Test Prep
Visit **www.eduplace.com/kids/mhm**
for more *Test Prep Practice.*

Copyright © Houghton Mifflin Company. All rights reserved.

Half-Dollars

Name _____

Half-Dollars

Standards: Review Grade 1 Standards

Learn About It

When a group of coins has a **half-dollar**, start counting with 50¢.

New Vocabulary: half-dollar

A half-dollar = 50¢

Start with 50. Then count by 10s.

__50__¢ __60__¢ __70__¢ __70__¢ total

Guided Practice

Write the total value of the coins.

1.

__50__¢ __75__¢ __80__¢ __85__¢ __86__¢   __86__¢ total

2.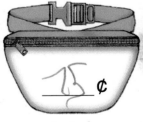

__5__¢ __10__¢ __5__¢ __5__¢ __5__¢   __75__¢ total

Explain Your Thinking What other coins could you use to show 50¢?

one hundred sixty-five **165**

Independent Practice

Write the total value of the coins.

A half-dollar has a value greater than a quarter. I count the half-dollar first.

1.

__95__ ¢

2.

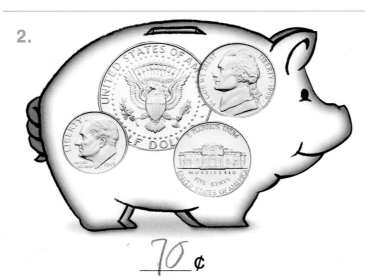

__70__ ¢

3.

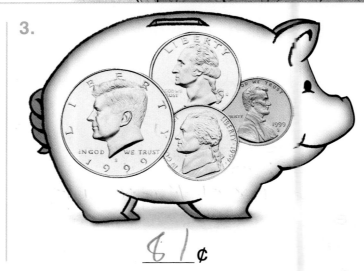

__81__ ¢

4.

__95__ ¢

5.

__56__ ¢

6. Color the bank with the greatest amount.

At Home Find items advertised for 99¢ or less. Ask your child to tell which coins could be used to buy each item.

Name _____

Standards
NS 5.0, 5.1
MR 1.2, 2.1

Use Coins to Show an Amount

Learn About It

Use coins with the greatest value to show an amount.

Use coins with the greatest value to make 40¢.

I cannot start with a half-dollar. It is more than 40¢.

Start with a quarter.   Add coins to make 40¢.

_25_ ¢   _35_ ¢   _40_ ¢

Guided Practice

Use coins of the greatest value to show each amount. Write how many of each coin

Think: Which coin should I start with?

	half-dollar	quarter	dime	nickel	penny
1. 56¢					
2. 19¢					
3. 38¢					

Explain Your Thinking How do you know if you used coins with the greatest value?

Independent Practice

Use coins of the greatest value to show
each amount. Then draw the coins.

I.  87¢

2.  79¢

3.  81¢

4.  75¢

Problem Solving • Reasoning

Logical Thinking

Each child has 50¢.
Draw the coins each
child could have.

5. Emily has 4 coins.

Draw or write to explain.

6. Bill has 2 coins.

Draw or write to explain.

 At Home Have your child explain how to make 32¢ with the fewest coins.

LESSON 10 One Dollar

Learn About It

When you write one **dollar**, use a
dollar sign and a **decimal point**.

New Vocabulary

dollar
dollar sign
decimal point

one dollar

100¢ or $1.00

↑   ↑
dollar sign   decimal point

one dollar

100¢ or $1.00

Guided Practice

Draw more coins to make one dollar.
Write the total value of the coins.

1. Use quarters.

25¢   25¢

__4__ quarters

100¢

$ 1.00

2. Use dimes.

____ dimes

____¢

$ 1.0

Explain Your Thinking What other coins could you use to show one dollar?

Independent Practice

Write the total value of the coins.
Circle the groups of coins that equal one dollar.

1. 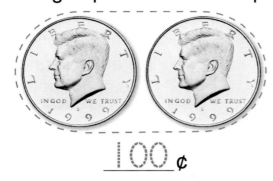 _100_ ¢

2.  _90_ ¢

3.  _100_ ¢

4.  _400_ ¢

Circle the correct way to write each amount.

5.   ¢30   30¢ $30

6.    1.00$ ¢100   ($1.00)

Problem Solving • Reasoning

Write About It

7. Megan has this coin.   Randy has these coins.

Both have $1.00. Explain why.

At Home Provide examples of things you can buy in a market for about one dollar. Ask your child to show the cost using different coin combinations.

	Standards
	NS 5.0, 5.1, 5.2

LESSON 11 Make Change

Learn About It

When you pay more than the price
for an item, you get change.

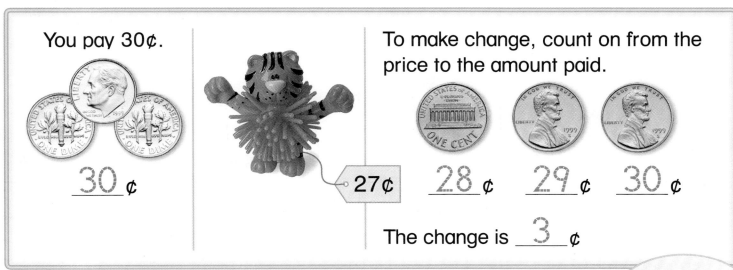

You pay 30¢.

__30__ ¢

27¢

To make change, count on from the
price to the amount paid.

__28__ ¢   __29__ ¢   __30__ ¢

The change is __3__ ¢

What will my change be?

Guided Practice

Write the amount paid. Count on from
the price to find the change.

Amount Paid	Price	Count On	Change
1. __20__ ¢	16¢	__17__ ¢ __18__ ¢ __19__ ¢ __20__ ¢	__4__ ¢
2. ___ ¢	32¢	__33__ ¢ ___ ¢ ___ ¢	___ ¢

Explain Your Thinking Tell how you could subtract to find the change.

Independent Practice

Write the amount paid. Count on from the price
to find the change.

Amount Paid	Price	Count On	Change
1. _50_ ¢	48¢	_49_ ¢ _50_ ¢	_2_ ¢
2. _40_ ¢	37¢	_1_ ¢ _1_ ¢ _1_ ¢	___ ¢
3. $___.___	98¢	___ ¢ ___ ¢	___ ¢
4. ___ ¢	32¢	___ ¢ ___ ¢ ___ ¢	___ ¢

Problem Solving • Reasoning

Using Vocabulary

5. Jamal pays for a puppet with
   1 **half dollar** and 1 **quarter**. How
   much change will he get?

71¢   _____ ¢

Draw or write to explain.

At Home Ask your child to explain how he or she counts change.

Name_____

LESSON 12

Problem Solving: Multistep Problems

Standards
NS **5.0, 5.1**
MR **1.1, 1.2**

Sometimes more than one step
is needed to solve a problem.

Joey had 90¢. He spent 20¢.
His sister borrowed a quarter.
How much money does Joey have left?

You can use coins to show each step in the problem.

Step 1 How much money did Joey have left
after he spent 20¢?
Show the coins Joey had after he spent 20¢.

Think:
How much did Joey
start with? Do I add or
subtract the 20¢?

Joey has _____ ¢.

Step 2 How much money did Joey have
after his sister borrowed a quarter?

Show the coins Joey had after he gave
his sister a quarter.

Think:
A quarter is 25¢. Do I
add or subtract 25¢?

Joey had _____ ¢ left.

Guided Practice

Solve. Use coins if you need to.

1 Kara had 3 dimes, 2 nickels, and 1 penny. She spent a nickel. Then her aunt gave her 2 dimes. How much money does Kara have?

Think: What should I do first?

Kara has _____ ¢

Draw or write to explain.

2 Carlos had 42¢. He earned 2 dimes. Then he got 12¢ from his mother. How much money does Carlos have?

Think: Do I add or subtract 2 dimes? Do I add or subtract 12¢?

Carlos has _____ ¢

3 Inez had 35¢. She gave 10¢ to her sister. Then she gave 15¢ to her brother. How much money does Inez have left?

Think: Do I add or subtract 10¢? Do I add or subtract 15¢?

Inez has _____ ¢ left

4 Bill had 85¢. He spent 50¢. How much more does he need to buy a notebook that costs 49¢?

Think: What are the steps to solve the problem?

He needs _____ ¢ more

At Home Have your child use coins to show you how he or she solved each problem.

Name_____

Choose a Strategy

Solve.

① Amber has 85¢. She buys 2
packs of laces for her roller
skates. Each pack costs 40¢.
How much does Amber have left?

_____ ¢

Draw or write to explain.

roller skates

② Pedro had 70¢. He earned 20¢.
Then he spent 40¢ on elbow
pads. How much money
does he have left?

_____ ¢

elbow pads

③ Reiko has 4 dimes. She gets
a quarter. She wants to buy
a helmet strap for 75¢. How
much more does she need?

_____ ¢

helmet

④ Jake has 30¢. He earns 2
nickels. The knee pads he wants
to buy cost 25¢ more than he has.
How much are the knee pads?

_____ ¢

knee pads

Mixed Practice

Memorize Your Facts

Add or subtract.

1.	8 + 8	2.	12 − 3	3.	9 − 7	4.	6 + 3	5.	10 + 1	6.	13 − 8

7.	11 − 3	8.	4 + 5	9.	3 + 6	10.	5 + 8	11.	17 − 8	12.	16 − 6

13.	14 − 7	14.	6 + 9	15.	12 − 5	16.	15 − 9	17.	4 + 8	18.	11 − 9

19. _____ = 6 + 7   20. _____ = 5 + 10   21. _____ = 7 + 9

22. 3 + 2 = _____ + 3   23. 8 + 5 = 5 + _____   24. 9 + 8 = _____

Brain Teaser Quarters, Dimes and Nickels

Cindy has 6 coins. She has quarters, dimes, and nickels. The total amount is 60¢. How many of each coin does she have?

_____ _____ _____

Safe Site

Internet Brain Teasers
Visit **www.eduplace.com/kids/mhm**
for more *Brain Teasers*.

Check Your Understanding of Lessons 7-12

Write the total amount.

1.

    _____¢

2.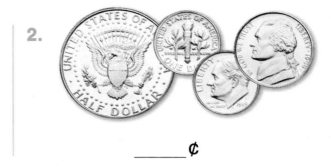

    _____¢

3. Draw coins with the greatest value to show the amount.

61¢

4. Circle the coins that make 46¢.

5. Count on from the price to find the change.
   Write the answers in the chart.

Amount Paid	Price	Count on	Change
 _____¢	27¢	_____¢ _____¢ _____¢	_____¢

Solve each problem.

6. Sal has 2 quarters and 1 nickel. He spends 42¢ for a notebook. How much more does he need to buy a pencil for 20¢?

    _____¢ more

7. Mary has 55¢. She spends 12¢ on a pencil. Then she gets 15¢. How much does she have now?

    _____¢

Test Prep • Cumulative Review
Maintaining the Standards

Fill in the ○ for the correct answer.

1 Mark the related number sentence for 9 + 3 = 12.

○ 12 + 3 = 15
○ 9 − 3 = 6
○ 6 + 3 = 9
○ 12 − 3 = 9

2 Mark the correct way to show the amount.

45¢ $45   ¢45   45$
○   ○   ○   ○

3 Jessie has these coins.

She spends 27¢. How much money does she have left?

27¢   13¢   18¢   8¢
○   ○   ○   ○

4 Choose a sign to make the sentence true.

89   89

>   <   =   ¢
○   ○   ○   ○

Use the pictograph to answer Questions 5 and 6.

Goals Scored				
Dana	☻	☻	☻	☻
Pete	☻	☻	☻	

Each ☻ stands for 1 goal.

5 How many goals did Dana score?

2   3   4   5
○   ○   ○   ○

6 How many goals were scored in all? _____ goals

Explain how you found your answer.

_____

_____

Copyright © Houghton Mifflin Company. All rights reserved.

Internet Test Prep
Visit **www.eduplace.com/kids/mhm**
for more *Test Prep Practice.*

Safe Site

Chapter Review

Name_____

Write the value for each coin.

	Coin	Amount
1.	penny	_1_ ¢
2.	nickel	_1_ ¢
3.	dime	_5_ ¢

	Coin	Amount
4.	quarter	_1_ ¢
5.	half-dollar	_50_ ¢
6.	dollar	_0_ ¢

7. Write one **dollar**.
Use a **dollar sign** and **decimal point**. _____

Write the total amount.

8.

_25_ ¢   _0_ ¢   _10_ ¢   _10_ ¢   _1_ ¢   _56_ ¢ total

9.

_100_ ¢ total

10. Draw coins to show two ways to make 25¢.

25¢   25 + 0 = 25   20 + 5

25¢   25 + 0 = 25

11. Write the total value of each group of coins.
Compare. Write >, <, or = in the ◯.

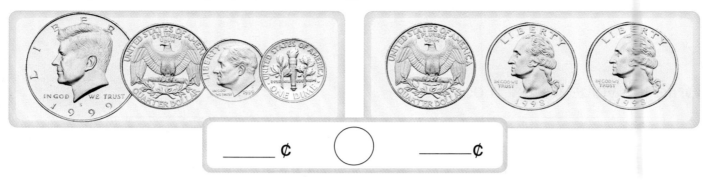

_____ ¢ ◯ _____ ¢

12. Show 40¢ with coins.
Draw the coins.

| 40¢ | |

13. Circle the coins you need.

35¢

14. Write the amount paid.
Count on from the price to find the change.

Amount Paid	Price	Count On			Change
_____ ¢	37¢	_____ ¢	_____ ¢	_____ ¢	_____ ¢

Solve each problem.

15. Eli has 2 quarters, 2 dimes and a nickel. How much more does she need to buy a pen for 89¢? _____ ¢

Draw or write to explain.

16. Lee has a quarter and 2 dimes. His aunt gives him 3 more dimes. Then he uses 35¢ to buy a toy. How much does he have now? _____ ¢

Chapter Test

Write the total amount.

1.

   25 ¢ 25 ¢ 10 ¢ ___ ¢   61 ¢
   total

2.

   40 ¢
   total

3. Draw coins to show two ways to make 35¢.

   35¢  35¢

   35 + 0 = 35
   3¢ + 8 = 35

   20 + 5 = 35
   35 + 0 = 35

4. Write each amount. Compare. Write **>**, **<**, or **=**.

   40 ¢ < 60 ¢

5. Show 39¢ with coins.
   Draw the coins.

   39¢

6. Circle the coins you need.

   31¢

Write the amount paid.
Count on from the price to find the change.

	Amount Paid	Price	Count On			Change
7.	_____ ¢	57¢	_____ ¢ _____ ¢ _____ ¢			_____ ¢
8.	_____ ¢	98¢	_____ ¢ _____ ¢			_____ ¢

Solve each problem.

Draw or write to explain.

9. Lee has 2 quarters, 2 dimes, and 1 penny. How much more money does he need to buy a toy for 79¢? _____ ¢

10. Maria has 67¢. Her aunt gives her 3 dimes. She buys a ruler for 22¢. How much does she have now? _____ ¢

Write About It

Mai makes a mistake counting her coins.
She counts them this way.
Explain what she does wrong.

50¢   60¢   70¢   80¢   85¢

_____

_____

Go for the Money

What You Need

game piece
number cube labeled 1, 2, 3, 1, 2, 3
nickels, dimes, and quarters

How to Play

① Put game pieces on start.

② Take turns tossing the number cube.
Move that many spaces.

③ Follow the directions on the space where you land.

④ The first player to collect $1.00 wins.

Take 10¢.	Take 20¢.	Take 3 nickels.	Put back 1 nickel.	Skip a turn.

START

Take 1 quarter.

Take 2 dimes.	Put back 15¢.	Take 2 nickels.	Take 1 dime.	Put back 10¢.

Name

Standards
NS 5.1

Enrichment

Ways to Show Amounts

Think:

and

equals 55¢.

Make each amount using the number
of coins shown.

55¢				
2 coins				
3 coins				
4 coins				
5 coins				
6 coins				

80¢				
3 coins				
4 coins				
5 coins				
6 coins				
7 coins				

Copyright © Houghton Mifflin Company. All rights reserved.

**Adding
Two-Digit
Numbers**

Dinosaurs Everywhere!

A Read-Aloud Story

written *by* **Sarah Curran**
illustrated *by* **Gary Johnson**

Accessing Prior Knowledge

This story will help
you review
- skip counting
  by 10s
- adding 10s

WAREHOUSE MANAGER

A Math Storybook for

_____

Ring! Ring! Ring!
HOW MANY stegosaurs will you bring?
10 per crate; 4 crates in all?
Where will I put them? They're really not small.

How many stegosaurs will arrive?

10, 20, 30 , 40

Ring! Ring! Ring!
HOW MANY triceratopses will you bring?
10 per crate; 7 crates in all?
There's not enough space—even in the hall!

How many triceratopses will arrive?

10, 20, 30, __40__, __50__, __60__, __70__

Ring! Ring! Ring!
HOW MANY tyrannosaurs will you bring?
10 per crate; 8 crates in all?
Where will they fit? They're big and tall!

How many tyrannosaurs will arrive?

10, 20, 30, 40, __50__, __60__, __70__, __8__

Ring! Ring! Not again! Oh, no!
HOW MANY apatosaurs are going to show?
10 per crate; 5 crates in all?
Where will I put them? This isn't a mall!

How many apatosaurs will arrive?

10, 20, 30 , 40 , 50

Wait, wait ... There MUST be a mistake!
There won't be room, for goodness' sake.
The museum director I will call
to find how many crates will be here in all.

How many crates will arrive?

_20_ crates

Copyright © Houghton Mifflin Company. All rights reserved.

Well, now I see that each dinosaur
is a MODEL to sell in the museum store!
There's plenty of room—no problem with space.
And dinosaurs WON'T take over the place!

Family Letter

Dear Family,

During the next few weeks, our math class will be learning about two-digit addition with and without regrouping.

You can expect to see work that provides practice with two-digit addition. There will also be work that provides practice with adding money.

As we learn about two-digit addition, you may wish to use the following as a guide.

Vocabulary

estimate To find an answer that is close to an exact answer.

number line A line that shows numbers in order.

regroup To rename a number by trading 10 ones for 1 ten.

sum The answer to an addition exercise.

To add

$$\begin{array}{r} 25 \\ +3 \end{array}$$

Step 1 Add the ones.

Tens	Ones
2	5
+	3
	8

Step 2 Add the tens.

Tens	Ones
2	5
+	3
2	8

To add

$$\begin{array}{r} 25 \\ +8 \end{array}$$

Step 1 Add the ones.

5 + 8 = 13 ones
Regroup 10 ones as 1 ten.

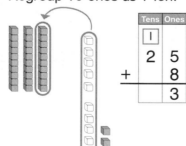

Tens	Ones
1	
2	5
+	8
	3

Step 2 Add the tens.

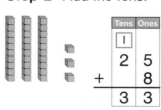

Tens	Ones
1	
2	5
+	8
3	3

Sincerely,
Your child's teacher

Standards
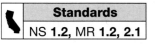
NS **1.2**, MR **1.2, 2.1**

Hands-On Activity

LESSON 3

Regroup Ones

Review
Vocabulary
regroup

Learn About It

Regroup 10 ones as 1 ten to show a number in another way.

Here is one way to show 35.

Workmat	
Tens	**Ones**

Regroup 10 ones as 1 ten.

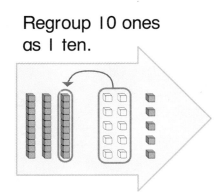

Here is another way to show 35.

Workmat	
Tens	**Ones**

2 tens 15 ones = 35

3 tens 5 ones = 35

Guided Practice

Use Workmat 3 with  and ⬜.
Regroup **10 ones** as 1 ten.

Think:
I am regrouping 10 ones as 1 ten.

1.

___3___ tens ___12___ ones

Regroup ➡

___4___ tens ___2___ ones = ___42___

2.

_____ tens _____ ones

Regroup ➡

_____ tens _____ ones = _____

Explain Your Thinking Why can you regroup 10 ones as 1 ten?

Independent Practice

Use Workmat 3 with 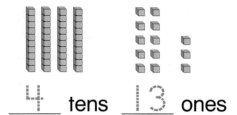 and ⬛.
Regroup **10 ones** as 1 ten.

1.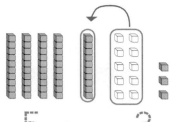

   Regroup ➡

   __4__ tens __13__ ones   __5__ tens __3__ ones = __53__

2. 3 tens 17 ones = __47__

3. 6 tens 15 ones = _____

4. 4 tens 10 ones = _____

5. 2 tens 16 ones = _____

6. 2 tens 14 ones = _____

7. 3 tens 12 ones = _____

8. 1 tens 13 ones = _____

9. 4 tens 15 ones = _____

10. 7 tens 10 ones = _____

11. 8 tens 11 ones = _____

12. 4 tens 14 ones = _____

13. 2 tens 12 ones = _____

Problem Solving • Reasoning

Number Sense

14. Circle the pictures that show 32.

15. **Write About It**   Explain why the pictures you circled show 32.

At Home Give your child a handful of objects such as cereal or macaroni. Have him or her count the objects by making groups of ten.

Name _____

Standards
NS **2.2, 5.1,** MR **1.2**

Decide When to Regroup

Learn About It

If there are 10 or more ones,
regroup 10 ones as 1 ten.

You have 3 tens and 5 ones.
You want to add 7 ones.

Step 1 Show 3 tens and 5 ones. Add 7 ones.	**Step 2** Regroup 10 ones as 1 ten.	**Step 3** How many in all?
Workmat	**Workmat**	**Workmat**
Tens | Ones	Tens | Ones	Tens | Ones
		4 tens 2 ones

Guided Practice

Use Workmat 3 with ▭▭▭▭ and ▫.

	Show this many.	**Add.**	**Do you need to regroup?**	**How many in all?**
1.	1 ten 3 ones	9 ones	(yes) no	_2_ tens _2_ ones
2.	4 tens 8 ones	4 ones	yes no	____ tens ____ ones
3.	6 tens 2 ones	5 ones	yes no	____ tens ____ ones

Explain Your Thinking How do you know when
you need to regroup?

Independent Practice

Use Workmat 3 with ▭▭▭▭▭▭ and ▫.

	Show this many.	Add.	Do you need to regroup?	How many in all?
1.	5 tens 7 ones	5 ones	(yes) no	__6__ tens __2__ ones
2.	6 tens 6 ones	8 ones	yes no	_____ tens _____ ones
3.	3 tens 4 ones	5 ones	yes no	_____ tens _____ ones
4.	2 tens 3 ones	7 ones	yes no	_____ tens _____ ones
5.	4 tens 2 ones	6 ones	yes no	_____ tens _____ ones
6.	7 tens 1 one	8 ones	yes no	_____ tens _____ ones
7.	2 tens 7 ones	6 ones	yes no	_____ tens _____ ones
8.	3 tens 5 ones	9 ones	yes no	_____ tens _____ ones

Problem Solving • Reasoning

Number Sense

9. Jan has 2 dimes and 5 pennies. She gets 9 more pennies. How many dimes and pennies does she have now?

_____ dimes _____ pennies

10. If Jan trades 10 pennies for 1 dime, how many dimes and pennies will she have?

_____ dimes _____ pennies

At Home Have your child look at the exercises on this page and explain why he or she did or did not need to regroup.

Name _____

Add One-Digit Numbers

Learn About It

Knowing when to regroup can help you add.

Find 26 + 8.

Step 1 Show 26 and 8. Add 6 ones and 8 ones.	**Step 2** Regroup 10 ones as 1 ten.	**Step 3** Add the tens.

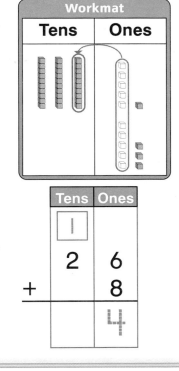

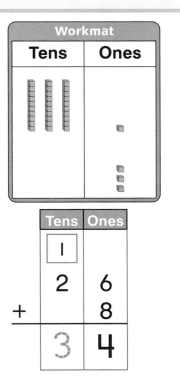

Guided Practice

Use Workmat 3 with ▭▭▭▭ and ▫. Add.

1.

Tens	Ones
1	
3	7
+	5
4	2

Think: Do I need to regroup when I add 7 ones and 5 ones?

2.

Tens	Ones
5	3
+	9

3.

Tens	Ones
4	5
+	3

Explain Your Thinking Did you regroup in Exercise 2? Why or why not?

Independent Practice

Use Workmat 3 with  and ▪.
Add. Regroup if you need to.

Think: Do I need to regroup when I add the ones?

1.

Tens	Ones
[1]	
3	4
+	7
4	1

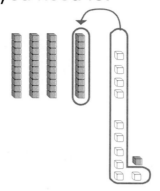

2.

Tens	Ones
[ ]	
4	5
+	9

3.

Tens	Ones
[ ]	
4	6
+	4

4.

Tens	Ones
[ ]	
	3
+ 6	3

5.

Tens	Ones
[ ]	
1	7
+	9

6.

Tens	Ones
[ ]	
2	7
+	5

7.

Tens	Ones
[ ]	
	8
+ 3	5

8.

Tens	Ones
[ ]	
5	7
+	2

9.

Tens	Ones
[ ]	
	7
+ 8	4

10.

Tens	Ones
[ ]	
9	0
+	6

Problem Solving•Reasoning

Number Sense

11. Write these digits in the boxes to make two addition exercises. Then write each sum.

3 5 6

Add with regrouping. | **Add without regrouping.**

☐ ☐   ☐ ☐
+ ☐   + ☐

Draw or write to explain.

At Home Ask your child why he or she regrouped in Exercise 3 and not in Exercise 4.

Name _____

Standards
NS **2.2**, AF **1.0**
MR **1.2**

Add Two-Digit Numbers

Learn About It

Regroup when there are 10 or more ones.

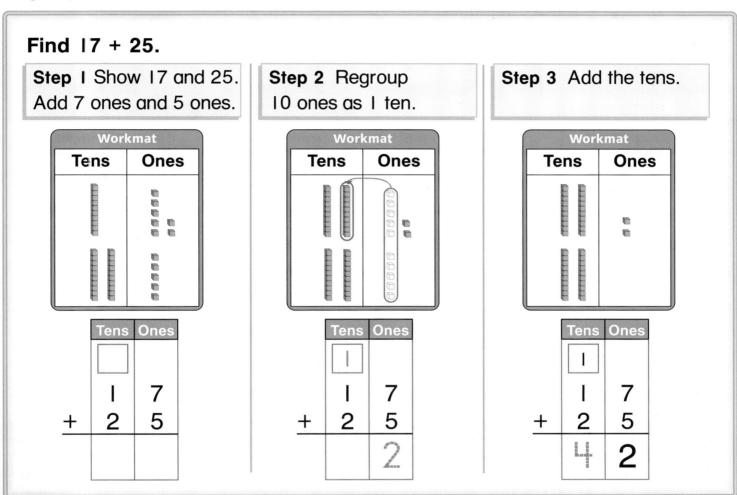

Find 17 + 25.

Step 1 Show 17 and 25. Add 7 ones and 5 ones.

Step 2 Regroup 10 ones as 1 ten.

Step 3 Add the tens.

Tens	Ones
1	7
+ 2	5

Tens	Ones
1	
1	7
+ 2	5
	2

Tens	Ones
1	
1	7
+ 2	5
4	2

Guided Practice

Use Workmat 3 with ▭▭▭▭ and ▫. Add.

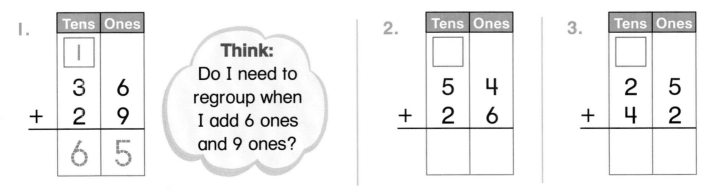

1.

Tens	Ones
1	
3	6
+ 2	9
6	5

Think: Do I need to regroup when I add 6 ones and 9 ones?

2.

Tens	Ones
5	4
+ 2	6

3.

Tens	Ones
2	5
+ 4	2

Explain Your Thinking 3 tens 16 ones is the same as 4 tens 6 ones. How does knowing this help you add?

Independent Practice

Use Workmat 3 with 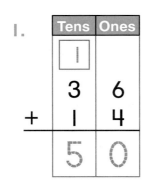 and ▪.
Add. Regroup if you need to.

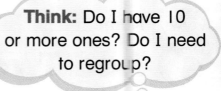

Think: Do I have 10 or more ones? Do I need to regroup?

1.

Tens	Ones
1	
3	6
+ 1	4
5	0

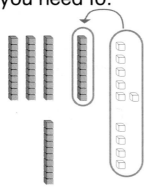

2.

Tens	Ones
4	5
+	8

3.

Tens	Ones
2	5
+ 4	5

4.

Tens	Ones
5	4
+ 3	7

5.

Tens	Ones
6	1
+ 2	8

6.

Tens	Ones
3	3
+ 1	8

7.

Tens	Ones
2	9
+ 2	1

8.

Tens	Ones
3	2
+	6

9.

Tens	Ones
2	6
+ 5	7

10.

Tens	Ones
1	9
+ 1	4

Problem Solving • Reasoning

Algebra Readiness · Number Sentences

11. Use two numbers from below.
Write a number sentence with
a sum of 30.

17   18   13   20

Think: Look for ones digits that add to 10.

_____ + _____ = 30

Draw or write to explain.

At Home Ask your child how he or she found the sums on this page and how he or she knew when to regroup.

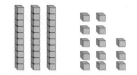

Quick ✓ Check

Check Your Understanding of Lessons 1–6

Add.

1. 30 + 20 = _____

2. 40 + 25 = _____

3. 71 + 20 = _____

Use Workmat 3 with ▭▭▭▭ and ◻.

4. Regroup to show one more ten.

Regroup 10 ones.

_____ tens _____ ones

Use Workmat 3 with ▭▭▭▭ and ◻.

	Show this many.	Add.	Do you need to regroup?	How many in all?
5.	3 tens 4 ones	7 ones	yes no	_____ tens _____ ones

Add. Regroup if you need to.

6.
Tens	Ones
□	
4	3
+	9

7.
Tens	Ones
□	
6	1
+	8

8.
Tens	Ones
□	
1	8
+	5

9.
Tens	Ones
□	
2	7
+	3

10.
Tens	Ones
□	
2	6
+ 1	5

11.
Tens	Ones
□	
5	0
+	9

12.
Tens	Ones
□	
3	2
+ 4	8

13.
Tens	Ones
□	
8	4
+ 1	3

Name_____

Test Prep • Cumulative Review
Maintaining the Standards

Fill in the ○ for the correct answer. NH means Not Here.

1 What number is seventy-three?

37   63   73   78
○   ○   ○   ○

2 Mark how much money Troy has.

33   42   47   65
○   ○   ○   ○

3 Add.
70 + 20 = ▨

9   70   90   NH
○   ○   ○   ○

4 Subtract.
11 − 7 = ▨

3   5   7   NH
○   ○   ○   ○

5 There are 9 muffins. 6 are apple. How many are not apple? Mark the number sentence that solves the problem.

○ 9 − 6 = 3
○ 6 + 9 = 15
○ 9 − 7 = 2
○ 15 − 6 = 9

6 Mark the value of the red digit.

48

4   8   40   80
○   ○   ○   ○

7 Sue has 15¢. She finds a nickel. Now how much money does she have? _____¢

Explain how you found your answer.

_____

_____

Copyright © Houghton Mifflin Company. All rights reserved.

Safe Site

Internet Test Prep
Visit www.eduplace.com/kids/mhm
for more *Test Prep Practice.*

LESSON 7

Practice Regrouping 10 to 12

Review Vocabulary
regroup

Learn About It

If there are 10, 11, or 12 ones,
regroup 10 ones as 1 ten.

At the museum our class
saw 34 shell fossils and
16 leaf fossils. How many
fossils did we see?

Tens	Ones
1	
3	4
+ 1	6
5	0

We saw 50 fossils.

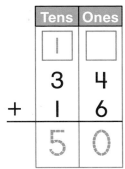

Remember to
regroup 10 ones
as 1 ten.

Guided Practice

Add. Regroup if you need to.

1.
Tens	Ones
1	
5	5
+ 2	6
8	1

2.
Tens	Ones
1	9
+ 4	3

3.
Tens	Ones
3	5
+ 2	5

Think:
Do I have 10 or
more ones? Do I need
to regroup?

4.
2	2
+ 6	0

5.
2	4
+	7

6.
4	7
+ 1	3

7.
3	6
+	6

Explain Your Thinking How many ones can you have
before you need to regroup? Tell why.

Independent Practice

Add. Regroup if you need to.

1. ₁
    3 3
    + 4 7
    8 0

2.
    5 1
    + 1 9

3.
    3 2
    +   7

4.
    2 6
    + 3 5

5.
    7 7
    +   5

6.
    4 8
    + 3 3

7.
    2 5
    + 1 5

8.
    1 0
    + 2 2

9. 5 1
    + 3 1
    8 2

10. 2 9
    + 5 2

11. 3 4
    +   8

12. 6 8
    + 1 2

13. 4 1
    + 3 4

Problem Solving·Reasoning

Using Data

14. How many children chose dinosaurs?

    _25_ children

15. Five children changed from planets to rockets. Now how many children chose rockets?

    _25_ children

16. **Write Your Own** Write a subtraction problem using information in the graph. Then solve.

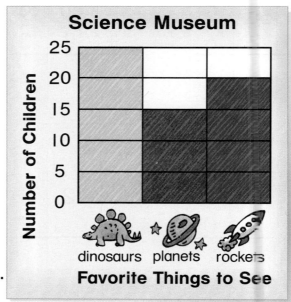

Science Museum

Number of Children

dinosaurs planets rockets

Favorite Things to See

At Home Ask your child to solve exercises such as 25 + 26 and 34 + 15. Have your child explain why regrouping is sometimes necessary.

Standards
NS **2.2**, AF **1.3**
SDP **2.2**

LESSON 8 Practice Regrouping 13 to 15

Learn About It

If there are 13, 14, or 15 ones,
regroup 10 ones as 1 ten.

A dinosaur has a neck that
is 35 feet long. The rest of
its body is 49 feet long.
How long is the dinosaur?

Tens	Ones
1	
3	5
+ 4	9
8	4

The dinosaur is 84 feet long.

Guided Practice

Add. Regroup if you need to.

1.
Tens	Ones
1	
3	6
+ 4	7
8	3

2.
Tens	Ones
1	
2	9
+ 6	5
9	4

→14

3.
Tens	Ones
1	
4	8
+ 2	7
7	5

→15

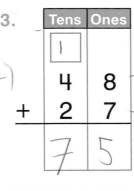

Think: What
questions should I ask
myself as I add?

4.
5	4
+ 3	1
8	5

5.
1	
4	7
+	7
5	4

→14

6.
1	
3	4
+ 4	9
8	3

→13

7.
1	
2	6
+	9
3	5

→15

Explain Your Thinking What addition facts can you use
to help you add 26 and 19? Why?

Independent Practice

Add. Regroup if you need to.

1.
4	7
+ 4	6
9	3

2.
5	3
+ 1	8
7	1

3.
3	0
+ 2	3
5	3

4.
2	9
+	6
3	5

5.
1	3
+ 3	2
4	5

6.
2	7
+ 3	7
6	4

7.
4	9
+	2
5	1

8.
4	8
+ 3	5
8	3

9.
```
  1 9
+ 7 5
  9 4
```

10.
```
  3 6
+ 3 4
  7 0
```

11.
```
  2 1
+ 6 1
  8 2
```

12.
```
  3 6
+ 0 7
  4 3
```

13.
```
  4 6
+   9
  5 5
```

14.
```
  3 7
+ 2 4
  6 1
```

15.
```
  2 5
+   8
  3 3
```

16.
```
  1 9
+ 5 5
  7 4
```

17.
```
  7 8
+ 1 7
  9 5
```

18.
```
  4 2
+ 3 0
  7 2
```

Problem Solving • Reasoning

Patterns

19. There are 4 stones in a box.
Kayla buys 5 boxes.
How many stones does she buy?
Complete the table to help you.

Boxes	1	2	3	4	5
Stones	4	8	12	16	20

_20_ stones

At Home Ask your child if regrouping is needed to answer these addition exercises and explain why: 56 + 13 (no); 48 + 15 (yes).

Standards
NS **2.2**

LESSON 9 Practice Regrouping 16 to 18

Learn About It

If there are 16, 17, or 18 ones,
regroup 10 ones as 1 ten.

Remember to regroup 10 ones as 1 ten.

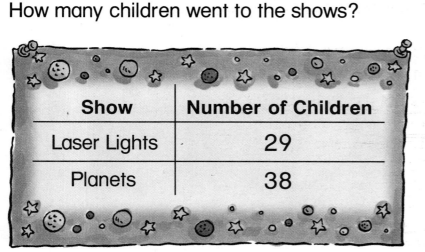

How many children went to the shows?

Show	Number of Children
Laser Lights	29
Planets	38

Tens	Ones
1	
2	9
+ 3	8
6	7

_67_ children

Guided Practice

Add. Regroup if you need to.

1. ⬜
   4 8
+ 3 8
   8 6

2. 1
   2 9 >17
+ 6 8
   9   7

3. ⬜
   3 7
+ 1 2
   4 9

4. 1
   2 9 >18
+ 5 9
   8 8

5. 1 7 >16
+ 2 9
  4 6

6. 4 6 >10
+   4
  5 0

7. 3 8 >17
+ 2 9
  6 7

8. 7 9 >16
+ 1 7
  9 6

9. 5 3 >
+ 3 4
  8 7

10. 3 1
+ 2 5
  5 6

11. 4 5
+ 1 9 >14
  6 9

12. 6 8 >16
+   8
  7 6

13. 2 7 >15
+ 5 8
  8 5

14. 1 9 >17
+ 4 8
  6 7

Explain Your Thinking Did you need to regroup in
Exercises 2 and 3? Explain why or why not.

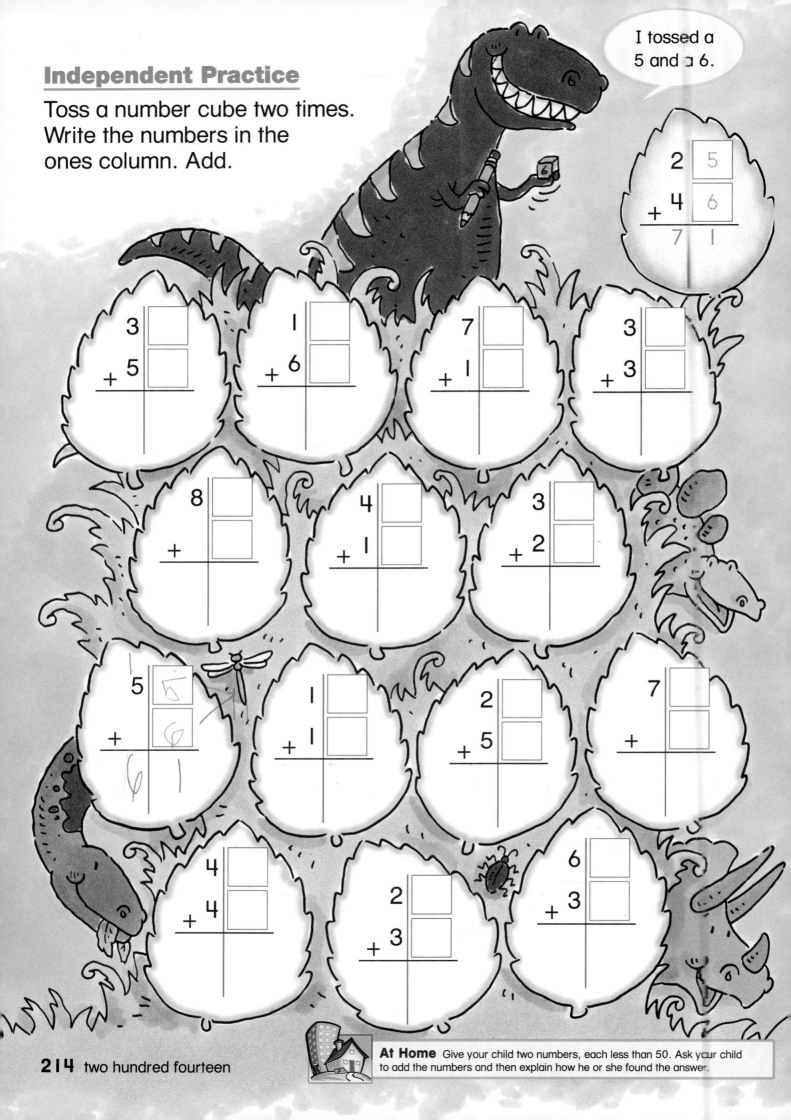

Independent Practice

Toss a number cube two times.
Write the numbers in the
ones column. Add.

I tossed a
5 and a 6.

```
  2 | 5
+ 4 | 6
-------
  7 | 1
```

```
3 |   |
+ 5 |   |
--------
```

```
1 |   |
+ 6 |   |
--------
```

```
7 |   |
+ 1 |   |
--------
```

```
3 |   |
+ 3 |   |
--------
```

```
8 |   |
+   |   |
--------
```

```
4 |   |
+ 1 |   |
--------
```

```
3 |   |
+ 2 |   |
--------
```

```
5 | 5 |
+   | 6 |
--------
  6 | 1
```

```
1 |   |
+ 1 |   |
--------
```

```
2 |   |
+ 5 |   |
--------
```

```
7 |   |
+   |   |
--------
```

```
4 |   |
+ 4 |   |
--------
```

```
2 |   |
+ 3 |   |
--------
```

```
6 |   |
+ 3 |   |
--------
```

214 two hundred fourteen

At Home Give your child two numbers, each less than 50. Ask your child
to add the numbers and then explain how he or she found the answer.

Name _____

LESSON 10 Estimate Sums

New
Vocabulary
number line
round
estimate

Learn About It

You can use a **number line** to **round** a number to the nearest ten. This can help you **estimate** a sum.

Use the number line to estimate.

Step 1 Round each number to the nearest ten.	**Step 2** Add.

<──┼──┼──┼──┼──┼──┼──┼──┼──┼──┼──>
30 31 32 33 34 35 36 37 38 39 **40**

39 nearest ten → 40
+32 nearest ten → +30

$$\begin{array}{r} 40 \\ +30 \\ \hline 70 \end{array}$$

Guided Practice

Use the number line. Round each number to the nearest ten. Estimate the sum.

Think: Which is the nearest ten?

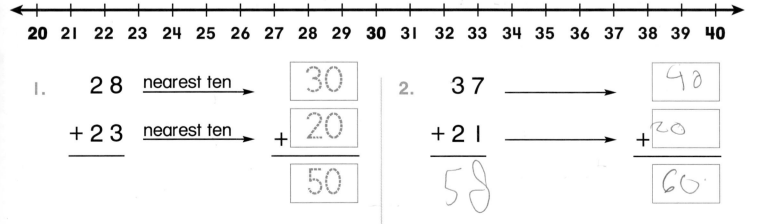

<──┼──>
20 21 22 23 24 25 26 27 28 29 **30** 31 32 33 34 35 36 37 38 39 **40**

1. 28 nearest ten → 30
   +23 nearest ten → +20
                      50

2. 37 ⟶ 40
   +21 ⟶ +20
          58   60

Explain Your Thinking How did you estimate the sum in Exercise 2?

two hundred fifteen **215**

Independent Practice

Use the number line. Round each number
to the nearest ten. Estimate the sum.

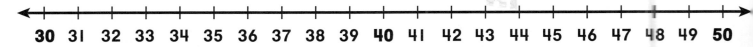

30 31 32 33 34 35 36 37 38 39 **40** 41 42 43 44 45 46 47 48 49 **50**

1.   3 8   nearest ten →   ⌜40⌝

     + 4 9   nearest ten → + ⌜50⌝

                            ⌜90⌝

2.   3 3   ————→   30

     + 3 1   ————→ + 30

            64   60

3.   4 7   ————→   50

     + 3 2   ————→ + 30

            80   80

4.   3 9   ————→   40

     + 3 7   ————→ + 40

                          88

5.   3 1   ————→   30

     + 4 3   ————→ + 40

            70   70

6.   4 2   ————→   40

     + 4 8   ————→ + 50

                          90

Problem Solving • Reasoning

7. **Estimate** The museum shop has
   32 nature posters and 43 planet
   posters. About how many posters
   are there?

   about 75 posters

8. **Write About It** The museum shop
   should always have about 55 posters.
   Do they need to order more? Explain.

Draw or write to explain.

At Home Discuss with your child the times when you
can estimate and the times when you need an exact answer.

Copyright © Houghton Mifflin Company. All rights reserved.

Name_____

Problem Solving: Guess and Check

You can guess which numbers to use to solve a problem. Then you can check your guess.

Jack buys 40 dinosaur stickers. Which two different packs of stickers does he buy?

Understand

What information would you use?

Jack buys _____ stickers.

He buys _____ different packs.

Plan

**Choose 2 different packs.
How can you check your guess?**

add   subtract

Solve

Try the large and jumbo packs.

Large   24
Jumbo   ⊕ 32
          ―――
           56

Think:
56 is too much.
Try again.

Medium ☐
Large ○ ☐
         ―――
        ☐

Look Back

**Did you find which two packs Jack bought?
How do you know?**

Guided Practice

Guess and check to solve each problem.

These bags of gems are sold in the museum store.

44
+21
65

+15
59

| 15 red | 21 blue | 37 green | 44 purple |

Remember:
► Understand
► Plan
► Solve
► Look Back

① Carl buys 52 gems. Which two different color gems did he buy?

Think: Which two bags have a total of 52?

_____red_____ and _____green_____

Draw or write to explain.

② Maria needs 65 gems to make a necklace. Which two different color gems should she get?

Think: Is my first guess correct? Do I need to try again?

___Purple___ and ___blue___

③ Marty gives 58 gems to his friend as a gift. Which two different color gems did he give?

Think: What two bags will I guess first?

___green___ and ___blue___

The museum shop sold two bags of gems on Friday. There were 74 gems in all. Which two bags were sold?

Think: Which two bags will give me a total of 74 gems?

_____ and _____

At Home Make up a problem like the ones on this page. Have your child solve it and explain the answer to you.

Name _____

Choose a Strategy

Solve.

Strategies

Use Models to Act It Out
Draw a Picture
Guess and Check

① Globes come in boxes of 12, 18, and 24. Mrs. Sung wants to buy 30 globes for her classroom. Which two boxes should she buy?

box of _____

box of _____

Draw or write to explain.

globe

② The museum shop has 12 model rockets. 4 are sold. How many model rockets are left?

_____ model rockets

rocket

③ Planet picture cards come in sets of 14, 28, and 36 cards. Leon buys a total of 64 cards. Which two sets did he buy?

set of _____

set of _____

planet

④ The museum shop has 6 fossils. Then it buys 38 more. How many fossils does the shop have now?

_____ fossils

fossil

Mixed Practice

Add or subtract.

1. $17 - 9 =$ _____   2. $9 + 9 =$ _____   3. $16 - 8 =$ _____

4. _____ $= 4 + 3$ 5. _____ $= 8 + 8$ 6. _____ $= 5 + 7$

Add. Regroup if you need to.

7. $\begin{array}{r} 1\,0 \\ +\,1\,0 \\ \hline \end{array}$
8. $\begin{array}{r} 3\,7 \\ +\ \ 9 \\ \hline \end{array}$
9. $\begin{array}{r} 4\,5 \\ +\,3\,8 \\ \hline \end{array}$
10. $\begin{array}{r} 3\,6 \\ +\,3\,1 \\ \hline \end{array}$
11. $\begin{array}{r} 6\,1 \\ +\,3\,3 \\ \hline \end{array}$

12. $\begin{array}{r} 1\,8 \\ +\,4\,1 \\ \hline \end{array}$
13. $\begin{array}{r} 5\,6 \\ +\ \ 9 \\ \hline \end{array}$
14. $\begin{array}{r} 3\,7 \\ +\,2\,4 \\ \hline \end{array}$
15. $\begin{array}{r} 3\,1 \\ +\,5\,0 \\ \hline \end{array}$
16. $\begin{array}{r} 4\,5 \\ +\,2\,8 \\ \hline \end{array}$

17. $\begin{array}{r} 6 \\ +\,9\,2 \\ \hline \end{array}$
18. $\begin{array}{r} 4\,4 \\ +\,2\,9 \\ \hline \end{array}$
19. $\begin{array}{r} 4\,3 \\ +\,1\,7 \\ \hline \end{array}$
20. $\begin{array}{r} 2\,0 \\ +\,4\,5 \\ \hline \end{array}$
21. $\begin{array}{r} 1\,5 \\ +\,1\,5 \\ \hline \end{array}$

 Brain Teaser

The page numbers on facing pages of a book have a sum of 25. What are the numbers?

_____ and _____

 **Internet Brain Teasers**
Visit www.eduplace.com/kids/mhm
for more *Brain Teasers*.

Quick ✓ Check

Check Your Understanding of Lessons 7–11

Add. Regroup if you need to.

1. 2 7
   + 4 3

2. 3 6
   +   6

3. 1 3
   + 1 5

4. 3 8
   + 4 7

5. 5 6
   + 2 7

6. 3 7
   + 3 7

7. 4 1
   + 2 8

8. 6 9
   + 2 8

9. 2 5
   + 4 6

10. 3 9
    +   9

Use the number line. Round each number
to the nearest ten. Estimate the sum.

30 31 32 33 34 35 36 37 38 39 **40** 41 42 43 44 45 46 47 48 49 **50**

11. 3 6 nearest ten ⟶ ☐
    + 4 2 nearest ten ⟶ + ☐
    ⎯⎯⎯   ⎯⎯⎯
                           ☐

12. 4 8 ⟶ ☐
    + 3 2 ⟶ + ☐
    ⎯⎯⎯   ⎯⎯⎯
              ☐

Solve the problem.

Second Grade Classes	
Room	**Number of Children**
Room A	28
Room B	32
Room C	27

Draw or write to explain.

13. Two classes went to the museum.
    There were 55 children in all. Which
    two classes went to the museum?

    _____ and _____

Test Prep • Cumulative Review

Maintaining the Standards

Fill in the ○ for the correct answer. NH means Not Here.

1 Mark the number that is greater than 94.

37   49   94   98
○   ○   ○   ○

2 Add.   5 7
              + 2 4

71   81   82   NH
○   ○   ○   ○

3 What number means 6 tens + 2?

62   60   26   8
○   ○   ○   ○

4 Estimate the sum.

28 + 34

○ about 20
○ about 40
○ about 60
○ about 80

5 Tom has two coins in his pocket. Their total value is 75¢. What coins are they?

○ 1 half-dollar, 1 quarter
○ 2 quarters
○ 2 half-dollars
○ 1 half-dollar, 1 dime

6   2 5   3 6
           + 3 6   + 2 5
         ┌──────┐   ┌──────┐
         │ ?   │   │ ?   │
         └──────┘   └──────┘

Will both sums be the same? **Explain** how you know.

_____

_____

_____

_____

_____

Copyright © Houghton Mifflin Company. All rights reserved.

Safe Site

Internet Test Prep
Visit www.eduplace.com/kids/mhm
for more *Test Prep Practice.*

Standards

NS **2.2, 2.3,** AF **1.1**

MR **1.1, 2.0**

LESSON 12 Different Ways to Add

64
+ 20

Which way would you choose to add?

I would use mental math...64, 74, 84.

I would use tens and ones blocks.

I would use paper and pencil.

I would use a hundred chart.

Guided Practice

Choose a way to add. Circle it.
Then add.

1. 33
   +60
   _93_

   mental math

   hundred chart

2. 48
   +20
   _68_

   mental math

   hundred chart

3. 37
   +18
   _55_

   tens and ones blocks

   paper and pencil

4. 56
   +23
   _74_

   tens and ones blocks

   paper and pencil

Add.

5. 62
   +31
   _93_

6. 22
   +49
   _71_

7. 71
   +20
   _91_

8. 50
   +30
   _80_

9. 19
   +29
   _48_

Explain Your Thinking Which ways did you choose
to add in Exercises 6 and 8? Tell why.

Independent Practice

Add.

Ways to Add

mental math
hundred chart
tens and ones blocks
paper and pencil

1. 52
  +18
  70

2. 36
  +61
  97

3. 79
  + 4
  93

4. 29
  +36
  65

5. 43
  +20
  63

6. 18
  +58
  77

7. 78
  +13
  91

8. 35
  +37
  77

9. 49
  +48
  97

10. 66
  + 5
  71

11. 29
  +50
  74

12. 36
  +54
  90

13. 57
  +21
  78

14. 79
  + 7
  6

15. 19
  +59

16. 37
  +48

17. 63
  +30

18. 24
  +57

Problem Solving • Reasoning

Algebra Readiness · Number Sentences

Draw the missing .
Complete the number sentence.

19.

43 + 30 = ____ + 43

20. **Write About It** Explain how you found your answer.

At Home Ask your child to name and explain the different ways to add.

LESSON 13 Horizontal Addition

Learn About It

Rewrite the numbers to help you add.

Find 47 + 26.

Step 1 Rewrite the numbers.	**Step 2** Add.

$$\begin{array}{cc} & 4 \;|\; 7 \\ + & 2 \;|\; 6 \\ \hline \end{array}$$

$$\begin{array}{cc} & {}^{1} \\ & 4 \;|\; 7 \\ + & 2 \;|\; 6 \\ \hline & 7 \;|\; 3 \end{array}$$

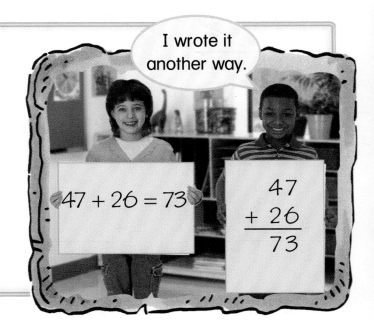

I wrote it another way.

$47 + 26 = 73$

$$\begin{array}{r} 47 \\ + 26 \\ \hline 73 \end{array}$$

Guided Practice

Rewrite the numbers. Then add.

1. 45 + 9

$$\begin{array}{cc} & 4 \;|\; 5 \\ + & \;|\; 9 \\ \hline & 5 \;|\; 4 \end{array}$$

Think: Do I write the 9 in the ones or the tens column?

2. 28 + 17

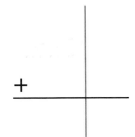

3. 64 + 8

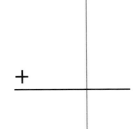

4. 36 + 16

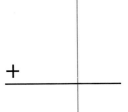

5. 18 + 72

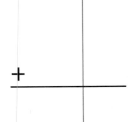

6. 63 + 25

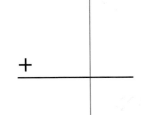

7. 28 + 53

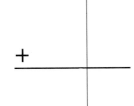

Explain Your Thinking To find 52 + 8, do you add 8 tens or 8 ones? How do you know?

Independent Practice

Rewrite the numbers. Then add.

1. 48 + 39

$$\begin{array}{r} 4\ 8 \\ +\ 3\ 9 \\ \hline 8\ 7 \end{array}$$

2. 59 + 15

+

3. 86 + 4

+

4. 27 + 34

+

5. 16 + 46

+

6. 25 + 46

+

7. 45 + 51

+

8. 39 + 9

+

9. 57 + 6

+

10. 65 + 19

+

11. 46 + 33

+

12. 23 + 67

+

Problem Solving • Reasoning

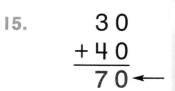

Using Vocabulary

Write a vocabulary word for each exercise.

| regroup | sum | round |

13.

67 $\xrightarrow{\text{nearest ten}}$ 70

_____

14.

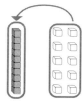

_____

15.

$$\begin{array}{r} 3\ 0 \\ +\ 4\ 0 \\ \hline 7\ 0 \end{array} \leftarrow$$

_____

At Home Choose a two-digit number less than 50. Ask your child to choose another number less than 50. Then have your child add the 2 numbers.

Name _____

	Standards
	NS **2.2, 5.0, 5.2**
	MR **2.0**

LESSON 14

Add Money

Learn About It

Use a cent sign when you add money.

Donna buys a  and a _____.
How much does she spend?

```
  1
  69¢
+ 19¢
─────
  88¢
```

Donna spends 88¢.

> Remember to write the ¢.

69¢   19¢   11¢

Guided Practice

Add.

1.
```
  29¢
+ 35¢
─────
  64¢
```

2.
```
  13¢
+ 42¢
─────
```

3.
```
  56¢
+ 37¢
─────
```

4.
```
  21¢
+ 49¢
─────
```

5.
```
  84¢
+  7¢
─────
```

Rewrite the numbers. Then add.

6. 17¢ + 69¢

```
    1 7¢
+   6 9¢
───────
    8 6¢
```

7. 36¢ + 6¢

8. 64¢ + 18¢

9. 38¢ + 7¢

Explain Your Thinking How is adding 39¢ and 19¢
like adding 39 and 19?

two hundred twenty-seven **227**

Independent Practice

Remember to write the ¢.

Add.

1.　57¢
　　+35¢
　　92¢

2.　48¢
　　+12¢

3.　27¢
　　+37¢

4.　69¢
　　+ 7¢

5.　47¢
　　+46¢

6.　62¢
　　+ 9¢

7.　47¢
　　+45¢

8.　12¢
　　+ 9¢

9.　36¢
　　+31¢

10.　24¢
　　+69¢

Rewrite the numbers. Then add.

11. 29¢ + 44¢

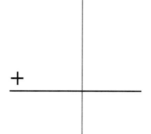

```
   2 9 ¢
 + 4 4 ¢
   7 3 ¢
```

12. 52¢ + 15¢

13. 75¢ + 5¢

14. 38¢ + 54¢

Problem Solving·Reasoning

Write About It

15. Tara has 75¢. She wants to buy the 🐞 and the 🔦. Does she have enough money? Explain how you know.

16. **Write Your Own** Write an addition problem about the pictures. Then solve.

55¢

24¢

31¢

47¢

At Home Help your child cut out two grocery ads for items each less than 50¢. Ask your child to find the total cost of the two items.

Standards
AF **1.1**, MR **2.0, 3.0**

LESSON 15
Algebra Readiness:
Add Three Numbers

Learn About It

You can add three numbers in
any order and get the same sum.

I look for 10s.
10 + 3 = 13

I look for a double fact.
7 + 6 = 13

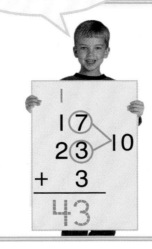
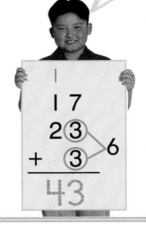

Add the ones.
Regroup if you need to.
Add the tens.

```
  1 7
  2 3
+   3
-----
  43
```

Guided Practice

Add.

1.
```
  3 2
  2 2
+ 1 6
-----
  70
```

2.
```
  2 6
  2 4
+ 2 3
-----
  73
```

3.
```
  1 6
  1 2
+ 3 4
-----
  62
```

4.
```
  1 6
  2 5
+ 3 5
-----
  76
```

5.
```
  4 2
    3
+ 1 4
-----
  58
```

6.
```
    8
  2 7
+ 4 2
-----
  77
```

7.
```
  1 9
  1 0
+ 2 3
-----
  52
```

8.
```
  2 1
  1 4
+ 3 3
-----
  68
```

9.
```
  2 6
  1 1
+ 1 6
-----
  53
```

10.
```
  5 2
    7
+ 1 3
-----
  72
```

11.
```
  2 6
  4 1
+ 1 0
-----
  77
```

12.
```
  1 6
  2 3
+   2
-----
```

13.
```
  4 5
  1 4
+ 2 4
-----
```

14.
```
  3 8
  2 1
+ 1 3
-----
```

15.
```
  2 7
  1 5
+ 2 2
-----
```

Explain Your Thinking Why can you add three numbers in any order?

Independent Practice

Add.

1. 19
    16
    +24
    ____
    59

2. 62
    19
    + 4
    ____

3. 17
    30
    +52
    ____

4. 61
     3
    +14
    ____

5. 27
    12
    +57
    ____

6. 14
    30
    +13
    ____

7. 53
    17
    + 8
    ____

8. 21
    42
    +13
    ____

9. 18
     4
    +36
    ____

10.   2
     34
    +27
    ____

11. 28
    11
    + 2
    ____

12. 41
    19
    +27
    ____

13. 9
    13
    +23
    ____

14. 12
    13
    +41
    ____

15. 34
    32
    +16
    ____

Problem Solving·Reasoning

Algebra Readiness · Properties

Complete the number sentences.

Think: Work inside the ( ) first

16. $(12 + 4) + 10 = $ __?__

    __16__ + 10 = ____

    $12 + (4 + 10) = $ __?__

    12 + ____ = ____

17. $(15 + 3) + 11 = $ __?__

    ____ + 11 = ____

    $15 + (3 + 11) = $ __?__

    15 + ____ = ____

18. **Write About It** Can adding the numbers in any order help you check your answer? Explain why.

At Home Have your child use three numbers to write his or her own addition problem and then solve it.

Copyright © Houghton Mifflin Company. All rights reserved.

Name _____

LESSON 16

Problem Solving:
Use Data From a Picture

Standards	
NS **5.0, 5.2**, AF **1.3**,	
MR **1.1, 3.0**	

You can use data from a
picture to solve a problem.

These gifts are on sale
in the museum shop.

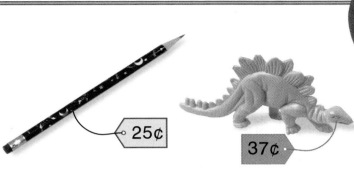

25¢   37¢   29¢

You can add to find the total amount spent.

Luke buys a globe and a pencil.
How much does he spend?

[　　] ¢ globe

+ [　　] ¢ pencil
———————
[　　] ¢ total cost

Think: Use the picture
to find the prices. Add
to find the total cost.

You can compare to see if there is enough money.

Anna has 65¢. Does she have enough
to buy a dinosaur and a pencil?

[　　] ¢ dinosaur

+ [　　] ¢ pencil
———————
[　　] ¢ total cost

Does Anna have enough money?   yes

no

Think: Find the
total cost of the
dinosaur and pencil.

Think: Is the total cost
greater than, less than,
or equal to the amount
Anna has?

Guided Practice

Use the pictures to solve each problem.

18¢   9¢   57¢   28¢   3(

① Gina buys a crystal and a rocket. How much does she spend?

Think: What information do I need from the picture?

_93_ ¢

Draw or write to explain.

② Jose wants to buy a flashlight and a patch. What is the total cost?

Think: How much does each item cost?

_____ ¢

③ Felix has 35¢. Does he have enough money to buy a dinosaur and a patch?

Think: What do I need to find?

The total cost is _____ ¢.
Does he have enough money?   yes   no

④ Lily has 60¢. Does she have enough money to buy a patch, a dinosaur, and a rocket?

Think: What do I need to do first?

The total cost is _____ ¢.
Does she have enough money?   yes   no

At Home Choose two items from the pictures above.
Ask your child how much money he or she would need to buy them.

Name _____

Choose a Strategy

Solve.

1 A toy stegosaur costs 43¢. Margo buys one for herself and one for her brother. How much does she spend?

Draw or write to explain.

_____ ¢

stegosaur

2 The museum shop has 15 toy triceratopses. 7 of them are sold. How many toy triceratopses are left?

_____

triceratops

3 Apatosaur stickers come in packs of 16, 24, and 34. Nina wants to buy 40 stickers. Which two packs should she buy?

pack of _____

pack of _____

apatosaur

4 Keith buys a tyrannosaur for 81¢. He pays with 3 quarters and 1 dime. How much change does he get?

_____ ¢

tyrannosaur

Mixed Practice

Add or subtract.

1. 10 + 9 = _____   2. 8 + 7 = _____   3. 5 + 0 = _____

4. 57   5. 84¢   6. 16   7. 77   8. 35
  +33   + 6¢   +51   +19   +15

9. 43¢   10. 72   11.   8   12. 19¢   13. 24
  +12¢   +15   +45   +54¢   +68

Rewrite each problem. Then add.

14. 10¢ + 12¢   15. 32 + 59   16. 25 + 50   17. 49 + 38

+ _____   + _____   + _____   + _____

Brain Teaser Find the Addends

Use four of the digits below to make a sum of 83. You can use a digit only once.

    3   4   5   6   7

+
‾‾‾‾‾
  8 3

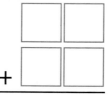

Internet Brain Teasers
Visit **www.eduplace.com/kids/mhm**
for more *Brain Teasers*.

Name _____

Check Your Understanding of Lessons 12–16

Add.

1. 7 3
   +2 0

2. 4 7 ¢
   +3 9 ¢

3. 2 8
   + 3

4. 7 1 ¢
   +1 9 ¢

5. 3 3
   +5 4

Rewrite the numbers. Then add.

6. 12 + 58

   +

7. 37 + 37

   +

8. 65¢ + 26¢

   +

Add.

9. 5 1
    1 1
   +2 9

10. 4 0
       8
    +1 2

11. 3 1
    3 2
   +3 3

12.   7
    2 1
   +4 5

13. 2 4
    3 7
   +1 0

Use the pictures to solve the problem.

41¢
fossil

35¢
globe

36¢
rocket

14. Marta has 75¢ to spend in the museum gift shop. What two items could she buy?

_____ and _____

Draw or write to explain.

Test Prep • Cumulative Review

Maintaining the Standards

Fill in the ○ for the correct answer. NH means Not Here.

1 Mark the one that is **not** a way to show thirty-six.

○ 30 + 6

○ 3 tens 6 ones

○ 3 tens 6 tens

○ 36

2 Add.   43¢
           + 19¢

62¢ 52¢ 51¢ NH
○   ○   ○   ○

3 Mark the number that will make the sentence true.

7 + 8 = 8 + ■

8   7   6   5
○   ○   ○   ○

4 Add.

28 + 48 = ■

66   70   74   NH
○   ○   ○   ○

Use the graph to answer Question 5.

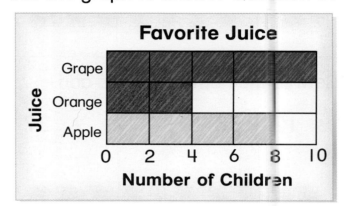

5 How many more children chose grape than orange?

3   4   6   10
○   ○   ○   ○

6 Make tally marks to show the number of books.

Books	~~||||~~ |||

Explain how the tally marks show how many books there are.

_____

_____

Internet Test Prep
Visit **www.eduplace.com/kids/mhm**
for more *Test Prep Practice*.

Safe Site

Copyright © Houghton Mifflin Company. All rights reserved.

Name _____

Chapter Review

Use the example to answer Exercises 1–3.

$\boxed{1}$

```
  5 7
+ 3 6
─────
  9 3
```

1. Which number is the **sum**? _____

2. When Julie added, she got 13 ones. Julie **regrouped** the 13 ones as _____ ten _____ ones.

3. Which number did Julie **add** to 57? _____

---

4. Pedro estimated to find 28 + 44. Circle the one that shows an **estimate**.

```
  3 0
+ 4 0
─────
  7 0
```

$\boxed{1}$
```
  2 8
+ 4 4
─────
  7 2
```

5. Here are 43 toy dinosaurs.

Kylie wants to **round** the number of dinosaurs to the nearest 10. What number should she get? _____

Add.

6.
```
  6 0
+ 2 0
─────
```

7.
```
  4 5
+   7
─────
```

8.
```
  5 3
+ 1 7
─────
```

9.
```
  3 5
+ 3 7
─────
```

10.
```
  7 1
+ 2 6
─────
```

Rewrite the numbers. Then add.

11. 68 + 17

12. 59¢ + 9¢

13. 28 + 48

14. 25¢ + 39¢

+

+

+

+

Add.

15.
```
  3 2
  4 2
+ 1 5
```

16.
```
  5 4
  1 6
+ 2 5
```

17.
```
  4 1
  3 3
+   9
```

18.
```
  2 6
  4 0
+ 2 6
```

19.
```
  3 5
  1 4
+ 1 1
```

Use the number line. Round each number to the nearest ten.
Estimate the sum.

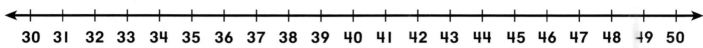

30 31 32 33 34 35 36 37 38 39 40 41 42 43 44 45 46 47 48 49 50

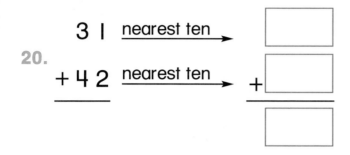

20.
```
  3 1   nearest ten →  [   ]
+ 4 2   nearest ten →  +[   ]
                        [   ]
```

21.
```
  4 8   ————→  [   ]
+ 3 1   ————→  +[   ]
                [   ]
```

Use the pictures to solve each problem.

21 blue   37 green   44 purple

22. Marc buys 81 stones. Which
    two different color gems does
    he buy?

Draw or write to explain.

_____ and _____

23. Kayla buys a dinosaur and a pencil.
    She pays with 85¢.
    What is her change?

35¢   47¢   63¢

Draw or write to explain.

_____ ¢

Copyright © Houghton Mifflin Company. All rights reserved.

Name _____

Chapter Test

Add.

1. 40
   +30

2. 57
   + 9

3. 34¢
   +34¢

4. 48
   +29

5. 26
   +44

6. 88
   + 7

7. 65
   +19

8. 36
   +45

9. 20¢
   +10¢

10. 28
    +28

Rewrite the numbers. Then add.

11. 50¢ + 37¢

   +

12. 39 + 29

   +

13. 57 + 5

   +

Use the number line to estimate the sum.

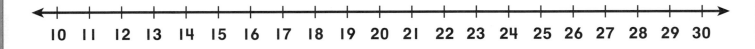

10 11 12 13 14 15 16 17 18 19 20 21 22 23 24 25 26 27 28 29 30

14. 11 <u>nearest ten</u> ⟶ ☐

    +29 <u>nearest ten</u> ⟶ + ☐
                                 ☐

15. 24 ⟶ ☐

    +27 ⟶ + ☐
              ☐

Add.

16.
```
  2 8
  1 3
+ 4 8
```

17.
```
  4 7
  3 3
+   6
```

18.
```
  1 5
  1 9
+ 2 5
```

Guess and check to solve the problem.
Use the pictures.

19. Bart buys 34 stickers.
Which two different
packs does Bart buy?

_____ pack   _____ pack

20. The total of the stickers is 87¢.
Bart pays with 90¢.
What is his change?

_____ ¢

Draw or write to explain.

Write About It

Two classes went to the museum.
Mr. Sun's class has 25 children. Miss
Gold's class has 28 children. How
many children went to the museum?

Ashley made a mistake when she
solved the problem this way.

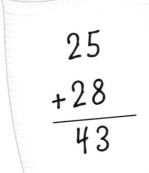

```
  25
+ 28
  43
```

What was Ashley's mistake?

_____

_____

Show how she can solve the
problem correctly.

Draw or write to explain.

Copyright © Houghton Mifflin Company. All rights reserved.

Add It Up!

Players
2

What You Need

- number cards (10–48)
- paper and pencil for each player

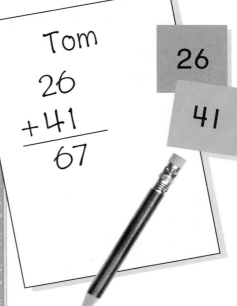

Tom
26
+41
67

26
41

How to Play

① Mix the cards. Place them face down. Each player takes two cards.

② Add the two numbers and find the sum.

③ The player with the greatest sum gets 1 point. When all the cards are used, mix them up and use them again.

④ The first player to get 10 points wins!

Enrichment

Comparing Sums

Find each sum.
Use >, <, or = to make
each sentence true.

1. 65 + 21 (?) 21 + 42

   __86__ (>) __63__

   | Draw or write to explain. |

2. 50 + 18 (?) 17 + 62

   ____ ◯ ____

3. 72 + 26 (?) 26 + 72

   ____ ◯ ____

4. 18 + 36 (?) 25 + 35

   ____ ◯ ____

5. 24 + 42 (?) 21 + 36

   ____ ◯ ____

6. 51 + 26 (?) 44 + 34

   ____ ◯ ____

Copyright © Houghton Mifflin Company. All rights reserved.

CHAPTER 6

Subtracting Two-Digit Numbers

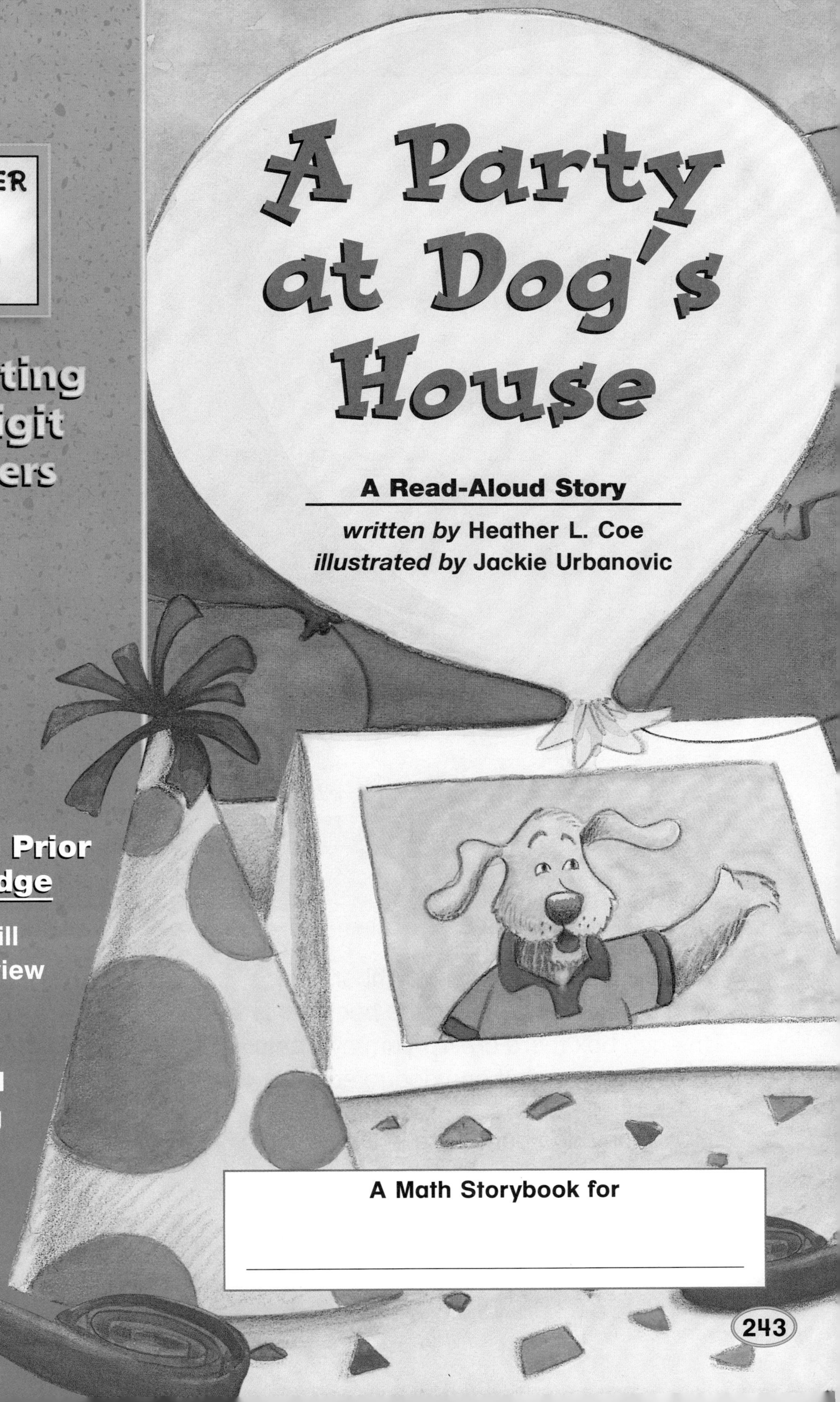

A Party at Dog's House

A Read-Aloud Story

written by Heather L. Coe
illustrated by Jackie Urbanovic

Accessing Prior Knowledge

This story will help you review

- Counting by tens
- Adding and subtracting

A Math Storybook for

____

A friend of Dog's is our neighbor Dan,
with 8 boxes of bones in the back of his van.
In each box there are 10 yummy treats.
That's a lot for just one dog to eat!

How many dog bones are in Dan's van?

10, 20, 30, __40__, __50__, __60__, __70__, __80__

As Dan was driving to a party for Dog,
his van ran over a very big log.
Bump! Bump! The van gave a jump,
and so 4 boxes fell out with a thump!

How many boxes fell out of the van? 4

How many bones is that? 40

Cat and Mouse each gave a shout
when they saw the 4 boxes of bones fall out.
They grabbed every box that they could see.

Mouse carried one box. Cat carried __3__ .

Down the road, Dan swerved past a tree.
The boxes bounced high—and out fell 3!
Bang! Bam! Boom! They crashed to the ground.
One box burst open, leaving bones all around.

How many boxes fell out of the van? _____

How many bones is that? _____

Frog and Fox saw the bones fly past.
They ran to the boxes and grabbed those bones fast.
Frog got 2 bones plus 1 full box,
and 8 bones plus 1 full box went to Fox.

How many bones does each animal have? Frog 12   Fox 18

Who has more bones? _fox does_

At Dog's party, poor Dan was quite blue.
He only had 1 box: "Oh, boo hoo!"
Then—surprise!—Cat and Mouse had brought 4.
And Fox and Frog came with 30 bones more.

How many bones were brought to Dog's house? __80__

Family Letter

SCHOOLVILLE USA

Vocabulary

difference The answer to a subtraction problem.

estimate To find an answer that is close to the exact number.

number line A line that shows numbers in order.

regroup To rename a number by trading 1 ten or 10 ones.

Dear Family,

During the next few weeks, our math class will be learning about two-digit subtraction with and without regrouping.

You can expect to see work that provides practice with two-digit subtraction. There will also be work that provides practice with using money.

As we learn about 2-digit subtraction, you may wish to use the following as a guide.

To subtract

$$38 - 5$$

Step 1 Subtract the ones.

Tens	Ones
3	8
−	5
	3

Step 2 Subtract the tens.

Tens	Ones
3	8
−	5
3	3

To subtract

$$32 - 5$$

Step 1 Regroup a ten.

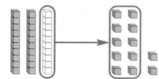

Take apart 1 ten to make 10 ones. $10 + 2 = 12$ ones

Step 2 Subtract.

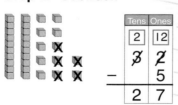

Tens	Ones
2	12
3	2
−	5
2	7

Sincerely,

Your child's teacher

250

Standards
NS **1.1, 2.3**, AF **1.3**

LESSON 1 · Mental Math: Subtract Tens

Learn About It

You can use mental math to find a **difference**.
When you **subtract** tens, think of a subtraction fact.

> **Review Vocabulary**
> **difference**
> **subtract**

5 tens − 3 tens = __2__ tens

> Think: 5 − 3 = 2

50 − 30 = 20
↑
difference

5 − 3 = 2

50 − 30 = 20

Guided Practice

Find each difference.

1. 8 tens − 4 tens = __4__ tens
   > Think: 8 − 4 = ?

   80 − 40 = 40

2. 6 tens − 3 tens = ____ tens
   > Think: 6 − 3 = ?

   60 − 30 = ____

3. 9 tens − 4 tens = ____ tens
   > Think: 9 − 4 = ?

   90 − 40 = ____

4. 7 tens − 5 tens = ____ tens
   > Think: 7 − 5 = ?

   70 − 50 = ____

5. 5 tens − 1 ten = ____ tens
   > Think: What fact should I use?

   50 − 10 = ____

6. 4 tens − 2 tens = ____ tens
   > Think: What fact should I use?

   ____ − ____ = ____

Explain Your Thinking How does knowing 4 − 2 = 2
help you solve 40 − 20?

Independent Practice

Find each difference.
Write the subtraction sentence.

Remember to use subtraction facts.

1. 9 tens − 7 tens = __2__ tens

   __90__ − __70__ = __20__

2. 3 tens − 1 ten = _____ tens

   _____ − _____ = _____

3. 8 tens − 3 tens = _____ tens

   _____ − _____ = _____

4. 5 tens − 2 tens = _____ tens

   _____ − _____ = _____

5. 3 tens − 2 tens = _____ ten

   _____ − _____ = _____

6. 7 tens − 2 tens = _____ tens

   _____ − _____ = _____

7. 8 tens − 1 ten = _____ tens

   _____ − _____ = _____

8. 9 tens − 3 tens = _____ tens

   _____ − _____ = _____

Problem Solving • Reasoning

Logical Thinking

Read the clues. Write each number.

Draw or write to explain.

9. You say it when you count by tens.
   It is greater than 50.
   It is less than 70. _____

10. You say it when you count by tens.
    It is less than 90.
    It is greater than 70. _____

At Home Give your child up to 9 dimes. Together create subtraction exercises. For example: 8 dimes − 3 dimes = 5 dimes; 80 − 30 = 50.

Copyright © Houghton Mifflin Company. All rights reserved.

	Standards
	NS 2.2, 2.3

LESSON 2 Subtract Without Regrouping

Learn About It

Sometimes you can use a tens and ones chart to help you subtract.

Tens	Ones
5	7
−	4
5	3

Sometimes you can use a hundred chart to help you subtract.

Find 57 − 30.

Step 1 Find 57 on the hundred chart.

Step 2 Count back 30 by subtracting 3 tens.

(57) 47, 37, 27

57 − 30 = _27_

1	2	3	4	5	6	7	8	9	10
11	12	13	14	15	16	17	18	19	20
21	22	23	24	25	26	27	28	29	30
31	32	33	34	35	36	37	38	39	40
41	42	43	44	45	46	47	48	49	50
51	52	53	54	55	56	57	58	59	60
61	62	63	64	65	66	67	68	69	70
71	72	73	74	75	76	77	78	79	80
81	82	83	84	85	86	87	88	89	90
91	92	93	94	95	96	97	98	99	100

Guided Practice

Subtract. Use the hundred chart.

Think:
Where do I start on the chart?
How many tens do I subtract?

1. 89 − 20 = _69_   2. 56 − 50 = ____

3. 77 − 40 = ____   4. 95 − 30 = ____

5. 43 − 30 = ____   6. 70 − 40 = ____

7. 3 9
   − 2 5
   _____

8. 6 2
   − 5 0
   _____

9. 3 5
   − 1 3
   _____

10. 9 3
    − 5 0
    _____

11. 5 8
    − 4 2
    _____

Explain Your Thinking Look at 61, 51, 41, and 31 on the hundred chart. Describe the pattern. What number comes next?

Independent Practice

Subtract.
Use the hundred chart.

1. 31 − 10 = _21_

2. 65 − 40 = ____

3. 74 − 30 = ____

4. 89 − 70 = ____

5. 55 − 20 = ____

6. 29 − 10 = ____

1	2	3	4	5	6	7	8	9	10
11	12	13	14	15	16	17	18	19	20
21	22	23	24	25	26	27	28	29	30
31	32	33	34	35	36	37	38	39	40
41	42	43	44	45	46	47	48	49	50
51	52	53	54	55	56	57	58	59	60
61	62	63	64	65	66	67	68	69	70
71	72	73	74	75	76	77	78	79	80
81	82	83	84	85	86	87	88	89	90
91	92	93	94	95	96	97	98	99	100

7.
```
  44
- 20
```

8.
```
  67
- 40
```

9.
```
  92
- 60
```

10.
```
  17
- 10
```

11.
```
  90
- 80
```

12.
```
  63
- 40
```

13.
```
  31
- 20
```

14.
```
  86
- 50
```

15.
```
  79
- 30
```

16.
```
  45
- 10
```

Problem Solving • Reasoning

17. There are 48 dog bones in a box.
Jane gives 10 bones to her dog.
How many bones are left?

_____ bones

Draw or write to explain.

At Home Have your child choose a number greater than 50 from the chart above and subtract 10, 20, 30, 40, and 50 from it.

Copyright © Houghton Mifflin Company. All rights reserved.

Standards
NS **1.2**, MR **1.2, 2.1**

Regroup Tens

Review
Vocabulary
regroup

Learn About It

Regroup 1 ten as 10 ones to show
a number in another way.

Here is one way to show 34.		Here is another way to show 34.

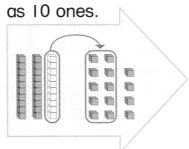

Regroup 1 ten
as 10 ones.

3 tens 4 ones = 34   2 tens 14 ones = 34

Guided Practice

Use Workmat 3 with and ▪ .
Regroup **1 ten** as 10 ones.

1. 53

Think:
I am regrouping
1 ten as 10 ones.

__5__ tens __3__ ones   Regroup   __4__ tens __13__ ones

2. 46

Regroup

_____ tens _____ ones   _____ tens _____ ones

Explain Your Thinking Why can you regroup 1 ten as 10 ones?

Independent Practice

Use Workmat 3 with 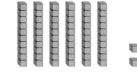 and ■.
Regroup **1 ten** as 10 ones.

1. | 62 | ⫼⫼⫼ : | Regroup ⟹ | __5__ tens __12__ ones |

2. 49 = __3__ tens __19__ ones

3. 32 = _____ tens _____ ones

4. 20 = _____ tens _____ ones

5. 54 = _____ tens _____ ones

6. 81 = _____ tens _____ ones

7. 75 = _____ tens _____ ones

8. 23 = _____ tens _____ ones

9. 68 = _____ tens _____ ones

10. 37 = _____ tens _____ ones

11. 90 = _____ tens _____ ones

12. 42 = _____ tens _____ ones

13. 56 = _____ tens _____ ones

Problem Solving•Reasoning

Write About It

14. Billy showed 37 this way. | Jill showed 37 this way.

Both are correct. Explain why.

Draw or write to explain.

At Home Your child is learning to regroup 1 ten as 10 ones. Ask your child to look at the exercises on this page and explain what he or she did.

Name _____

LESSON 4 Decide When to Regroup

Learn About It

If there are not enough ones to subtract, regroup 1 ten as 10 ones.

You have 2 tens and 4 ones.
You want to take away 5 ones.

Step 1 Show 2 tens and 4 ones. Are there enough ones to take away 5 ones?

Workmat	
Tens	**Ones**

Step 2 Regroup 1 ten as 10 ones.

Workmat	
Tens	**Ones**

Step 3 Take away 5 ones. How many are left?

Workmat	
Tens	**Ones**

1 ten 9 ones

Guided Practice

Use Workmat 3 with ▭▭▭▭ and ▫.

	Show this many.	Take away.	Do you need to regroup?	How many are left?
1.	4 tens 2 ones	7 ones	(yes) no	_3_ tens _5_ ones
2.	5 tens 4 ones	9 ones	yes no	____ tens ____ ones
3.	3 tens 6 ones	2 ones	yes no	____ tens ____ ones

Explain Your Thinking How do you know when you need to regroup?

Independent Practice

Use Workmat 3 with  and ▪.

	Show this many.	Take away.	Do you need to regroup?		How many are left?
1.	5 tens 6 ones	7 ones	(yes)	no	__4__ tens __9__ ones
2.	4 tens 3 ones	8 ones	yes	no	____ tens ____ ones
3.	3 tens 7 ones	7 ones	yes	no	____ tens ____ ones
4.	6 tens 5 ones	3 ones	yes	no	____ tens ____ ones
5.	2 tens 4 ones	7 ones	yes	no	____ tens ____ ones
6.	7 tens 2 ones	9 ones	yes	no	____ tens ____ ones
7.	9 tens 8 ones	5 ones	yes	no	____ tens ____ ones
8.	3 tens 4 ones	6 ones	yes	no	____ tens ____ ones

Problem Solving • Reasoning

Draw or write to explain.

Write About It

9. Rita has 2 dimes and 5 pennies.
   She wants to give a friend 8 pennies.
   Explain how she can do this.

10. Rita gave her friend the 8 pennies.
    Find how much money Rita has left.

    _____ ¢

At Home Have your child explain one problem on this page. Then ask how he or she knew whether to regroup or not in Exercises 3 and 5.

LESSON 5

Subtract One-Digit Numbers

Learn About It

Knowing when to regroup can help you subtract.

Find 43 − 5.

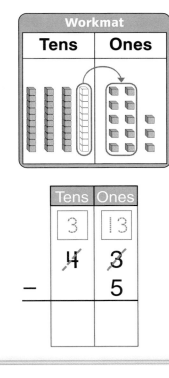

Step 1 Show 43. Can you take away 5 ones?

Tens	Ones
4	3
−	5

Step 2 Regroup 1 ten as 10 ones.

Tens	Ones
3	13
4	3
−	5

Step 3 Subtract.

Tens	Ones
3	13
4	3
−	5
3	8

Guided Practice

Use Workmat 3 with ▭▭▭▭ and ▪. Subtract.

1.

Tens	Ones
2	12
3	2
−	4
2	8

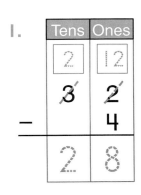

Think:
Are there enough ones to take away 4 ones? Do I need to regroup?

2.

Tens	Ones
5	4
−	6

3.

Tens	Ones
4	6
−	3

Explain Your Thinking Did you regroup in Exercise 1? Why or why not?

Independent Practice

Use Workmat 3 with 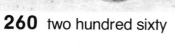 and ▫.
Subtract. Regroup if you need to.

Think:
Can I take away the ones?
Do I need to regroup?

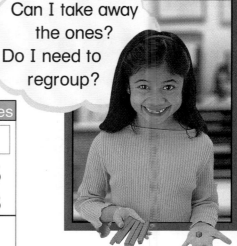

1.

Tens	Ones
~~4~~ 5	~~11~~ ~~1~~
−	4
4	7

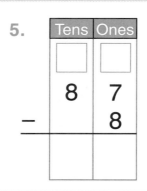

2.

Tens	Ones
6	5
−	8

3.

Tens	Ones
4	3
−	7

4.

Tens	Ones
2	6
−	3

5.

Tens	Ones
8	7
−	8

6.

Tens	Ones
7	9
−	6

7.

Tens	Ones
6	2
−	3

8.

Tens	Ones
3	6
−	2

9.

Tens	Ones
7	1
−	5

10.

Tens	Ones
9	4
−	9

Problem Solving • Reasoning

Use 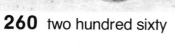 and ▫ to solve.

Draw or write to explain.

11. The pet shop had 46 fish.
On Tuesday, 8 fish were sold.
How many fish were still at the pet shop?

_____ fish

At Home Ask your child to tell you in which problems on this page he or she needed to regroup.

Subtract Two-Digit Numbers

LESSON 6

Learn About It

Regroup when there are not enough ones to subtract.

Find 32 − 18.

Step 1 Can you take away 8 ones?	**Step 2** Regroup 1 ten as 10 ones.	**Step 3** Subtract the ones.	**Step 4** Subtract the tens.

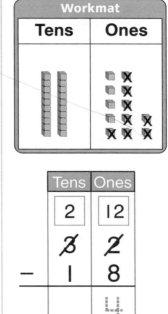

Workmat

Tens	Ones

	Tens	Ones
	3	2
−	1	8

	Tens	Ones
	2	12
	3̸	2̸
−	1	8

	Tens	Ones
	2	12
	3̸	2̸
−	1	8
		4

	Tens	Ones
	2	12
	3̸	2̸
−	1	8
	1	4

Guided Practice

Use Workmat 3 with ▭▭▭▭ and ▪. Subtract.

1.

	Tens	Ones
	1	15
	2̸	5̸
−	1	6
		9

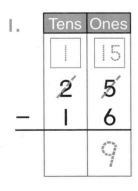

Think:
Are there enough ones to take away 6 ones? Do I need to regroup?

2.

	Tens	Ones
	4	9
−	2	5

3.

	Tens	Ones
	5	0
−	3	7

Explain Your Thinking 3 tens 2 ones is the same as 2 tens 12 ones. How does knowing this help you subtract?

Independent Practice

Use Workmat 3 with ▭ and ▫.
Subtract. Regroup if you need to.

Think:
Can I take away the ones?
Do I need to regroup?

1.
Tens	Ones
5	13
6̷	3̷
− 2	9
3	4

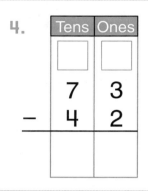

2.
Tens	Ones
7	5
− 2	8

3.
Tens	Ones
4	1
− 1	6

4.
Tens	Ones
7	3
− 4	2

5.
Tens	Ones
3	5
− 1	3

6.
Tens	Ones
9	0
− 4	7

7.
Tens	Ones
8	9
− 2	7

8.
Tens	Ones
2	4
− 1	9

9.
Tens	Ones
5	8
− 4	2

10.
Tens	Ones
6	2
− 3	6

Problem Solving • Reasoning

Number Sense

11. Show 43 with your blocks. Pick a number to subtract from 43 in which you need to regroup. Write the subtraction exercise and solve.

12. **Write About It** How did you know you needed to regroup?

Draw or write to explain.

At Home Name a two-digit number. Ask your child to name another two-digit number that can be subtracted from it without regrouping.

Name _____

LESSON 7

Problem Solving: Use Models to Act It Out

Standards
MR **1.1, 1.2**

You can solve some problems by acting them out with tens and ones blocks.

Dogs can be trained to help people.
One dog-training class has 22 dogs in it.
Only 13 dogs finish the class.
How many dogs do not finish the class?

Understand

Tell what you need to find out.

What information will you use?   _____ dogs are in the class.

             _____ dogs finish the class.

Plan

How would you solve the problem?   add   subtract

Use tens and ones blocks to help.

Solve

Write the numbers to solve the problem.
Show the numbers with blocks.

Do you need to regroup?

     yes   no

○ ☐
☐
———
☐ dogs

Look Back

How many dogs do not finish the class?   _____ dogs

Explain how you know your answer makes sense.

Guided Practice

Solve each problem.
Use blocks if you need to.

Remember:
► Understand
► Plan
► Solve
► Look Back

Remember to use the 4 steps.

① Guide dogs helped 25 people on Monday and 17 people on Tuesday. How many people were helped on both days?

Think: What do I need to find out?

Draw or write to explain.

___42___ people

② 47 mules went down a steep path. 19 mules had packs. How many mules did not have packs?

Think: Do I add or subtract to solve the problem?

_____ mules

③ There are 23 horses in the barn. 8 leave to take children on rides. How many are still in the barn?

Think: Do I add or subtract to solve the problem?

_____ horses

④ Rescue dogs saved 32 people in May, June, and July. They saved 15 in May and 7 in June. How many did they save in July?

Think: What should I do first to solve the problem?

_____ people

At Home Make up a story problem for your child. Then have him or her solve the problem and explain the answer.

Name ______________________________

Choose a Strategy

Strategies

Draw a Picture
Use Models to Act It Out
Write a Number Sentence

Solve.

1. There are 15 turtles by the pond. 7 walk away. How many turtles are still by the pond?

   _____ turtles

Draw or write to explain.

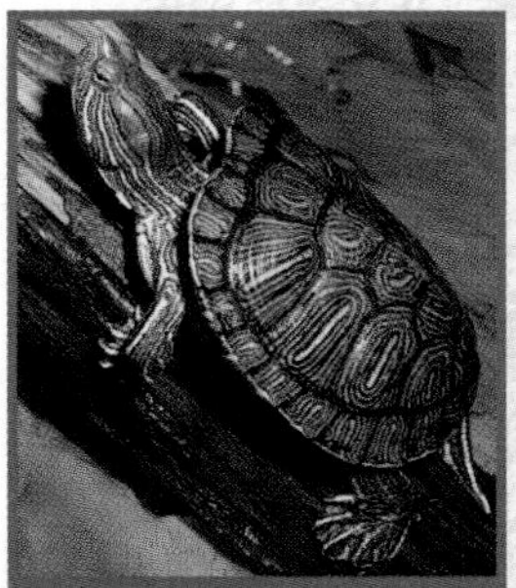
turtle

2. Max saw 21 parrots. Emily saw 12 parrots. How many more parrots did Max see than Emily?

   _____ parrots

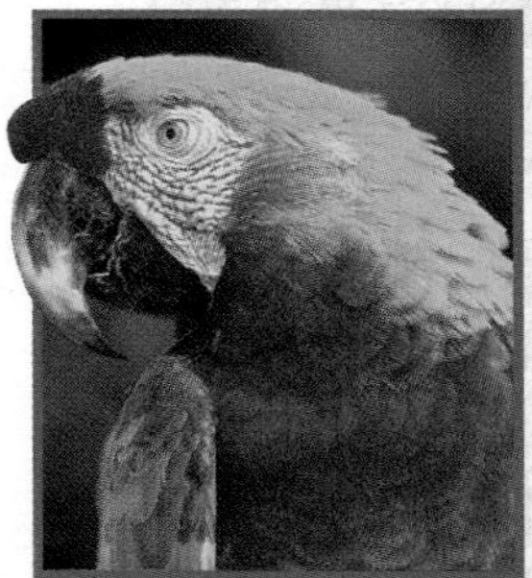
parrot

3. There are 4 polar bears. Each polar bear has 2 cubs. How many cubs are there?

   _____ cubs

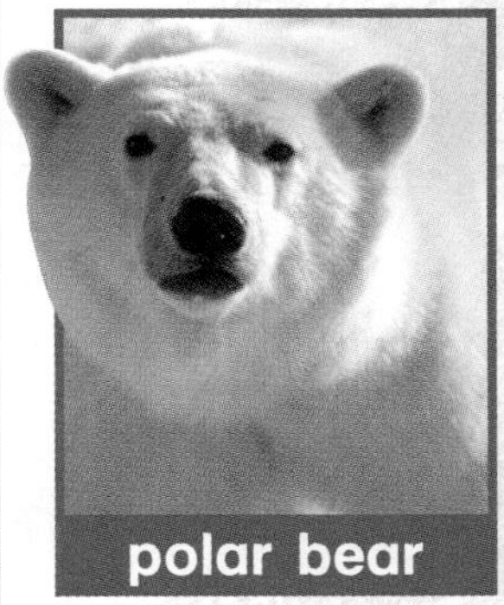
polar bear

4. A tiger jumps 14 feet in one jump. Then it runs another 30 feet. How far does it go?

   _____ feet

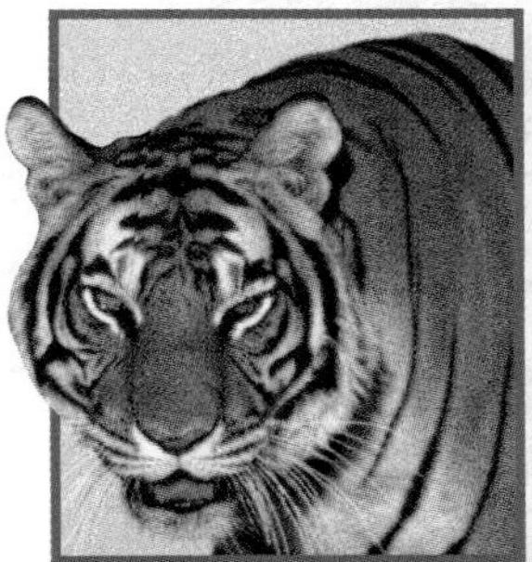
tiger

Name _____

Mixed Practice

Add. Regroup if you need to.

	1.	2.	3.	4.	5.
	25 + 7	81 +14	15 +49	29 +12	45 +22

Subtract. Regroup if you need to.

6.

Tens	Ones
☐	☐
2	7
− 1	3

7.

Tens	Ones
☐	☐
4	2
− 2	8

8.

Tens	Ones
☐	☐
9	3
− 7	6

9.

Tens	Ones
☐	☐
5	1
− 1	0

10.

Tens	Ones
☐	☐
4	7
−	5

11.

Tens	Ones
☐	☐
8	6
− 5	8

12.

Tens	Ones
☐	☐
8	3
− 2	4

13.

Tens	Ones
☐	☐
7	8
− 4	5

 Brain Teaser Find the Difference

Write 6, 7, 8, and 9 in the first set of boxes to get the **greatest** possible difference. Write 6, 7, 8, and 9 in the second set of boxes to get the **least** possible difference.

Greatest

☐ ☐
− ☐ ☐

Least

☐ ☐
− ☐ ☐

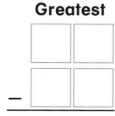 **Internet Brain Teasers**
Visit **www.eduplace.com/kids/mhm**
for more *Brain Teasers*.

Quick ✓ Check

Check Your Understanding of Lessons 1–7

Subtract.

1. 50 – 30 = _____

2. 34 – 10 = _____

3. 41 – 20 = _____

Use Workmat 3 with  and ▫.

4. Regroup to show one fewer ten.

34

| Regroup 1 ten. |

_____ tens _____ ones

Use Workmat 3 with ▭▭▭ and ▫.

Show this many.	Take away.	Do you need to regroup?	How many are left?
5. 72	5	yes no	_____ tens _____ ones

Subtract. Regroup if you need to.

6.
Tens	Ones
6	5
–	8

7.
Tens	Ones
4	3
–	6

8.
Tens	Ones
3	5
– 1	4

9.
Tens	Ones
5	7
– 2	8

Use Workmat 3 with ▭▭▭ and ▫.

10. The pet store had 25 birds.
It sold 8 birds on Friday.
How many birds does the store
have now?

_____ birds

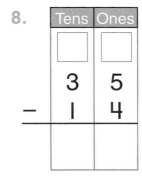

Draw or write to explain.

Test Prep • Cumulative Review
Maintaining the Standards

Name_____

Fill in the ○ for the correct answer. NH means Not Here.

1 Mark another way to show 45.

- ○ 3 tens 5 ones
- ○ 5 tens 4 ones
- ○ 3 tens 15 ones
- ○ 4 tens 15 ones

2 Subtract.

$$40 - 10 = \blacksquare$$

50　40　3　NH
○　　○　○　○

3 Abby has the money shown. She buys a game for 59¢. Mark how much money she has left.

29¢　14¢　8¢　4¢
○　　○　　○　　○

4 Ty sees 55 geese in the park. Kim sees 29 geese in the pond. How many geese do they see in all?

84　74　26　24
○　○　○　○

5 Mark the number that comes between.

63		84

48　59　72　85
○　○　○　○

6 Add.
$$\begin{array}{r} 6\,5 \\ +\ \ 7 \\ \hline \end{array}$$

72　62　58　NH
○　○　○　○

7 **Explain** how you can find the missing number.

$$80 - \blacksquare = 60$$

_____

_____

Copyright © Houghton Mifflin Company. All rights reserved.

Safe Site

Internet Test Prep
Visit **www.eduplace.com/kids/mhm**
for more *Test Prep Practice*.

Practice Regrouping With 10 or 11

Learn About It

Sometimes when you subtract, you **regroup** to make 10 or 11 ones.

Review
Vocabulary
regroup

Pete caught 40 fish. He tossed 13 back into the pond. How many fish did he keep?

Tens	Ones
4	0
− 1	3

Regroup 1 ten as 10 ones.

Tens	Ones
3	10
4	0
− 1	3
2	7

Pete kept 27 fish.

Guided Practice

Subtract. Regroup if you need to.

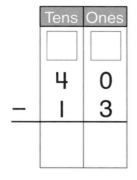

Think:
Can I subtract the ones?
Do I need to regroup?

1.

Tens	Ones
4	10
5	0
− 3	5
1	5

2.

Tens	Ones
4	1
− 1	6

3.

Tens	Ones
6	1
−	7

4.

9	1
−	1

5.

7	0
− 5	4

6.

6	0
− 3	2

7.

8	1
−	3

Explain Your Thinking What numbers can you subtract from 21 so that you do not need to regroup? How do you know?

Independent Practice

Subtract. Regroup if you need to.

1. $\begin{array}{c} \boxed{7}\ \boxed{11} \\ \not{8}\ \not{1} \\ -\ 1\ 9 \\ \hline 6\ 2 \end{array}$

2. $\begin{array}{c} \boxed{}\ \boxed{} \\ 9\ 0 \\ -\ \ 3 \\ \hline \end{array}$

3. $\begin{array}{c} \boxed{}\ \boxed{} \\ 4\ 1 \\ -\ 1\ 1 \\ \hline \end{array}$

4. $\begin{array}{c} \boxed{}\ \boxed{} \\ 3\ 1 \\ -\ 2\ 6 \\ \hline \end{array}$

5. $\begin{array}{c} \boxed{}\ \boxed{} \\ 4\ 0 \\ -\ 3\ 2 \\ \hline \end{array}$

6. $\begin{array}{c} \boxed{}\ \boxed{} \\ 6\ 1 \\ -\ 2\ 4 \\ \hline \end{array}$

7. $\begin{array}{c} \boxed{}\ \boxed{} \\ 7\ 0 \\ -\ 3\ 7 \\ \hline \end{array}$

8. $\begin{array}{c} \boxed{}\ \boxed{} \\ 5\ 0 \\ -\ \ 9 \\ \hline \end{array}$

9. $\begin{array}{c} 6\ 0 \\ -4\ 5 \\ \hline \end{array}$

10. $\begin{array}{c} 5\ 1 \\ -3\ 1 \\ \hline \end{array}$

11. $\begin{array}{c} 8\ 0 \\ -\ 7 \\ \hline \end{array}$

12. $\begin{array}{c} 7\ 1 \\ -2\ 8 \\ \hline \end{array}$

13. $\begin{array}{c} 4\ 0 \\ -\ 9 \\ \hline \end{array}$

Problem Solving•Reasoning

Using Data

14. Which color bird was seen most often?

    _____

15. How many more blue birds were seen than brown birds?

    _____ more blue birds

16. **Write Your Own** Write a subtraction problem using information in the graph. Then solve.

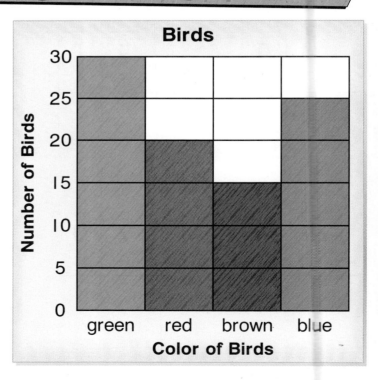

At Home Ask your child to solve exercises such as 60 – 27 and 51 – 34. Encourage your child to explain how he or she found the answer.

	Standards
	NS **2.2**, AF **1.3**

LESSON 9 Practice Regrouping With 12 to 14

Learn About It

Sometimes when you subtract, you regroup to make 12, 13, or 14 ones.

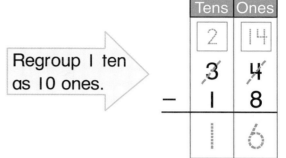

There are 34 flies.
Frog caught 18 flies.
How many flies are left?

Tens	Ones
3	4
− 1	8

Regroup 1 ten as 10 ones.

Tens	Ones
2	14
3	4
− 1	8
1	6

16 flies are left.

Guided Practice

Subtract. Regroup if you need to.

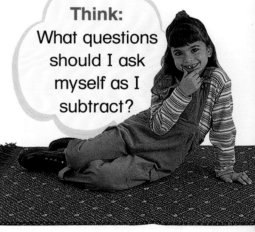

Think:
What questions should I ask myself as I subtract?

1.
Tens	Ones
4	13
5	3
− 3	6
1	7

2.
Tens	Ones
3	2
− 1	7

3.
Tens	Ones
7	4
− 2	5

4.
9	3
− 2	2

5.
7	4
− 1	5

6.
8	2
−	4

7.
6	3
− 4	8

Explain Your Thinking Did you need to regroup
in Exercise 7? Tell why or why not.

Independent Practice

Subtract. Regroup if you need to.

1.
```
  [2] [14]
   3   4
-  1   5
―――――――
   1   9
```

2.
```
 [ ] [ ]
  6   2
-     6
```

3.
```
 [ ] [ ]
  9   4
-  6   2
```

4.
```
 [ ] [ ]
  7   3
-  5   6
```

5.
```
 [ ] [ ]
  4   1
-  1   9
```

6.
```
 [ ] [ ]
  5   4
-  3   1
```

7.
```
 [ ] [ ]
  6   3
-  2   7
```

8.
```
 [ ] [ ]
  8   4
-     6
```

9.
```
  74
- 34
―――
  40
```

10.
```
  40
-  9
```

11.
```
  83
- 48
```

12.
```
  64
- 35
```

13.
```
  52
- 18
```

14.
```
  43
- 13
```

15.
```
  92
- 73
```

16.
```
  24
- 17
```

17.
```
  93
-  5
```

18.
```
  80
- 47
```

Problem Solving • Reasoning

Algebra Readiness · Number Sentences

19. Someone spilled juice on the zookeeper's records. Find the numbers that can no longer be read.

Animals at the Zoo	Pounds of Food Eaten		
	Saturday	Sunday	Total
Tigers		19	83
Lions	73	21	
Bears	67		94
Monkeys	71	11	

At Home Have your child guess which is greater, the answer to 52 – 37 or the answer to 63 – 19. Then check by doing the exercises together.

Standards
NS **2.2**

Practice Regrouping With 15 to 18

Learn About It

Sometimes when you subtract, you regroup to make 15, 16, 17, or 18 ones.

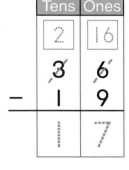

Cat sees 36 birds in a tree. 19 birds fly away. How many birds are still in the tree?

Tens	Ones
3	6
− 1	9

Regroup 1 ten as 10 ones.

Tens	Ones
2	16
3̸	6̸
− 1	9
1	7

__17__ birds

Guided Practice

Subtract. Regroup if you need to.

1.
7	17
8̸	7̸
− 1	8
6	9

2.
7	5
−	9

3.
6	5
−	8

4.
7	6
− 1	7

5. 96
  −49

6. 98
  − 2

7. 56
  −18

8. 47
  −16

9. 55
  − 7

10. 75
  −36

11. 97
  −47

12. 58
  − 9

13. 67
  −48

14. 26
  − 7

Explain Your Thinking In a subtraction exercise, will you ever need to regroup to make 19 ones? Why or why not?

Independent Practice

Use a paper clip and a pencil.
Spin the spinner. Write each
number in the box. Subtract.

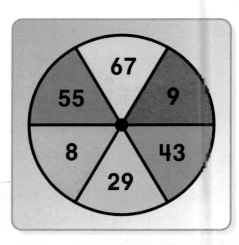

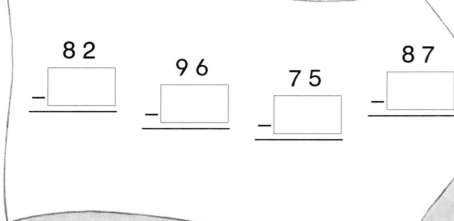

82
– [   ]

96
– [   ]

75
– [   ]

87
– [   ]

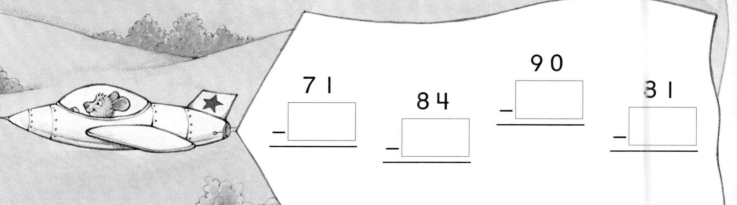

71
– [   ]

84
– [   ]

90
– [   ]

31
– [   ]

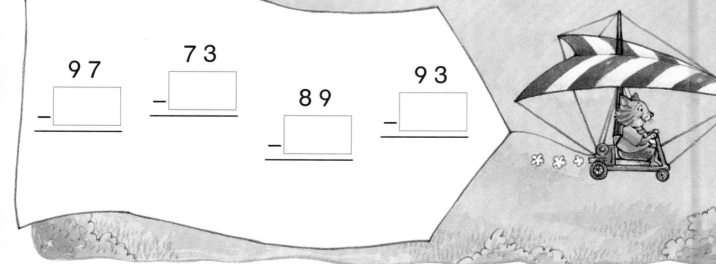

97
– [   ]

73
– [   ]

89
– [   ]

93
– [   ]

At Home Give your child 2 two-digit numbers. Ask him or her to subtract the
lesser number from the greater number and then tell if regrouping was needed.

Standards
NS **2.0, 6.0**

Estimate Differences

**Review
Vocabulary**

**number line
round
estimate**

Learn About It

You can use a **number line** to **round** a number to the nearest ten. This can help you **estimate** a difference.

Use the number line to estimate.

Step 1 Round each number to the nearest ten.	**Step 2** Subtract.

20 21 22 23 24 25 26 27 28 29 30

28 nearest ten → 30
-21 nearest ten → -20

$$\begin{array}{r} 30 \\ -20 \\ \hline 10 \end{array}$$

Guided Practice

Use the number line. Round each number to the nearest ten. Estimate the difference.

Think: Which is the nearest ten?

30 31 32 33 34 35 36 37 38 39 40 41 42 43 44 45 46 47 48 49 50

1. 49 nearest ten → 50
   -31 nearest ten → -30
   20

2. 41 ⟶ ☐
   -32 ⟶ $-$ ☐
   ☐

Explain Your Thinking How did you find the nearest ten for each number in Exercise 2?

Independent Practice

Use the number line. Round each number
to the nearest ten. Estimate the difference.

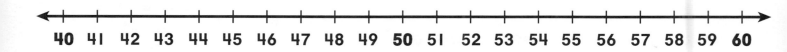

40 41 42 43 44 45 46 47 48 49 **50** 51 52 53 54 55 56 57 58 59 **60**

1. 5 8 <u>nearest ten</u> → 60

    − 4 2 <u>nearest ten</u> → − 40

    20

2. 5 3 ⎯⎯⎯→ ☐

    − 4 1 ⎯⎯⎯→ − ☐

3. 4 9 ⎯⎯⎯→ ☐

    − 4 3 ⎯⎯⎯→ − ☐

4. 5 7 ⎯⎯⎯→ ☐

    − 4 4 ⎯⎯⎯→ − ☐

5. 5 9 ⎯⎯⎯→ ☐

    − 4 7 ⎯⎯⎯→ − ☐

6. 4 4 ⎯⎯⎯→ ☐

    − 4 1 ⎯⎯⎯→ − ☐

Problem Solving•Reasoning

7. **Estimate** Luis had 51 shells.
    He gave Bill 42 shells. About how
    many shells did Luis keep?

    about _____ shells

    Draw or write to explain.

At Home Ask your child to tell you the nearest ten for 59 (60) and for 42 (40)
and then estimate to find 59 − 42 (60 − 40 = 20).

Quick ✓ Check

Check Your Understanding of Lessons 8–11

Subtract. Regroup if you need to.

| 1. | 90
−34 | 2. | 65
− 3 | 3. | 30
−22 | 4. | 42
−28 | 5. | 75
−25 |

| 6. | 27
−19 | 7. | 56
−43 | 8. | 24
− 8 | 9. | 33
−19 | 10. | 84
−40 |

Use the number line. Round each number
to the nearest ten. Estimate the difference.

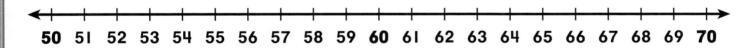

50 51 52 53 54 55 56 57 58 59 **60** 61 62 63 64 65 66 67 68 69 **70**

11. 63 nearest ten → ☐
   − 54 nearest ten → − ☐
   _____
   ☐

12. 68 ————→ ☐
   − 51 ————→ − ☐
   _____
   ☐

Solve the problem.

13. A pet shop has 35 birds and
    16 dogs. How many birds
    and dogs are in the pet shop?

    _____ birds and dogs

    Draw or write to explain.

Name_____

Test Prep • Cumulative Review

Maintaining the Standards

Fill in the ○ for the correct answer. NH means Not Here.

① Subtract.
$$\begin{array}{r} 5\,7 \\ -\,2\,9 \\ \hline \end{array}$$

28	32	38	NH
○	○	○	○

② Which is correct?

 <

 >

 >

 >

③ What number is 20 more than 56?

36	58	76	86
○	○	○	○

④ Subtract.
$$\begin{array}{r} 8\,2 \\ -\ \ 7 \\ \hline \end{array}$$

74	75	84	NH
○	○	○	○

⑤ Add.
$$\begin{array}{r} 4\,6 \\ +\,3\,5 \\ \hline \end{array}$$

11	71	72	NH
○	○	○	○

⑥ There are 66 ducks flying. 27 ducks land in a pond.

$$\begin{array}{r} {\scriptstyle 5\ \ 16} \\ \cancel{6}\,\cancel{6} \\ -\,2\,7 \\ \hline 3\,9 \end{array}$$

Explain why this subtraction exercise shows how many ducks are still flying.

_____

_____

_____

Copyright © Houghton Mifflin Company. All rights reserved.

Safe Site

Internet Test Prep
Visit **www.eduplace.com/kids/mhm**
for more *Test Prep Practice.*

Different Ways to Subtract

```
  5 5    Which way would you
- 3 0    choose to subtract?
```

I would use mental math...**55**, 45, 35, 25.

I would use tens and ones blocks.

I would use paper and pencil.

I would use a hundred chart.

Guided Practice

Choose a way to subtract. Circle it.
Then subtract.

1.
```
  3 6
- 1 0
  2 6
```
mental math

hundred chart

2.
```
  5 8
- 3 0
```
mental math

hundred chart

3.
```
  5 6
- 3 7
```
tens and ones blocks

paper and pencil

4.
```
  8 4
- 5 9
```
tens and ones blocks

paper and pencil

Subtract.

5.
```
  4 9
- 2 1
```

6.
```
  9 2
- 4 6
```

7.
```
  6 0
- 4 0
```

8.
```
  9 0
- 4 5
```

9.
```
  7 5
- 6 0
```

Explain Your Thinking For Exercise 2, which way
did you choose to subtract? Tell why.

Independent Practice

Subtract.

Ways to Subtract

mental math

hundred chart

tens and ones blocks

paper and pencil

1. 1 1 8
    2 8
    − 1 9
    ———
      9

2.   7 9
    − 4 0
    ———

3.   6 3
    −   8
    ———

4.   9 6
    − 6 6
    ———

5.   3 9
    − 1 2
    ———

6.   5 0
    − 2 4
    ———

7.   8 4
    −   9
    ———

8.   7 5
    − 3 1
    ———

9.   7 2
    − 5 5
    ———

10.   9 8
    − 7 0
    ———

11.   8 7
    − 5 4
    ———

12.   6 0
    − 3 8
    ———

13.   7 3
    − 4 3
    ———

14.   5 1
    − 4 3
    ———

15.   3 5
    −   7
    ———

16.   4 9
    − 2 0
    ———

17.   7 2
    − 3 7
    ———

18.   6 6
    − 2 9
    ———

Problem Solving • Reasoning

Patterns

Find each difference. Look for a pattern.
Write the next exercise in the box.

19.   8 4
    −   7
    ———

      8 4
    − 1 7
    ———

      8 4
    − 2 7
    ———

      8 4
    − 3 7
    ———

    ┌───┐
    │   │
    └───┘
    ┌───┐
    │   │
  − └───┘
    ┌───┐
    │   │
    └───┘

At Home Ask your child to explain the different ways to subtract.

Horizontal Subtraction

Learn About It

Rewrite the numbers to help you subtract.

I wrote it another way.

Find 85 − 59.

Step 1 Rewrite the numbers.	**Step 2** Subtract.
$\begin{array}{c c} 8 & 5 \\ - 5 & 9 \end{array}$	$\begin{array}{c c} 7 & 15 \\ \not{8} & \not{5} \\ - 5 & 9 \\ \hline 2 & 6 \end{array}$

$85 - 59 = 26$

$\begin{array}{r} 85 \\ -59 \\ \hline 26 \end{array}$

Guided Practice

Rewrite the numbers. Then subtract.

1. $48 - 9$

$\begin{array}{c c} 3 & 18 \\ \not{4} & \not{8} \\ - & 9 \\ \hline 3 & 9 \end{array}$

2. $63 - 7$

3. $84 - 55$

Think: Which number do I write first?

4. $81 - 32$

5. $77 - 58$

6. $78 - 69$

7. $65 - 4$

Explain Your Thinking To find $45 - 7$, do you subtract 7 ones or 7 tens? How do you know?

Independent Practice

Rewrite the numbers. Then subtract.

1. $36 - 19$

$$
\begin{array}{c|c}
2 & 16 \\
3 & 6 \\
- 1 & 9 \\
\hline
1 & 7 \\
\end{array}
$$

2. $58 - 24$

3. $68 - 32$

4. $72 - 9$

5. $64 - 47$

6. $42 - 3$

7. $71 - 25$

8. $38 - 17$

9. $96 - 34$

10. $81 - 4$

11. $60 - 35$

12. $45 - 27$

Problem Solving•Reasoning

13. Meg's dog weighs 95 pounds. Her dog weighs 18 pounds more than Bob's dog weighs. How much does Bob's dog weigh?

_____ pounds

Draw or write to explain.

14. **Write Your Own** Write an addition problem about the two dogs. Then solve.

At Home Start with a two-digit number such as 52. Ask your child to choose a two-digit number that is less than 52 and then subtract. Repeat with other numbers.

Standards
NS 2.2, 5.0, MR 2.1

LESSON 14 Add and Subtract Money

Learn About It

You add and subtract money just as you add and subtract two-digit numbers.

Use ¢ when you add or subtract money.

15¢

Add.		Subtract.	
1 5	1 5¢	$\overset{4}{\cancel{5}}\overset{10}{\cancel{0}}$	$\overset{4}{\cancel{5}}\overset{10}{\cancel{0}}$¢
+ 1 5	+ 1 5¢	− 1 5	− 1 5¢
30	30¢	35	35¢

Lemonade

Guided Practice

Add or subtract.

1. $\overset{4\,12}{\cancel{5}\cancel{2}}$¢
    − 1 8¢
    34¢

2. 6 4 ¢
    − 2 7 ¢

3. 1 5 ¢
    + 5 ¢

4. 7 4 ¢
    − 2 8 ¢

5. 4 3 ¢
    + 3 6 ¢

Rewrite the numbers. Then add or subtract.

6. 33¢ + 48¢

    3 3 ¢
  + 4 8 ¢
    8 1 ¢

7. 96¢ − 8¢

8. 47¢ − 19¢

9. 56¢ + 13¢

Explain Your Thinking When you add 19¢ and 20¢, is your answer in cents? Why or why not?

Independent Practice

Remember to watch the signs.

Add or subtract.

1.
```
   6 10
   7̸ 0̸ ¢
 - 1 8 ¢
   5 2 ¢
```

2.
```
   2 6 ¢
 + 4 8 ¢
```

3.
```
   3 2 ¢
 + 4 0 ¢
```

4.
```
   7 8 ¢
 -   9 ¢
```

5.
```
   6 7 ¢
 - 4 8 ¢
```

6.
```
   5 9 ¢
 - 3 4 ¢
```

7.
```
   4 7 ¢
 +   5 ¢
```

8.
```
   5 0 ¢
 + 2 8 ¢
```

9.
```
   3 4 ¢
 - 1 9 ¢
```

10.
```
   5 8 ¢
 - 3 7 ¢
```

Rewrite the numbers. Then add or subtract.

11. 90¢ − 75¢
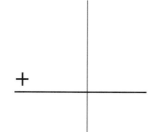
```
   8  10
   9̸  0̸ ¢
 - 7   5 ¢
   1   5 ¢
```

12. 57¢ + 12¢
```
 +
```

13. 85¢ − 66¢
```
 -
```

14. 27¢ + 6¢
```
 +
```

Problem Solving • Reasoning

15. How much money do you need to buy 2 treats?

_____ ¢

treat 29¢   bowl 48¢

16. You have 9 dimes. You buy a treat and a bowl. How much money do you have left?

_____ ¢

Draw or write to explain.

17. **Write About It** Explain how you solved Problem 16.

At Home Give your child a few coins. Ask your child to tell you if there is enough to buy either of the items shown above.

Standards
NS **2.1, 2.2,** MR **2.0**

LESSON 15

Algebra Readiness:
Check Subtraction

Review
Vocabulary

difference

Learn About It

After you find the **difference**, you can add to check your subtraction.

Subtract.

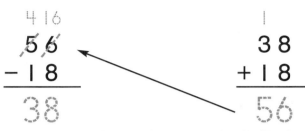

```
  4 16
  5 6          3 8
- 1 8        + 1 8
  3 8          5 6
```

To check, start with the difference, 38. Add the number you subtracted, 18.

If the sum equals the number you subtracted from, your answer is correct.

Guided Practice

Subtract. Check by adding.

1.
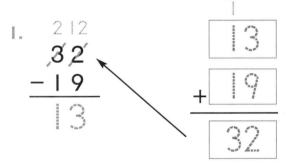
```
   2 12
   3 2          1 3
  - 1 9       +  1 9
    1 3          3 2
```

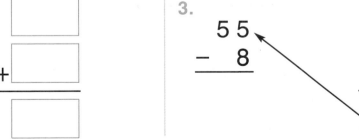

Think: Which two numbers do I add to check?

2.
```
   9 0
  - 4 7        +
```

3.

```
   5 5
  -  8         +
```

4.
```
   8 1
  - 6 6        +
```

5.
```
   7 2
  - 6 4        +
```

Explain Your Thinking Explain why you can use addition to check subtraction.

Independent Practice

Subtract. Check by adding.

1.
$$\begin{array}{r} 68 \\ -42 \\ \hline 26 \end{array}$$
$$\begin{array}{r} 26 \\ +42 \\ \hline 68 \end{array}$$

2.
$$\begin{array}{r} 40 \\ -5 \\ \hline \end{array}$$
$$+\underline{}$$

3.
$$\begin{array}{r} 54 \\ -19 \\ \hline \end{array}$$
$$+\underline{}$$

4.
$$\begin{array}{r} 85 \\ -6 \\ \hline \end{array}$$
$$+\underline{}$$

5.
$$\begin{array}{r} 49 \\ -28 \\ \hline \end{array}$$
$$+\underline{}$$

6.
$$\begin{array}{r} 74 \\ -10 \\ \hline \end{array}$$
$$+\underline{}$$

7.
$$\begin{array}{r} 53 \\ -7 \\ \hline \end{array}$$
$$+\underline{}$$

8.
$$\begin{array}{r} 98 \\ -51 \\ \hline \end{array}$$
$$+\underline{}$$

Problem Solving • Reasoning

Using Vocabulary

9. After you **regroup**, you have 2 tens 16 ones. What number did you start with?

_____

10. **Write Your Own** Write a subtraction exercise that has a **difference** of 20.

Draw or write to explain.

At Home Ask your child to show you how to use addition to check the answer to a subtraction exercise. Try an exercise such as 47 − 18 = ■.

Name _____

LESSON 16

Problem Solving: Use a Table

Standards
AF **1.3**, MR **3.0**

You can use information in a table to solve a problem.

Veterinarians help keep animals healthy. This table shows animals that were treated by a veterinarian.

Animals	Number Treated
Rabbits	43
Cats	64
Dogs	29

You can use a table and add to solve a problem.

How many cats and dogs were treated?

[ ] cats

⊕ [ ] dogs
_____
[ ] cats and dogs treated

Think:
Find the numbers in the table. Add, because you need to find a total.

You can use a table and subtract to solve a problem.

How many more cats were treated than rabbits?

[ ] cats

⊖ [ ] rabbits
_____
[ ] more cats treated

Think:
Find the numbers in the table. Subtract, because you need to compare.

Day	Number Treated
Monday	64
Tuesday	50
Wednesday	45

Guided Practice

Use the table to solve each problem.

Draw or write to explain.

1 How many animals were treated on Tuesday and Wednesday?

Think: Do I add or subtract?

_95_ animals

2 How many more animals were treated on Monday than on Wednesday?

Think: Do I add or subtract?

_____ animals

3 17 of the animals treated on Wednesday were dogs. How many were not dogs?

Think: Which numbers should I use?

_____ other animals

4 On Tuesday, Dr. Kim treated 18 animals. Dr. Clark treated 14 animals. Dr. Sam treated the rest. How many animals did Dr. Sam treat?

Think: What should I do first?

_____ animals

At Home Use the table on this page to make up a story problem for your child. Then have your child solve it and explain the answer.

Name_____

Kind of Dog	Number in Show
Collie	24
Poodle	37
Beagle	16
Bulldog	18

collie

Choose a Strategy

Use the table to solve each problem.

1 How many collies and poodles are there in the show?

_____ collies and poodles

Draw or write to explain.

2 After the first day, 9 poodles drop out of the show. How many stay in the show?

_____ poodles

poodle

3 Each beagle in the show has two floppy ears. How many ears are on all the beagles?

_____ ears

beagle

4 During the show, 21 bulldogs join the others. How many bulldogs are there now?

_____ bulldogs

bulldog

Name _____

Mixed Practice

Add or subtract.

1.
```
  [ ][ ]
    2 3
  - 1 7
```

2.
```
  [ ]
    3 6
  +   9
```

3.
```
  [ ][ ]
    4 5
  - 2 6
```

4.
```
  [ ]
    6 6
  + 1 7
```

5.
```
    4 0
  - 2 8
```

6.
```
    3 7
  - 1 6
```

7.
```
    8 1
  + 1 4
```

8.
```
    8 2
  - 2 8
```

9.
```
    2 5
  +   7
```

10.
```
    9 8
  - 3 4
```

11.
```
    6 7
  + 1 5
```

12.
```
    5 3
  - 3 3
```

13.
```
    4 2
  - 2 9
```

14.
```
    2 8
  + 5 6
```

15.
```
    8 4
  -   9
```

16.
```
    7 5
  - 4 8
```

17.
```
    5 1
  - 1 0
```

18.
```
    9 3
  - 7 6
```

19.
```
    4 1
  -   9
```

 Brain Teaser Mystery Locker

My locker number is between 56 and 68.
The sum of its two digits is equal to 10 + 2.
It is an even number. What is my locker
number?

_____

Safe Site

Internet Brain Teasers
Visit **www.eduplace.com/kids/mhm**
for more *Brain Teasers*.

Quick ✓ Check

Check Your Understanding of Lessons 12–16

Subtract.

1. $\begin{array}{r} 23 \\ -15 \\ \hline \end{array}$

2. $\begin{array}{r} 89¢ \\ -73¢ \\ \hline \end{array}$

3. $\begin{array}{r} 74 \\ -\ \ 9 \\ \hline \end{array}$

4. $\begin{array}{r} 37 \\ -19 \\ \hline \end{array}$

5. $\begin{array}{r} 64 \\ -21 \\ \hline \end{array}$

Rewrite the numbers. Then add or subtract.

6. 86 − 27

7. 36¢ + 58¢

8. 79¢ − 6¢

Subtract. Check by adding.

9. $\begin{array}{r} 73 \\ -25 \\ \hline \end{array}$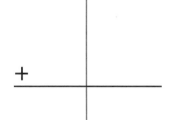

10. $\begin{array}{r} 62 \\ -39 \\ \hline \end{array}$

Use the table to answer the question.

11. How much more does the large bag weigh than the medium bag?

_____ pounds

Bags of Dog Food	
Size	**Weight**
small	10 pounds
medium	18 pounds
large	35 pounds

Test Prep • Cumulative Review

Maintaining the Standards

Fill in the ○ for the correct answer. NH means Not Here.

1 There are 35 penguins on the ice. 17 jump into the water. How many penguins are still on the ice?

52　　37　　18　　16
○　　　○　　　○　　　○

2 Extend the pattern.

1, 4, 7, 10, 13, 16,

_____, _____, _____

18, 21, 24　　　19, 21, 22
　　○　　　　　　　○

19, 22, 25　　　22, 26, 30
　　○　　　　　　　○

3 How many more tadpoles hatched in May than in April?

Month	Tadpoles Hatched
April	28
May	50
June	39

11　　22　　78　　89
○　　　○　　　○　　　○

4 Subtract.　　$\begin{array}{r} 8\ 1 \\ -\ 1\ 8 \\ \hline \end{array}$

62　　73　　99　　NH
○　　　○　　　○　　　○

5 Mai has 1 dime, 1 nickel, and 1 penny. How much money does she have?

31¢　21¢　16¢　11¢
○　　　○　　　○　　　○

6 Subtract.　　$\begin{array}{r} 6\ 5 \\ -\ 2\ 8 \\ \hline \end{array}$

Explain how you know you are right.

_____

_____

_____

_____

Copyright © Houghton Mifflin Company. All rights reserved.

Safe Site

Internet Test Prep
Visit **www.eduplace.com/kids/mhm**
for more *Test Prep Practice.*

Name _____

Chapter Review

Use the example to answer Exercises 1-3.

$$\begin{array}{r} \boxed{2}\,\boxed{14} \\ 3\ 4 \\ -\ 1\ 5 \\ \hline 1\ 9 \end{array}$$

1. Which number is the **difference**? _____

2. Alan had to **regroup**.
   He regrouped 34 as _____ tens _____ ones.

3. Which number did Alan **subtract** from 34? _____

---

4. Kim estimated to find 61 − 23.
   Circle the one that shows an
   estimate.

$$\begin{array}{r} 6\ 0 \\ -\ 2\ 0 \\ \hline 4\ 0 \end{array}$$

$$\begin{array}{r} \boxed{5}\,\boxed{11} \\ 6\ 1 \\ -\ 2\ 3 \\ \hline 3\ 8 \end{array}$$

5. Here are 32 books.

Jim wants to **round** the number
of books to the nearest 10.
What number should he get? _____

Subtract.

6. $\begin{array}{r} 2\ 3 \\ -\ 7 \\ \hline \end{array}$ 7. $\begin{array}{r} 6\ 6 \\ -4\ 5 \\ \hline \end{array}$ 8. $\begin{array}{r} 9\ 5 \\ -3\ 6 \\ \hline \end{array}$ 9. $\begin{array}{r} 4\ 1 \\ -1\ 4 \\ \hline \end{array}$ 10. $\begin{array}{r} 7\ 2 \\ -5\ 0 \\ \hline \end{array}$

Rewrite the numbers. Then add or subtract.

11. 90¢ − 61¢   12. 67 − 8   13. 70¢ + 20¢   14. 55 − 19

Subtract. Check by adding.

15.
```
   7 6
 − 3 8      + ___
 _____
```

16.
```
   4 3
 − 1 7      + ___
 _____
```

17.
```
   9 4
 − 8 0      + ___
 _____
```

Use the number line. Round each number to the nearest ten.
Estimate the difference.

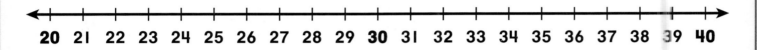

20 21 22 23 24 25 26 27 28 29 **30** 31 32 33 34 35 36 37 38 39 **40**

18.
```
  2 9  nearest ten →  [    ]
− 2 1  nearest ten → −[    ]
_____
```

19.
```
  3 8  ————→  [    ]
− 2 4  ————→ −[    ]
_____
```

Use the table to answer the question.

20. How many more cats were
    adopted than dogs?

    _____ cats

Pets	Number Adopted
Cats	26
Dogs	12
Hamsters	35

Solve the problem.

21. In the morning a zookeeper gave
    16 pears to the monkeys. At night
    he gave them 23 apples. How
    many pears and apples did the
    monkeys get that day?

    _____ pears and apples

Draw or write to explain.

Copyright © Houghton Mifflin Company. All rights reserved.

Chapter Test

Subtract.

| 1. 6 4
   −4 7 | 2. 5 0
   −2 6 | 3. 3 9
   − 5 | 4. 8 3
   − 4 | 5. 9 7
   −6 8 |

| 6. 5 2
   −4 6 | 7. 8 0
   −5 0 | 8. 7 8
   − 9 | 9. 4 5
   −1 5 | 10. 3 6
   − 8 |

Rewrite the numbers. Subtract.

11. 76¢ − 39¢

12. 62 − 16

13. 55¢ − 35¢

Subtract. Check by adding.

14.   4 8
     −2 9

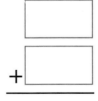

15.   7 1
     −6 2

Use the number line to estimate the difference.

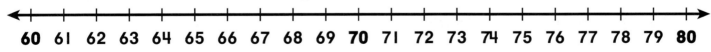

60 61 62 63 64 65 66 67 68 69 **70** 71 72 73 74 75 76 77 78 79 **80**

16.   7 1 <u>nearest ten</u> →

   − 6 3 <u>nearest ten</u> → −

17.   7 7 <u>nearest ten</u> →

   − 6 2 <u>nearest ten</u> → −

Sea Animals	Number Seen
Whales	26
Dolphins	35
Eels	28

Solve the problem.

Draw or write to explain.

18. How many dolphins and eels were seen altogether?

_____ dolphins and eels

19. How many more dolphins were seen than whales?

_____ more dolphins

20. Later in the day, 15 more eels were seen. How many eels were seen in all?

_____ eels

Write About It

Jason made this mistake in subtraction:

$$
\begin{array}{r}
5\,8 \\
-\ 1\,9 \\
\hline
4\,1
\end{array}
$$

Explain what Jason did wrong.

_____

_____

_____

Show how he can subtract correctly.

Draw or write to explain.

Name _____

Subtract From 99

What You Need

• bag with number cards 0–25
• paper and pencil for each player

$$\begin{array}{r} 99 \\ -\ 16 \\ \hline \end{array}$$

16

How to Play

1. Write the number 99 at the top of your paper.

2. Take turns drawing a number card from the bag.

3. Subtract your number from 99.

4. Take turns drawing new numbers from the bag. Subtract each new number from the last difference on your paper.

5. The player with the least difference after four turns wins.

Enrichment
Subtraction Combinations

| Bugs 36¢ | Post Cards 6¢ | Dinosaurs 65¢ | Sea Animals 21¢ | Stickers 15¢ |

Each child had 90¢ to spend at the museum shop.
Guess and then check to find what each child bought.

1. Carlos had 25¢ left. What did he buy?

   _____

   _____

   Draw or write to explain.

2. Rosa had 54¢ left. What did she buy?

   _____

   _____

3. Jan had 19¢ left. Which 2 items did she buy?

   _____

   _____

4. Tim had 48¢ left. Which 2 items did he buy?

   _____

   _____

5. **Write Your Own** Write a problem about the museum gift shop. Ask a friend to solve it.

Copyright © Houghton Mifflin Company. All rights reserved.

CHAPTER 7

Geometry, Fractions, and Probability

Accessing Prior Knowledge

This story will help you review

- Circles
- Squares
- Triangles
- Rectangles

The Clubhouse

A Read-Aloud Story

written by Linda Brett Dorf
illustrated by Megan Halsey

A Math Storybook for

Rozellyn Jaird

What can we do on a rainy day? We can build a clubhouse inside and play.

There are lots of things that we can use. Draw the shapes that you would choose.

Draw some shapes you would choose.

Copyright © Houghton Mifflin Company. All rights reserved.

300

Draw rectangles.

The sides of this box
are wide and tall.
The faces are rectangles—
like a wall!

This clubhouse will fit
both you and me.
Now draw the rectangles
that you see.

Draw circles and squares.

Some windows are round, and others are square. Some windows can open to let in fresh air.

This clubhouse will be for you and me. Draw the circles and squares that you see.

Copyright © Houghton Mifflin Company. All rights reserved.

Draw triangles.

Here's a perfect tent, but it's in a tangle. Let's make a room made of triangles.

This clubhouse is just right for you and me. Now draw the triangles that you see.

Our Clubhouse

Draw shapes you might see inside the clubhouse.

Are there other things that just might fit? We have room inside— we're not cramped a bit!

We've finished our clubhouse— our work is done. Now it's time to have some fun!

Copyright © Houghton Mifflin Company. All rights reserved.

Oh, look! Our friends have come
to play. They've brought some
toys with them today.

It's better by far—and much
more fun—to share our
clubhouse with everyone!

Family Letter

Dear Family,

During the next few weeks, our math class will be learning about geometry, fractions, and probability.

You can expect to see work that provides practice with shapes, fractions, and probability.

As we learn about geometry and fractions, you may wish to use the following sample as a guide.

Copyright © Houghton Mifflin Company. All rights reserved.

Vocabulary

face The flat surface of a solid shape.

edge The segment where two faces of a solid shape meet.

line of symmetry A line that separates a shape into two matching parts.

congruent Two shapes that are the same size and shape.

Solid Shapes

Cone   Cube   Cylinder   Rectangular Prism   Pyramid   Sphere

Plane Shapes

Square   Rectangle   Triangle   Circle

Fractions

$\frac{1}{3}$ $\frac{1}{4}$ $\frac{1}{2}$ $\frac{1}{5}$

Sincerely,

Your child's teacher

LESSON 1 Plane Shapes

New **Vocabulary**
triangle
square
rectangle
circle

Learn About It

The plane shapes, **triangle**, **square**, **rectangle**, and **circle**, come in different sizes.

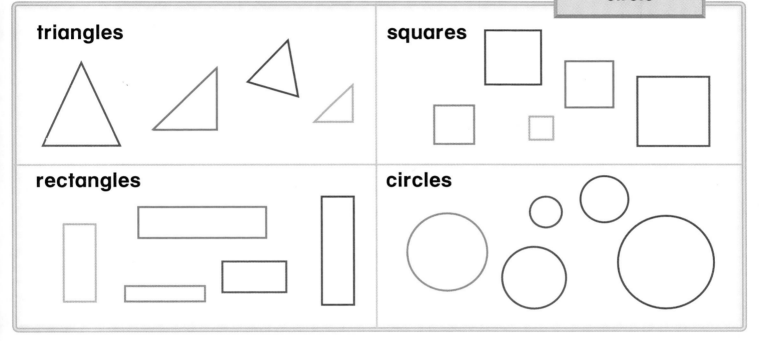

triangles

squares

rectangles

circles

Guided Practice

1. Circle the triangles.

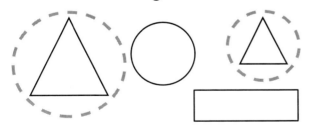

2. Circle the squares.

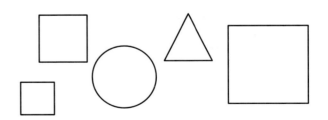

3. Circle the rectangles.

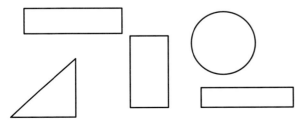

4. Circle the circles.

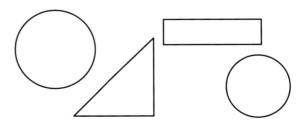

Explain Your Thinking How can you sort the shapes in Exercise 3 into two different groups?

Independent Practice

Circle the shapes that match each name.

1. rectangle

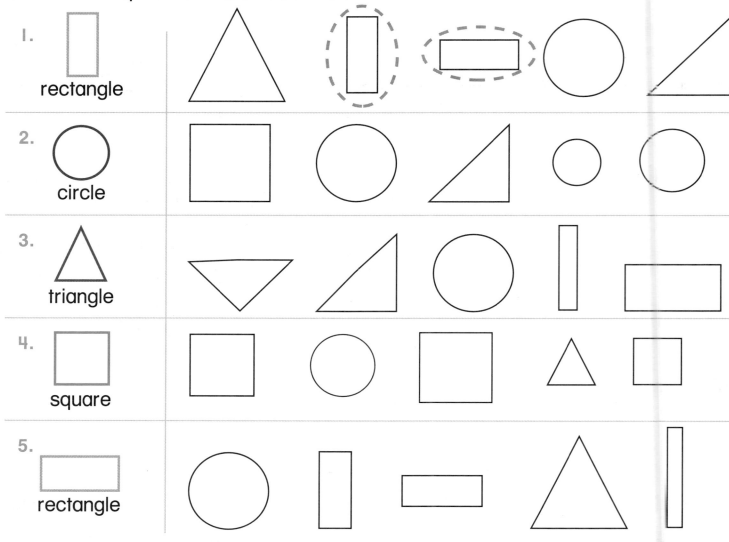

2. circle

3. triangle

4. square

5. rectangle

Problem Solving • Reasoning

Visual Thinking

6. Circle all the shapes below that are ovals. Put an X on the shapes that are not ovals.

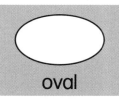

oval

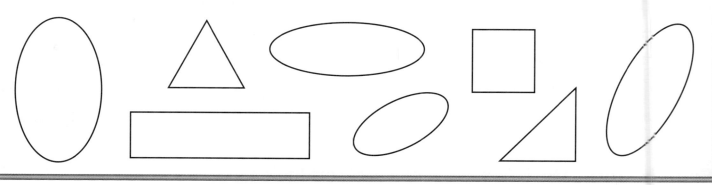

At Home Help your child find at home each of the plane shapes shown on this page.

LESSON 2 Sides and Vertices

New Vocabulary
sides
vertex/vertices

Learn About It

You can describe plane shapes by the number of **sides** and **vertices**.

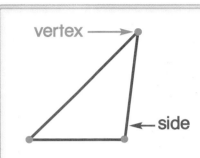

vertex ——→
←— side

This shape has
3 sides and
3 vertices.

This shape has
4 sides and
4 vertices.

Guided Practice

Write how many sides and vertices.

1.

___4___ sides

___4___ vertices

2.

_____ sides

_____ vertices

3.

_____ sides

_____ vertices

4.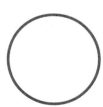

_____ sides

_____ vertices

5.

_____ sides

_____ vertices

6.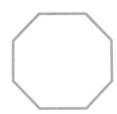

_____ sides

_____ vertices

Explain Your Thinking Tell what you notice about the number of sides and vertices in each shape.

Independent Practice

Draw each figure.

1. 4 sides   4 vertices

2. 3 sides   3 vertices

3. 5 sides   5 vertices

4. 0 sides   0 vertices

5. 6 sides   6 vertices

6. 4 equal sides   4 vertices

Problem Solving•Reasoning

Logical Thinking

7. Who drew each shape?

   • Rick drew a shape with 4 sides.
   • Lea did not draw the square.
   • Mary drew a shape with 3 vertices.

Next to each shape, write the name
of the child who drew it.

At Home Draw several shapes for your child and ask him or her to
identify the number of sides and vertices.

Name _____

Solid Shapes

Learn About It

You can describe solid shapes by the number of faces, edges, and vertices.

New Vocabulary	
face	sphere
edge	pyramid
vertex	cylinder
cube	cone
rectangular prism	

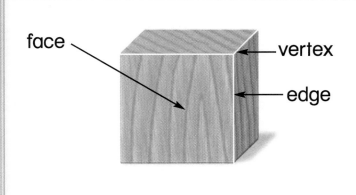

face → vertex → edge

A **face** is flat.

An **edge** is where 2 faces meet.

A **vertex** is the place where 3 or more edges meet.

Guided Practice

Use solid shapes. Count the faces, edges, and vertices.

		Faces	Edges	Vertices
1.	cube	6	12	8
2.	rectangular prism			
3.	pyramid			

4. Draw a line to match the word with the shape.

cylinder	sphere	cone

Explain Your Thinking How can you sort the solid shapes in Exercises 1–4 into two different groups?

Independent Practice

Circle the objects that match the solid shape.

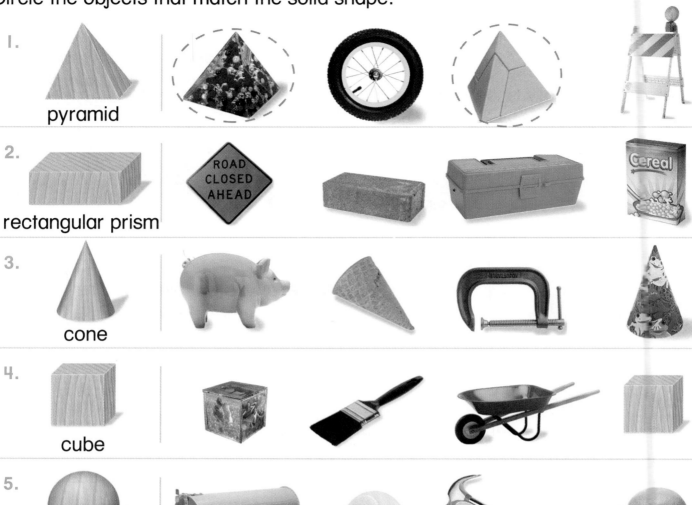

1. pyramid

2. rectangular prism

3. cone

4. cube

5. sphere

Problem Solving • Reasoning

Some solids slide.
Some solids roll.

6. Roll and slide each solid.
   Circle the solids that roll.
   Put an X on the solids that slide.

7. **Write About It** Do any solids roll
   and slide? Explain your answer.

At Home Find objects in your home that are like the solid shapes. Ask your child to name the solid shapes.

Standards
MG **2.0**, MR **1.2**

LESSON 4 Congruent Shapes

New Vocabulary

congruent

Learn About It

Shapes are **congruent** if they have the same shape and size.

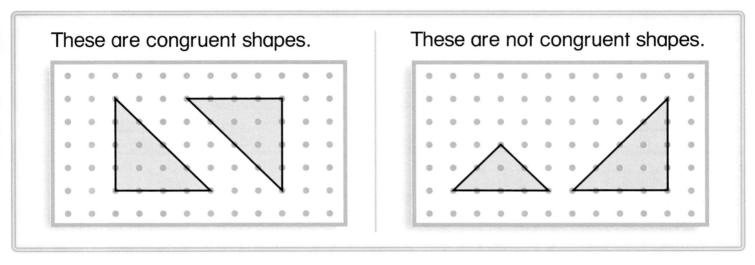

These are congruent shapes.

These are not congruent shapes.

Guided Practice

Circle the shape that is congruent to the first shape.

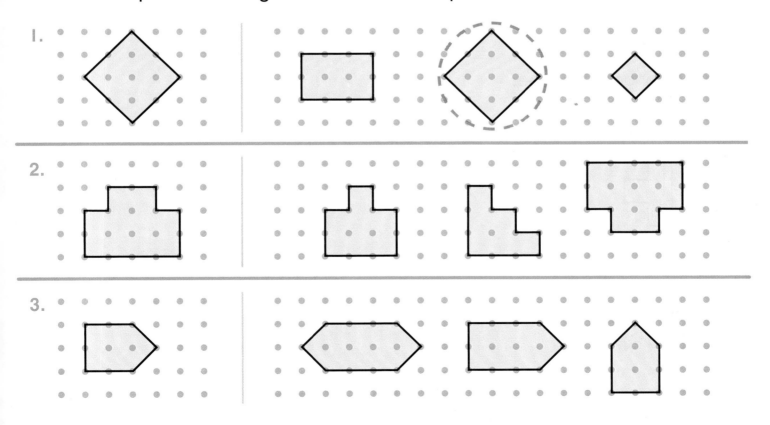

1.

2.

3.

Explain Your Thinking Are two squares always congruent? Why or why not?

Independent Practice

Circle the shape that is congruent to the first shape.

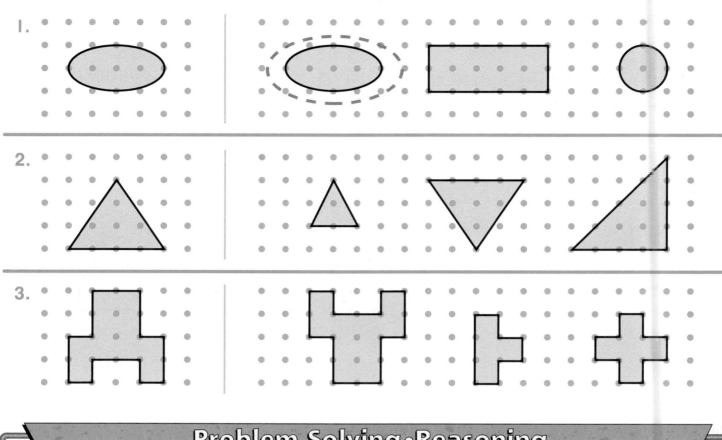

1.

2.

3.

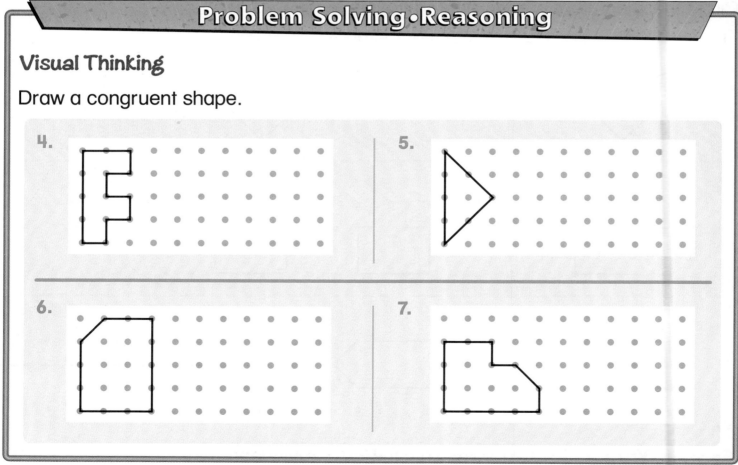

Problem Solving•Reasoning

Visual Thinking

Draw a congruent shape.

4.

5.

6.

7.

At Home Ask your child to explain how he or she knows which shape is congruent to the first shape in each exercise.

Standards
MG **2.2**, MR **1.2**, **2.0**

Make New Shapes

Learn About It

You can take shapes apart or put them together
to make new shapes.

| Use these blocks. | Make this shape. | Then make this shape. |

Guided Practice

Use the pattern blocks shown. Make the first shape.
Then make the next shape. Trace your shapes.

1. Use these blocks.

4

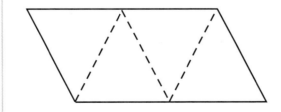

2. Use these blocks.

2

1

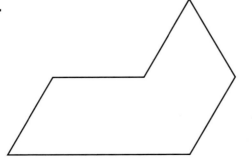

Explain Your Thinking What other blocks could you
use to make the first shape in Exercise 2?

Independent Practice

Use the pattern blocks. Make the shape shown.
Trace around the blocks.
Make a new shape. Trace around the blocks.

1. Use these blocks.

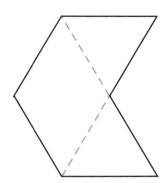

2. Use these blocks.

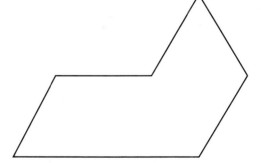

3. Use these blocks.

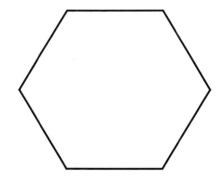

Problem Solving • Reasoning

Write About It

4. Trace and cut out the shape. Use
   the two triangles to make new
   shapes. Draw the shapes you make.

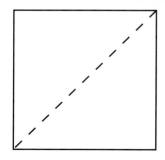

At Home Cut 2 or 3 shapes out of paper and ask your child to use the shapes to make another shape.

LESSON 6 Symmetry

Learn About It

Shapes with a **line of symmetry** have equal parts.

New Vocabulary

line of symmetry

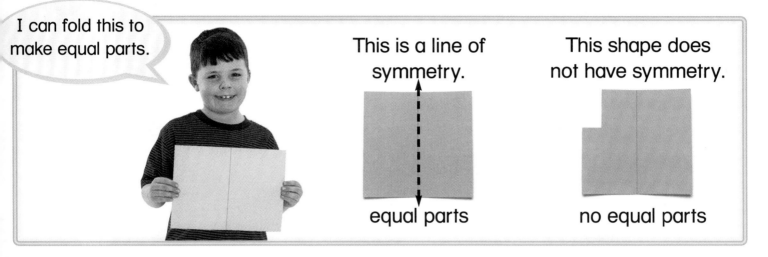

I can fold this to make equal parts.

This is a line of symmetry.

equal parts

This shape does not have symmetry.

no equal parts

Guided Practice

Circle the shapes that have a line of symmetry. Draw the line. Cross out the shapes that do not have symmetry.

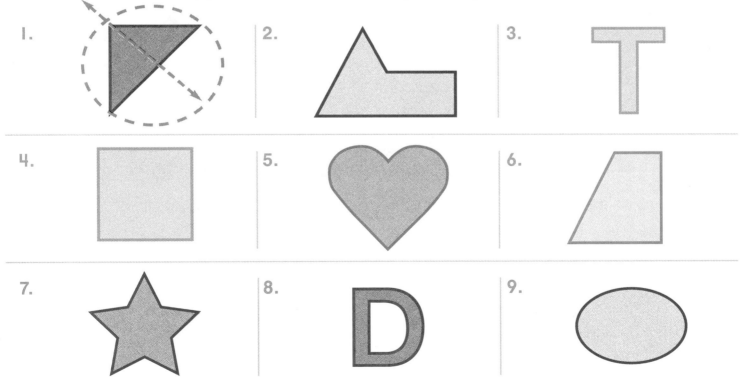

1.

2.

3.

4.

5.

6.

7.

8.

9.

Explain Your Thinking How does folding a shape help prove there is a line of symmetry?

Independent Practice

Draw a line of symmetry.
Cross out pictures that do not have symmetry.

1.

2.

3.

4.

5.

6.

7.

8.

9.

10.

11.

12.

Problem Solving·Reasoning

13. Draw 1 line of symmetry.

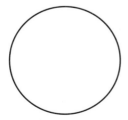

How many equal parts
did you make? _____

14. Draw 4 lines of symmetry.

How many equal parts
did you make? _____

At Home Ask your child to explain why each object does or does not have a line of symmetry.

Name _____

Standards
MG **2.0**, SDP **2.0**
MR **2.2**, **3.0**

LESSON 7 Problem Solving: Find a Pattern

You can describe the shapes in a pattern to tell what is likely to come next.

What are the next two shapes likely to be?

● ▢ ▢ ● ▢ ▢ ● ▢   ? ?
_____ _____

 Understand

Circle what you need to find out.

How many shapes are there in the pattern?

What are the next two shapes likely to be?

Plan

Circle the order of the shapes in the pattern.

Solve

Circle the two shapes that are likely to come next.

Look Back

Say the pattern. Do the shapes you circled continue the pattern?

Guided Practice

Circle the two shapes that are likely to come next in the pattern.

Remember:
► Understand
► Plan
► Solve
► Look Back

Remember to use the 4 steps.

① Mike saw this pattern on a folder.

Think: What shape comes after the triangle?

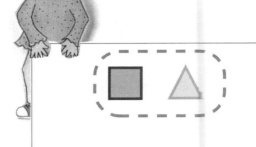

② Rita saw this pattern on a cup.

Think: What is the pattern?

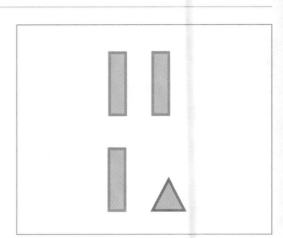

③ Gail saw this pattern on a hat.

Think: How many circles are before each triangle?

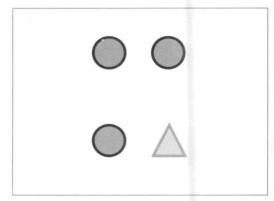

④ Rob saw this pattern on a shirt.

Think: What shape comes after the square?

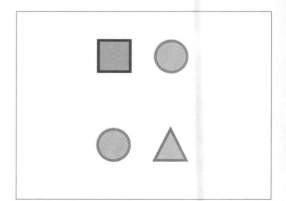

 At Home Ask your child to draw his or her own shape pattern and then explain how to find the shape that comes next.

Name_____

Choose a Strategy

Solve.

① Tim drew the pattern for a quilt. Circle the two shapes that are likely to come next.

Draw or write to explain.

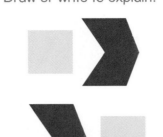

quilt

② Ellie has 65¢. She buys a drum for 48¢ and a bell for 15¢. How much change should she get?

_____ ¢

drum

③ Linda drew this pattern for a rug. Circle the one that is likely to come next.

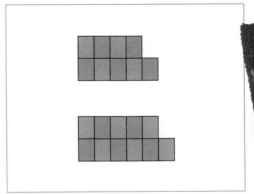

rug

④ A bookcase has 2 shelves. Each shelf has 8 candles. How many candles are in the bookcase?

_____ candles

candle

Name _____

Mixed Practice

Write the missing numbers.

1. 3 + 4 = 4 + _____

2. 2 + _____ = 5 + 2

3. 4 + _____ = 5 + 4

4. 3 + 8 = 8 + _____

Add or subtract.

5. 9 + 8 = _____

6. 5 + 7 = _____

7. 14 − 6 = _____

8.　　1 2
　　+3 8

9.　　2 8
　　−　9

10.　　5 7
　　−4 2

11.　　3 1¢
　　+1 7¢

12.　　7 4
　　+1 3

13.　　4 5¢
　　−1 6¢

14.　　8 0¢
　　−5 4¢

15.　　6 2
　　−1 7

16.　　6 1
　　+1 0

17.　　8 6
　　+　9

18.　　2 7
　　−2 3

19.　　7 6
　　+2 3

20.　　4 2¢
　　−2 4¢

21.　　1 7
　　+6 7

22.　　9 0
　　−　3

 Brain Teaser Twice as Much

Ben is twice as old as Kate.
Drew is twice as old as Ben.
If Kate is 4 years old, how old are Ben
and Drew?

Ben _____　　　Drew _____

 Safe Site

Internet Brain Teaser
Visit **www.eduplace.com/kids/mhm**
for more *Brain Teasers*.

322 three hundred twenty-two

Copyright © Houghton Mifflin Company. All rights reserved.

Name_____

Check Your Understanding of Lessons 1–7

Use solid shapes. Count the faces, edges, and vertices.

		Faces	Edges	Vertices
1.				
2.				

3. Circle the shapes that match the name.

Triangle

Write how many sides and vertices. | Draw a line of symmetry.

4. _____ sides

_____ vertices

5. 6.

7. Circle the shape that is congruent to the first shape.

8. Circle the shape you could make with these blocks.

I

I

9. Circle the two shapes that are likely to come next.

Test Prep • Cumulative Review

Maintaining the Standards

Fill in the ○ for the correct answer. NH means Not Here.

1 Mark the shape with 3 sides and 3 vertices.

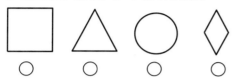

○   ○   ○   ○

2 Add.

$$27$$
$$+48$$

60   65   74   NH
○   ○   ○   ○

Use the bar graph to answer Question 3.

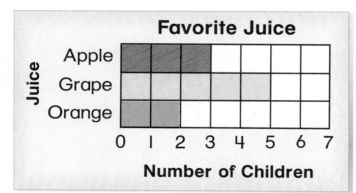

3 Which tally marks show the number of children who like grape juice?

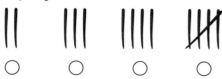

○   ○   ○   ○

4 Subtract. $68 - 21 = $ ■

57   48   47   NH
○   ○   ○   ○

5 Mark the shape that is a cube.

○   ○   ○   ○

6 Add. $53 + 39 = $ ■

82   92   96   NH
○   ○   ○   ○

7

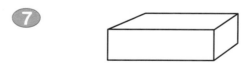

Explain how you can find the number of edges on a rectangular prism.

_____

_____

_____

_____

Copyright © Houghton Mifflin Company. All rights reserved.

Safe Site

Internet Test Prep
Visit **www.eduplace.com/kids/mᴎm**
for more *Test Prep Practice.*

LESSON 10 Wholes and Parts

Learn About It

A fraction can name one whole or more than one whole.

The whole square is purple.

$\frac{4}{4} = 1$

$\frac{4}{4}$ are purple.
Four fourths are purple.

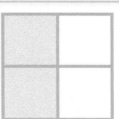

6 parts are yellow.

$\frac{6}{4}$ are yellow.
Six fourths are yellow.

Guided Practice

Circle the fraction that names the shaded part.

1.

$\frac{1}{4}$ $\frac{3}{3}$ $\left(\frac{4}{3}\right)$

2.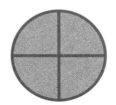

$\frac{3}{4}$ $\frac{4}{4}$ $\frac{2}{3}$

3.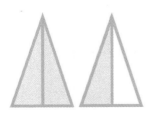

$\frac{3}{2}$ $\frac{1}{2}$ $\frac{2}{3}$

4.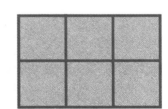

$\frac{3}{4}$ $\frac{6}{6}$ $\frac{5}{5}$

5.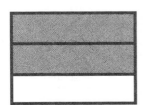

$\frac{3}{3}$ $\frac{4}{3}$ $\frac{2}{3}$

6.

$\frac{7}{4}$ $\frac{7}{7}$ $\frac{3}{4}$

Explain Your Thinking How do you know that $\frac{5}{5}$ is equal to one whole?

Independent Practice

Write the fraction for the shaded parts.

$\frac{5}{5}$ is shaded.

That is one whole.

1.

$\frac{5}{5}$

2.

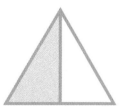

_____

3.

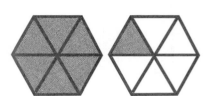

_____

4.

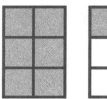

_____

5.

_____

6.

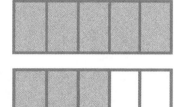

_____

7.

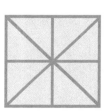

_____

Problem Solving • Reasoning

8. These fractions fell off the chart. Where do they belong? Write each fraction on the chart.

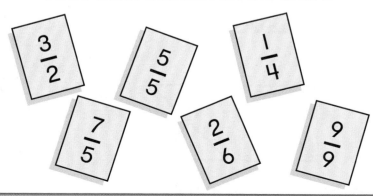

$\frac{3}{2}$ $\frac{5}{5}$ $\frac{1}{4}$ $\frac{7}{5}$ $\frac{2}{6}$ $\frac{9}{9}$

Less than 1 whole	One whole	More than 1 whole

At Home Ask your child to name each fraction and explain if it is less than, equal to, or more than 1 whole.

Standards
NS **4.2**

LESSON 13 Fractional Parts of a Group

Learn About It

You can show a fractional part of a group.

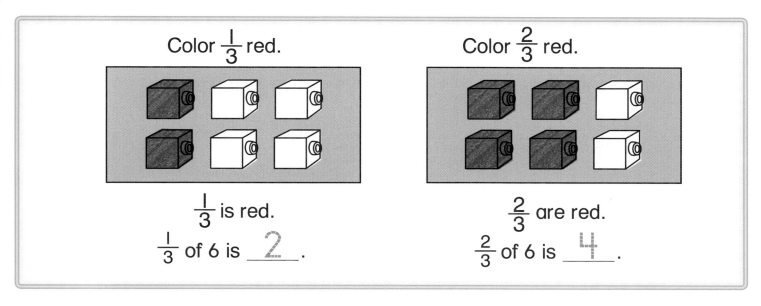

Color $\frac{1}{3}$ red.

$\frac{1}{3}$ is red.

$\frac{1}{3}$ of 6 is ___2___ .

Color $\frac{2}{3}$ red.

$\frac{2}{3}$ are red.

$\frac{2}{3}$ of 6 is ___4___ .

Guided Practice

Color to show the fraction.

1. $\frac{4}{8}$

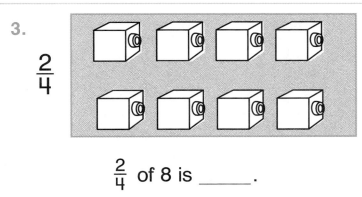

$\frac{4}{8}$ of 8 is ___4___ .

2. $\frac{1}{4}$

$\frac{1}{4}$ of 8 is _____ .

3. $\frac{2}{4}$

$\frac{2}{4}$ of 8 is _____ .

4. $\frac{4}{10}$

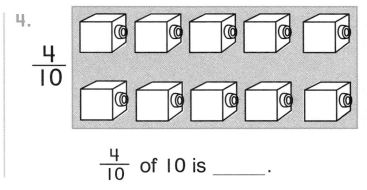

$\frac{4}{10}$ of 10 is _____ .

Explain Your Thinking How can you find an equal part of a group?

Independent Practice

Color to show each fraction.
Write the number.

1.

$\frac{2}{3}$

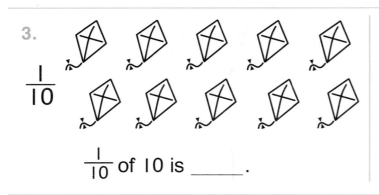

$\frac{2}{3}$ of 6 is __4__ .

2.

$\frac{7}{8}$

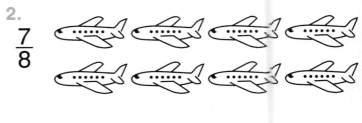

$\frac{7}{8}$ of 8 is _____ .

3.

$\frac{1}{10}$

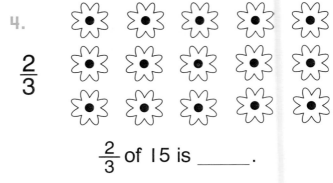

$\frac{1}{10}$ of 10 is _____ .

4.

$\frac{2}{3}$

$\frac{2}{3}$ of 15 is _____ .

5.

$\frac{1}{2}$

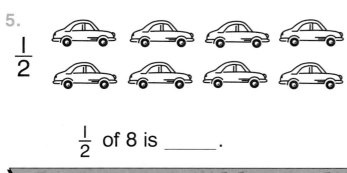

$\frac{1}{2}$ of 8 is _____ .

6.

$\frac{4}{6}$

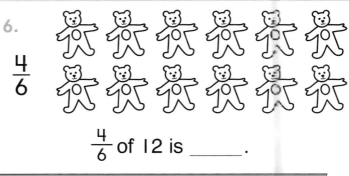

$\frac{4}{6}$ of 12 is _____ .

Problem Solving • Reasoning

7. Color the balls. Write how many.

Color $\frac{1}{2}$ of the balls ( ) .

Color $\frac{1}{4}$ of the balls ( ) .

Color $\frac{1}{4}$ of the balls ( ) .

_____ blue balls   _____ red balls   _____ yellow balls

$\frac{1}{2}$ of 12 is _____ . $\frac{1}{4}$ of 12 is _____ . $\frac{1}{4}$ of 12 is _____ .

At Home Ask your child to explain how he or she decided
how to color each fraction in the exercises on this page.

	Standards
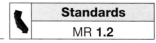	MR **1.2**

More Likely or Less Likely

New Vocabulary

more likely
less likely

Learn About It

Sometimes you need to decide if an event
is **more likely** or **less likely** to happen.

Color	Times Picked
Blue	ⵘ⅃ I
Red	III

There are 6 blue and 2 red cubes
in the bag.

You are more likely to pick a .

I picked a
blue cube
more times.

Guided Practice

Pick one cube from a bag.
Record the color. Return the cube.
Repeat 9 more times.

1. Place 3 and 6 in a bag.

Color	Times Picked
Blue	
Red	

Circle the cube that you are
more likely to pick.

2. Place 2 and 8 in a bag.

Color	Times Picked
Blue	
Red	

Circle the cube that you are
less likely to pick.

Explain Your Thinking What do you think your results
would be if you repeated Exercise 1 another 10 times?

Independent Practice

Spin the spinner. Record the color.
Repeat 9 times.

1.

Color	Results
Red	
Green	
Blue	

Circle the color that the spinner
is **most likely** to land on.

red   green   blue

2.

Color	Results
Red	
Green	
Yellow	

Circle the color that the spinner
is **most likely** to land on.

red   green   yellow

At Home Ask your child to draw a spinner
where the result is most likely to be blue.

Name_____

Problem Solving: Use Data From a Picture

You can use information in a picture to solve a problem.

Paul, Mark and Leah cut a pizza into 8 equal pieces.

You can use a picture to find a fraction.

Mark ate 3 pieces of pizza. What fraction of the pizza did he eat?

☐ number of pieces Mark ate
___
☐ total number of equal pieces

Mark ate _____ of the pizza.

Think:
How many pieces were in the whole pizza?
How many pieces did Mark eat?

You can use a picture to compare two fractions.

Paul ate $\frac{3}{8}$ of the pizza. Leah ate $\frac{2}{8}$ of the pizza. Who ate more pizza, Paul or Leah?

$$\frac{3}{8} \bigcirc \frac{2}{8}$$

_____ ate more of the pizza.

Think: Use the picture to find $\frac{3}{8}$. Use the picture to find $\frac{2}{8}$. Which is greater?

Guided Practice

Use the picture to solve each problem.

1. Mike ate 1 slice of pie. What fraction of the pie did Mike eat?

   $\dfrac{1}{8}$ of the pie

   Think: How many equal slices are there in all?

   Draw or write to explain.

2. Amy ate $\dfrac{1}{8}$ of the pie. Ty ate $\dfrac{2}{8}$ of the pie. Who ate more pie?

   Think: Which is greater, $\dfrac{1}{8}$ or $\dfrac{2}{8}$?

   _____ ate more

3. Andy ate 3 slices of pie. What fraction of the pie did Andy eat?

   Think: How many slices are there in all?

   _____ of the pie

4. $\dfrac{7}{8}$ of the pie was eaten. How many slices are left for Carlos?

   Think: How many slices were there to begin with?

   _____ slice

At Home Make up a word problem for your child about slices of pie.

Name _____

Choose a Strategy

Solve.

Strategies

Draw a Picture
Use Models to Act It Out
Write a Number Sentence

Draw or write to explain.

1. Max cut his waffle into 4 equal pieces. He ate $\frac{1}{2}$ of the pieces. How many pieces did he eat?

   _____ pieces

   waffle

2. Mary cut her muffin into 3 equal pieces. She ate 2 pieces. What fraction of the muffin did she eat?

   _____ of the muffin

   muffin

3. Tim made 4 pancakes. He ate 1 of them. Kate ate 2 of them. How many pancakes are left?

   _____ pancake

   pancake

4. Jan buys 2 bagels. She cuts each of them in half. Then she cuts those pieces in half again. How many pieces of bagel does she have?

   _____ pieces of bagel

   bagel

Mixed Practice

Write the missing numbers.

1. $3 + 5 = \underline{\quad} + 3$ 2. $4 + 2 = \underline{\quad} + 4$ 3. $5 + 4 = \underline{\quad} + 5$

Add or subtract.

4. $17 - 8 = \underline{\quad}$ 5. $\underline{\quad} = 8 + 7$ 6. $12 - 4 = \underline{\quad}$

7.
$$\begin{array}{r} 43 \\ -29 \\ \hline \end{array}$$

8.
$$\begin{array}{r} 54 \\ -8 \\ \hline \end{array}$$

9.
$$\begin{array}{r} 38 \\ +37 \\ \hline \end{array}$$

10.
$$\begin{array}{r} 90¢ \\ -41¢ \\ \hline \end{array}$$

11.
$$\begin{array}{r} 67 \\ +31 \\ \hline \end{array}$$

12.
$$\begin{array}{r} 89 \\ -53 \\ \hline \end{array}$$

13.
$$\begin{array}{r} 45 \\ +17 \\ \hline \end{array}$$

14.
$$\begin{array}{r} 42 \\ -33 \\ \hline \end{array}$$

15.
$$\begin{array}{r} 75¢ \\ -48¢ \\ \hline \end{array}$$

16.
$$\begin{array}{r} 36 \\ +19 \\ \hline \end{array}$$

17.
$$\begin{array}{r} 15 \\ 24 \\ +35 \\ \hline \end{array}$$

18.
$$\begin{array}{r} 6 \\ 13 \\ +24 \\ \hline \end{array}$$

19.
$$\begin{array}{r} 57 \\ 23 \\ +12 \\ \hline \end{array}$$

20.
$$\begin{array}{r} 31 \\ 7 \\ +12 \\ \hline \end{array}$$

21.
$$\begin{array}{r} 42 \\ 13 \\ +28 \\ \hline \end{array}$$

 Brain Teaser Tell the Truth

Use each digit from 0 to 6 once to
make this subtraction problem true.

 0   1   2 3 4 5 6

Safe Site

Internet Brain Teasers
Visit **www.eduplace.com/kids/mhm**
for more *Brain Teasers*.

Quick ✓ Check

Check Your Understanding of Lessons 8–15

Write the fraction for the shaded parts.

1.

_____

2.

_____

3.

_____

4.
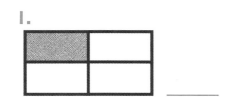
_____

5.

_____

6.
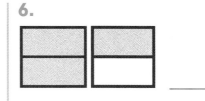
_____

Compare the shaded parts. Write **>** or **<**.

7.
   $\dfrac{1}{2}$ ◯ $\dfrac{1}{3}$

8.
 $\dfrac{1}{4}$ ◯ $\dfrac{1}{6}$

9. Write a fraction for each color.

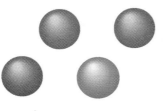

_____ red   _____ blue

10. Color to show each fraction.

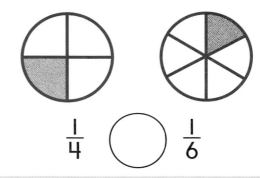

$\dfrac{1}{3}$ yellow $\dfrac{2}{3}$ green

11. Look at the table. Circle the color that is **less likely** to be picked.

Color	Cubes in Bag
purple	⁙
orange	𝍱 ‖‖

purple   orange

12. Annie ate $\dfrac{1}{6}$ of the pie. Paul ate 3 pieces of the pie. Who ate more?

_____ ate more.

Name _____

Test Prep • Cumulative Review

Maintaining the Standards

Fill in the ○ for the correct answer. NH means Not Here.

1 Mark the fraction of the shape that is shaded.

$\frac{1}{5}$	$\frac{1}{4}$	$\frac{3}{4}$	$\frac{4}{4}$
○	○	○	○

2 Mark the number that comes between.

27		41

14	23	37	51
○	○	○	○

3 Choose a sign to make the sentence true.

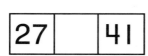

$\frac{1}{3}$ ○ $\frac{1}{2}$

>	<	=	¢
○	○	○	○

4 Subtract.

$$\begin{array}{r} 7\,2 \\ -\,4\,9 \\ \hline \end{array}$$

23	37	41	NH
○	○	○	○

5 Mark the fraction of the cubes that are yellow.

$\frac{6}{8}$	$\frac{1}{2}$	$\frac{2}{6}$	$\frac{2}{8}$
○	○	○	○

6 Pat ate 2 slices of waffle. What fraction of the waffle did she eat?

_____

Explain how you can check if your answer is correct.

_____

_____

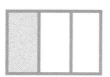

Internet Test Prep
Visit **www.eduplace.com/kids/nhm**
for more *Test Prep Practice.*

Copyright © Houghton Mifflin Company. All rights reserved.

Chapter Review

Match each letter to the correct word.

1.

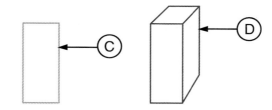

edge _____   face _____   side _____   vertices _____

2. Circle the squares.

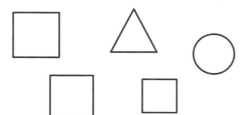

3. Write how many sides and vertices.

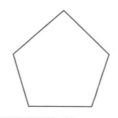

_____ sides

_____ vertices

4. Circle the shape that is congruent to the first shape.

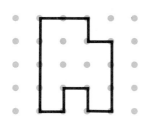 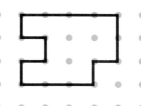 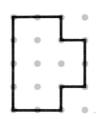

5. Circle the shapes that can be used to make this shape.

6. Draw a line of symmetry.

7. Draw the two shapes that are likely to come next.

_____ _____

Write the fraction for the shaded part.

8.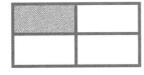

_____

9.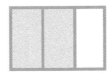

_____

10.

_____

Compare the shaded parts.
Write > or <.

11.

$\frac{1}{3}$ ◯ $\frac{1}{2}$

12.

$\frac{1}{4}$ ◯ $\frac{1}{8}$

13. Write a fraction for each color.

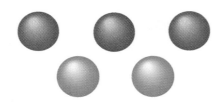

_____ red   _____ blue

14. Color to show the fraction.
Write the number.

$\frac{2}{3}$  $\frac{2}{3}$ of 6 is _____.

15. These cubes are in a bag.

Circle the cube you are **most likely** to pick.

16. Use the picture to solve the problem.
Lea ate 2 slices of the pizza. Rick ate $\frac{1}{2}$ of the pizza. Who ate more?

_____ ate more.

346 three hundred forty-six

Copyright © Houghton Mifflin Company. All rights reserved.

Name _____

Chapter Test

1. Circle the objects that match the solid shape.

2. Circle the shapes that match the name.

 square

3. Write how many sides and vertices.

_____ sides

_____ vertices

4. Circle the pattern blocks used to make this shape.

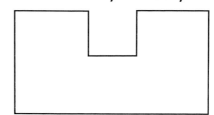

5. Draw a congruent shape.

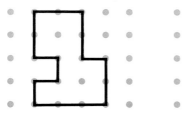

6. Draw a line of symmetry.

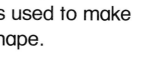

7. Draw the two shapes that are likely to come next.

      _____ _____

Write the fraction for the shaded part.

8.

_____

9.

_____

10.

_____

Write the fraction for the shaded part.

11. _____

12. _____

13. _____

14. Compare the shaded parts. Write **>** or **<**.

   $\frac{1}{4}$ ◯ $\frac{1}{8}$

15. Write a fraction for each color.

_____ blue _____ red

Color to show the fraction.

16. $\frac{1}{3}$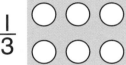

$\frac{1}{3}$ of 6 is _____.

17. $\frac{1}{2}$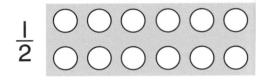

$\frac{1}{2}$ of 12 is _____.

18. These cubes are in a bag.

Circle the cube you are **most likely** to pick.

Use the picture to solve each problem.

19. Tom ate $\frac{1}{2}$ of the pizza. How many slices did he eat? _____ slices

20. Jane ate 3 slices. Rob ate $\frac{1}{4}$ of the pizza. How many slices are left? _____ slices

 Write About It

What does the fraction $\frac{2}{5}$ mean? _____

_____

348 three hundred forty-eight

Copyright © Houghton Mifflin Company. All rights reserved.

Fraction Match

What You Need

- 8 counters for each player
- fraction cards

How to Play

1. Mix the cards. Place them facedown. Take turns picking one fraction card.

2. Match the fraction on the card with a picture on the game board. Put a counter on the picture.

3. The first player to get 4 counters in a row in any direction wins.

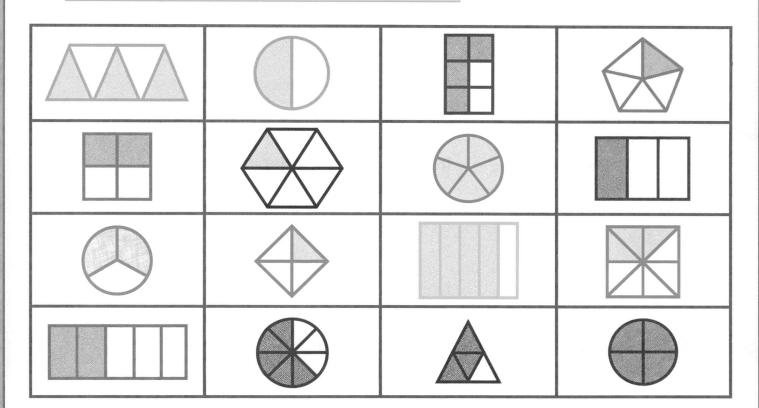

Enrichment

Decimals

You can show tenths as a
fraction or as a decimal.

Fraction

$\dfrac{1}{10}$

one tenth

Decimal

ones	tenths
0 .	**1**

one tenth

↑— decimal point

Write a fraction and a decimal for the shaded part.

1.

   two tenths

   $\dfrac{2}{10}$

   fraction

ones	tenths
0 .	2

   decimal

2.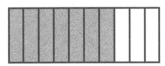

   seven tenths

   _____
   fraction

ones	tenths
0 .	

   decimal

3.

   nine tenths

   _____
   fraction

ones	tenths
0 .	

   decimal

4.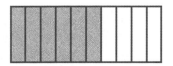

   six tenths

   _____
   fraction

ones	tenths
0 .	

   decimal

5. **Write About It** How could you color the
   counters to show 0.5? Explain.

   ◯ ◯ ◯ ◯ ◯
   ◯ ◯ ◯ ◯ ◯

Copyright © Houghton Mifflin Company. All rights reserved.

Multiplication and Division

Accessing Prior Knowledge

This story will help you review
- skip counting
- counting equal groups

Too Much Trash!

A Read-Aloud Story

written by Janet Ann Burgess
illustrated by Nathan Y. Jarvis

A Math Storybook for

_____

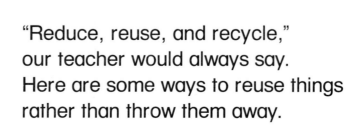

"Reduce, reuse, and recycle,"
our teacher would always say.
Here are some ways to reuse things
rather than throw them away.

Copyright © Houghton Mifflin Company. All rights reserved.

We took some empty cartons
and added seeds and soil mix.
Oh, look! We've made 3 groups of 2.

2 + 2 + 2 = _____ in all

We filled these empty bottles
with colored sand, and then—
Oh, look! We've made 2 groups of 5.

5 + 5 = _____ in all

Copyright © Houghton Mifflin Company. All rights reserved.

An egg carton becomes a box for rocks.
We painted it ourselves.
Oh, look! We see 6 groups of 2.

$2 + 2 + 2 + 2 + 2 + 2 =$ _____ in all

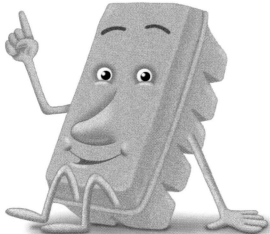

With potato printing you can make a gift-wrap that looks great. Oh, look! We've made 4 groups of 2.

2 + 2 + 2 + 2 = _____ in all

Copyright © Houghton Mifflin Company. All rights reserved.

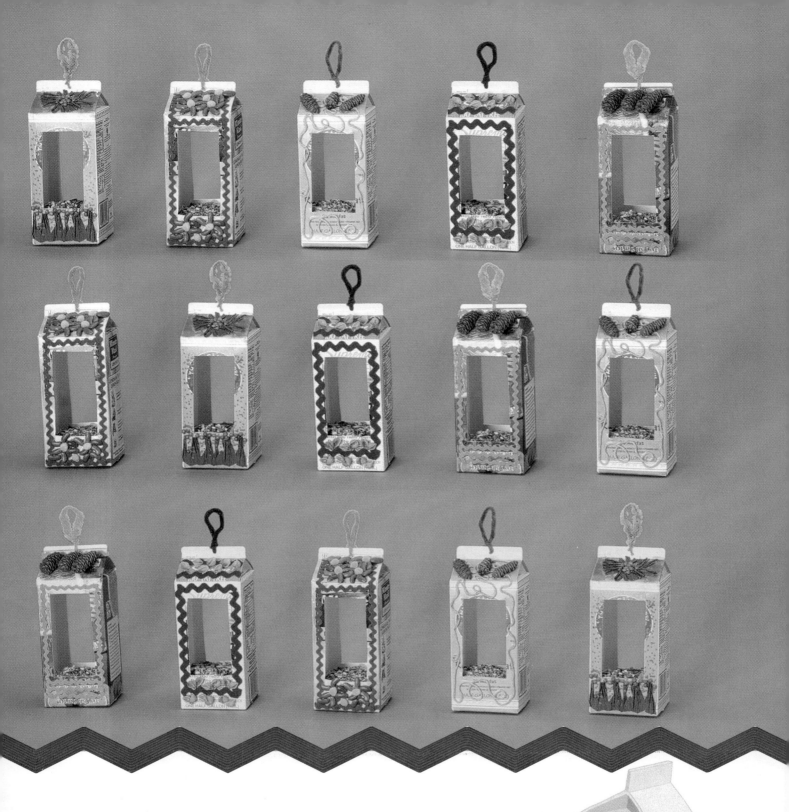

We turned milk cartons into feeders where birds can eat and be seen. Oh, look! We've made 3 groups of 5.

5 + 5 + 5 = _____ in all

Family Letter

Vocabulary

divide To find the number of equal groups.

equal groups Groups that have the same number of objects.

multiply To find the total number of objects in groups of equal size.

product The answer to a multiplication problem.

remainder The number that is left after dividing.

skip count To count equal groups.

Dear Family,

During the next few weeks, our math class will be learning about multiplication and division.

You can expect to see work that provides practice with multiplication and division.

As we learn about multiplication, you may wish to use the following sample as a guide.

3 groups of 2

$$3 \times 2 = 6$$

groups   in each group   product

$$
\begin{array}{r}
2 \\
\times\, 3 \\
\hline
6
\end{array}
$$
2 in each group
× 3 groups
6 product

Sincerely,
Your child's teacher

LESSON 3 Multiply With 2

New
Vocabulary

multiply
product

Learn About It

You can add equal groups. You can **multiply** equal groups to find the **product**.

There are 2 counters in each group. How many counters are in 3 groups?

3 groups of 2

Add.

$$2 + 2 + 2 = \underline{6}$$
↑
sum

Multiply.

$$3 \times 2 = \underline{6}$$
↑   ↑   ↑
number   number in   product
of groups   each group

3 times 2 equals 6.

Guided Practice

Write the sum. Then write the product.

1. 4 groups of 2

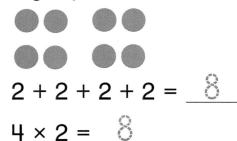

$$2 + 2 + 2 + 2 = \underline{8}$$

$$4 \times 2 = \underline{8}$$

2. 5 groups of 2

$$2 + 2 + 2 + 2 + 2 = \underline{}$$

$$5 \times 2 = \underline{}$$

3. 6 groups of 2

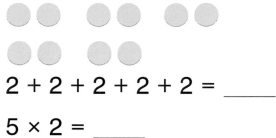

$$2 + 2 + 2 + 2 + 2 + 2 = \underline{}$$

$$6 \times 2 = \underline{}$$

4. 2 groups of 2

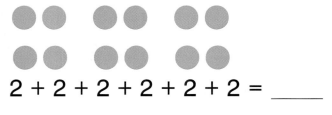

$$2 + 2 = \underline{}$$

$$2 \times 2 = \underline{}$$

Explain Your Thinking How is 3×2 the same as $2 + 2 + 2$?

Independent Practice

Write how many counters in all. Then write the product.

1.

    8 groups of 2 = __16__

    8 × 2 = __16__

2.

    5 groups of 2 = _____

    5 × 2 = _____

3.

    9 groups of 2 = _____

    9 × 2 = _____

4.

    10 groups of 2 = _____

    10 × 2 = _____

Multiply.

5. 4 × 2 = _____   6. 9 × 2 = _____   7. 7 × 2 = _____

8. 8 × 2 = _____   9. 10 × 2 = _____   10. 6 × 2 = _____

Problem Solving • Reasoning

Using Data

11. The children of King School recycled for 3 days. How many bottles were recycled each day?

    Monday _____

    Tuesday _____

    Wednesday _____

Bottles Recycled Last Week

Monday

Tuesday

Wednesday

Each 🍶 stands for 2 bottles

At Home Ask your child to explain how he or she would multiply 3 by 2 and 6 by 2.

Standards
NS **3.0, 3.1, 5.0**
MR **2.1**

LESSON **4** ## Multiply With 5

Learn About It

You can write a **multiplication sentence** to show how many in all.

New
Vocabulary

multiplication sentence

There are 5 fish in each group.
How many fish are in 2 groups?

2 groups of 5

$5 + 5 = \underline{10}$

$\underline{2} \times \underline{5} = \underline{10}$

multiplication sentence

Guided Practice

Write the sum.
Then write the multiplication sentence.

1. 3 groups of 5

$5 + 5 + 5 = \underline{15}$

$\underline{3} \times \underline{5} = \underline{15}$

2. 4 groups of 5

$5 + 5 + 5 + 5 = \underline{}$

$\underline{} \times \underline{} = \underline{}$

3. 6 groups of 5

$5 + 5 + 5 + 5 + 5 + 5 = \underline{}$

$\underline{} \times \underline{} = \underline{}$

4. 5 groups of 5

$5 + 5 + 5 + 5 + 5 = \underline{}$

$\underline{} \times \underline{} = \underline{}$

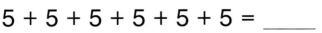

Explain Your Thinking How can skip counting by 5s help you multiply by 5?

Independent Practice

Write how many in all.
Then write the multiplication sentence.

1.

4 groups of 5 = 20

4 × 5 = 20

2.

6 groups of 5 = _____

_____ × _____ = _____

3.

2 groups of 5 = _____

_____ × _____ = _____

4.

5 groups of 5 = _____

_____ × _____ = _____

5.

8 groups of 5 = _____

_____ × _____ = _____

6.

7 groups of 5 = _____

_____ × _____ = _____

Multiply.

7. 3 × 5 = _____

8. 5 × 5 = _____

9. 6 × 5 = _____

10. 8 × 5 = _____

11. 9 × 5 = _____

12. 7 × 5 = _____

Problem Solving • Reasoning

Write About It

13. How can you use multiplication to find the total amount the coins are worth?

At Home Use small objects like macaroni to make 3 groups of 5. Ask your child to write a multiplication sentence to show how many in all.

Standards
NS **3.1**, MR **1.0**

LESSON 6 Multiply With 10

Learn About It

You can skip count to help you multiply by 10.

I can skip count by 10s. 10, 20, 30, 40, 50.

There are 10 pencils in each can.
How many are in 5 cans?

____5____ tens

$5 \times 10 = $ ____50____

Guided Practice

Write how many tens. Multiply.

1.

____2____ tens

$2 \times 10 = $ ____20____

2.

_____ tens

$4 \times 10 = $ _____

3.

_____ tens

$6 \times 10 = $ _____

4.

_____ tens

$8 \times 10 = $ _____

Explain Your Thinking How can skip counting
by 10s help you multiply by 10?

Independent Practice

Multiply. Memorize each fact.

Multiply by 2

3	6
4	
5	
6	
7	

Multiply by 5

5	
6	
7	
8	
9	

Multiply by 10

2	
3	
4	
5	
6	

Toss a number cube.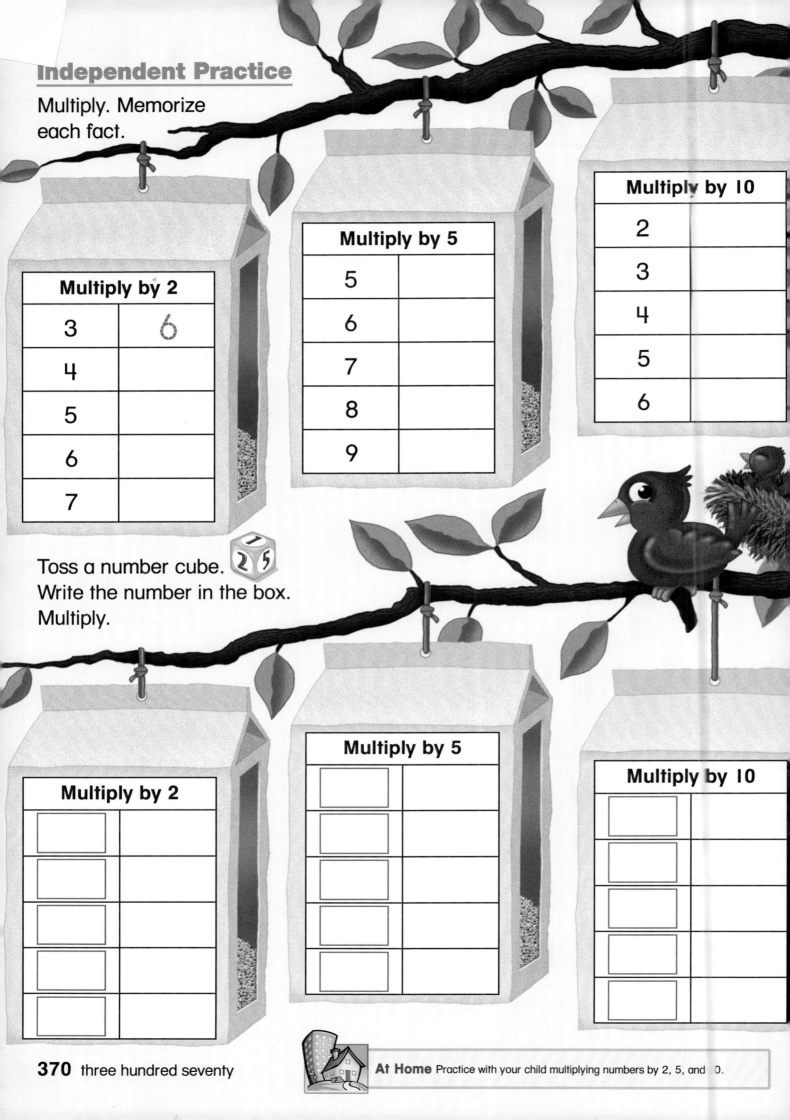
Write the number in the box.
Multiply.

Multiply by 2

Multiply by 5

Multiply by 10

At Home Practice with your child multiplying numbers by 2, 5, and 0.

Quick ✓ Check

Check Your Understanding of Lessons 1–6

Skip count. Write the numbers.

1.

_____, _____, _____, _____   _____ in all

Make equal groups with counters. Draw the counters. Then add.

2. **4 equal groups of 2**

____ + ____ + ____ + ____ = ____

Color to make equal rows. Find the product.

3. **4 rows of 5**   **5 rows of 4**   4. **3 rows of 2**   **2 rows of 3**

4 × 5 = ____   5 × 4 = ____   3 × 2 = ____   2 × 3 = ____

Multiply.

5. 10 × 3 = ____   6. 5 × 7 = ____   7. 2 × 8 = ____

8. 5 × 4 = ____   9. 10 × 7 = ____   10. 6 × 2 = ____

11. 2 × 7 = ____   12. 3 × 5 = ____   13. 4 × 10 = ____

Name _____

Test Prep • Cumulative Review

Maintaining the Standards

Fill in the ○ for the correct answer. NH means Not Here.

1 Add.

$$47$$
$$+29$$

66	74	76	NH
○	○	○	○

2 Mark the value of the coins.

10¢	30¢	50¢	70¢
○	○	○	○

3 Which one shows $\frac{1}{3}$?

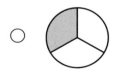

4 Multiply. $4 \times 2 =$ ▪

8	6	4	NH
○	○	○	○

5 Megan has 4 bags of fish. Each bag has 5 fish. How many fish does she have?

15	20	25	30
○	○	○	○

6 Mark the shape that is <u>not</u> a triangle.

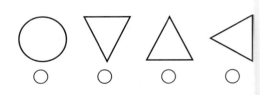

○   ○   ○   ○

7 Matt has 61 cans to recycle. He gets 20 more cans. How many cans does he have?

_____ cans

Explain how you found the answer.

_____

_____

_____

Copyright © Houghton Mifflin Company. All rights reserved.

Safe Site

Internet Test Prep
Visit **www.eduplace.com/kids/mhm**
for more *Test Prep Practice.*

Multiply in Vertical Form

Learn About It

You can write multiplication facts in two ways.

How many stamps in all?

2 groups of 5

$2 \times 5 = \underline{10}$

groups   in each   in all
         group

$$\begin{array}{r} 5 \\ \times 2 \\ \hline 10 \end{array}$$ in each group
groups
in all

Guided Practice

Find each product.

1.

$3 \times 2 = \underline{6}$

$$\begin{array}{r} 2 \\ \times 3 \\ \hline 6 \end{array}$$

2.

$2 \times 4 = \underline{}$

$$\begin{array}{r} 4 \\ \times 2 \\ \hline \end{array}$$

3.

$3 \times 5 = \underline{}$

$$\begin{array}{r} 5 \\ \times 3 \\ \hline \end{array}$$

4.

$2 \times 6 = \underline{}$

$$\begin{array}{r} 6 \\ \times 2 \\ \hline \end{array}$$

5. $\begin{array}{r} 8 \\ \times 2 \\ \hline \end{array}$ 6. $\begin{array}{r} 2 \\ \times 5 \\ \hline \end{array}$ 7. $\begin{array}{r} 5 \\ \times 6 \\ \hline \end{array}$ 8. $\begin{array}{r} 2 \\ \times 7 \\ \hline \end{array}$ 9. $\begin{array}{r} 5 \\ \times 5 \\ \hline \end{array}$ 10. $\begin{array}{r} 9 \\ \times 2 \\ \hline \end{array}$

Explain Your Thinking Which multiplication fact would you use to show 4 groups of 5? Explain.

Independent Practice

Find each product. Memorize each fact.

1.

   $5 \times 4 = \underline{20}$

   $\begin{array}{r} 4 \\ \times 5 \\ \hline 20 \end{array}$

2.

   $2 \times 5 = \underline{}$

   $\begin{array}{r} 5 \\ \times 2 \\ \hline \end{array}$

3. $\begin{array}{r} 2 \\ \times 2 \\ \hline \end{array}$
4. $\begin{array}{r} 8 \\ \times 5 \\ \hline \end{array}$
5. $\begin{array}{r} 5 \\ \times 9 \\ \hline \end{array}$
6. $\begin{array}{r} 2 \\ \times 6 \\ \hline \end{array}$
7. $\begin{array}{r} 2 \\ \times 8 \\ \hline \end{array}$
8. $\begin{array}{r} 5 \\ \times 3 \\ \hline \end{array}$

9. $\begin{array}{r} 7 \\ \times 2 \\ \hline \end{array}$
10. $\begin{array}{r} 6 \\ \times 5 \\ \hline \end{array}$
11. $\begin{array}{r} 2 \\ \times 4 \\ \hline \end{array}$
12. $\begin{array}{r} 5 \\ \times 5 \\ \hline \end{array}$
13. $\begin{array}{r} 7 \\ \times 5 \\ \hline \end{array}$
14. $\begin{array}{r} 2 \\ \times 5 \\ \hline \end{array}$

15. $\begin{array}{r} 4 \\ \times 2 \\ \hline \end{array}$
16. $\begin{array}{r} 2 \\ \times 9 \\ \hline \end{array}$
17. $\begin{array}{r} 5 \\ \times 7 \\ \hline \end{array}$
18. $\begin{array}{r} 2 \\ \times 3 \\ \hline \end{array}$
19. $\begin{array}{r} 6 \\ \times 2 \\ \hline \end{array}$
20. $\begin{array}{r} 6 \\ \times 5 \\ \hline \end{array}$

Problem Solving • Reasoning

Algebra Readiness · Number Sentences

Write a number sentence to solve.

21. There are 3 groups of cans.
    There are 15 cans in all.
    How many cans are in
    each group?

    $3 \times \underline{} = 15$

22. There are 6 boxes.
    Each box holds 5 bottles.
    How many bottles are
    there?

    $\underline{} \times \underline{} = \underline{}$

At Home Ask your child to write the multiplication facts in Exercises 10 and 17 another way.

Copyright © Houghton Mifflin Company. All rights reserved.

Standards
NS **3.1**
MR **2.0, 3.3**

LESSON 8

Multiply With 1 and 0

Learn About It

Review
Vocabulary
product

You can multiply by 1 and by 0 to find a **product**.

When you multiply by 1, the product is always the other number.

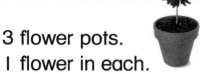

3 flower pots.
1 flower in each.
How many flowers are there?

3 groups of 1 = ___3___

3 × 1 = ___3___ flowers

↑
product

When you multiply by 0, the product is always 0.

3 flower pots.
0 flowers in each.
How many flowers are there?

3 groups of 0 = ___0___

3 × 0 = ___0___ flowers

↑
product

Guided Practice

Find each product.

1.

4 × 0 = ___0___

2.

7 × 1 = _____

3.

$\begin{array}{r} 1 \\ \times\,6 \\ \hline \end{array}$

4.

$\begin{array}{r} 0 \\ \times\,5 \\ \hline \end{array}$

Explain Your Thinking How does knowing 6 x 1 = 6 help you find 65 x 1?

Independent Practice

Find each product.

1.

   $2 \times 1 = \underline{2}$

2.

   $2 \times 0 = \underline{}$

3. $1 \times 1 = \underline{}$
4. $6 \times 0 = \underline{}$
5. $0 \times 10 = \underline{}$

6. $0 \times 8 = \underline{}$
7. $1 \times 10 = \underline{}$
8. $9 \times 1 = \underline{}$

9. $\underline{} = 5 \times 1$
10. $\underline{} = 1 \times 7$
11. $\underline{} = 0 \times 7$

12. $\begin{array}{r} 5 \\ \times 3 \\ \hline \end{array}$
13. $\begin{array}{r} 1 \\ \times 8 \\ \hline \end{array}$
14. $\begin{array}{r} 2 \\ \times 6 \\ \hline \end{array}$
15. $\begin{array}{r} 5 \\ \times 8 \\ \hline \end{array}$
16. $\begin{array}{r} 9 \\ \times 0 \\ \hline \end{array}$
17. $\begin{array}{r} 1 \\ \times 3 \\ \hline \end{array}$

18. $\begin{array}{r} 0 \\ \times 4 \\ \hline \end{array}$
19. $\begin{array}{r} 2 \\ \times 0 \\ \hline \end{array}$
20. $\begin{array}{r} 3 \\ \times 2 \\ \hline \end{array}$
21. $\begin{array}{r} 4 \\ \times 1 \\ \hline \end{array}$
22. $\begin{array}{r} 5 \\ \times 0 \\ \hline \end{array}$
23. $\begin{array}{r} 5 \\ \times 7 \\ \hline \end{array}$

Problem Solving • Reasoning

Write About It

24. Circle the number sentence that matches the picture.

    $4 \times 1 = 4$

    $4 + 1 = 5$

Explain how you know you are right.

At Home Ask your child to explain what he or she knows about multiplying a number by 0 and by 1.

Standards
NS **3.0, 3.1, 3.3**
SDP **1.4** MR **1.1, 1.2**

Name _____

Different Ways to Multiply

2
× 6   Which way would you multiply to find the answer?

I would skip count: 2, 4, 6, 8, 10, 12.

I would use counters.

I would draw a picture.

Guided Practice

Choose a way to multiply. Circle it.
Then multiply.

1. 2
   × 7
   14
   use counters
   draw a picture
   skip count

2. 4
   × 5
   use counters
   draw a picture
   skip count

3. 6
   × 1
   use counters
   draw a picture
   skip count

4. 8
   × 2
   use counters
   draw a picture
   skip count

Multiply.

5. 0
   × 8

6. 2
   × 2

7. 1
   × 3

8. 5
   × 7

9. 2
   × 4

10. 3
   × 5

Explain Your Thinking Why did you choose to multiply
the way you did in Exercises 1–4?

Independent Practice

Choose a way to solve each problem.
Then solve. Memorize each fact.

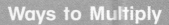

Ways to Multiply

Use counters.

Draw a picture.

Skip count.

1. 5
    × 6

2. 9
    × 1

3. 2
    × 9

4. 1
    × 7

5. 5
    × 3

6. 6
    × 0

7. 6
    × 2

8. 5
    × 9

9. 0
    × 2

10. 4
     × 1

11. 2
     × 3

12. 5
     × 5

13. 2
     × 5

14. 1
     × 1

15. 0
     × 2

16. 5
     × 8

17. 8
     × 1

18. 5
     × 2

19. 2
     × 8

20. 4
     × 0

21. 2
     × 7

22. 5
     × 1

23. 10 × 8 = _____

24. 2 × 1 = _____

25. 10 × 7 = _____

26. 0 × 0 = _____

27. 3 × 10 = _____

28. 9 × 10 = _____

Problem Solving·Reasoning

Using Data

29. Each can was worth 5¢. How much
    more money did Dana earn than Chen?

    _____ ¢

30. **Write Your Own** Write an addition
    problem by using the information in
    the graph. Then solve.

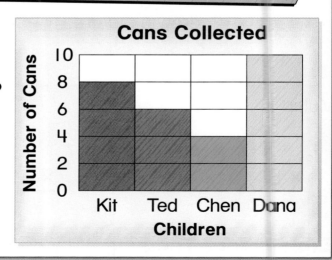

Cans Collected

At Home Ask your child how many cans Kit collected and
how much money he earned.

Name _____

Problem Solving: Draw a Picture

Standards
NS **3.0, 3.3**
MR **1.1, 1.2, 2.2**

You can draw a picture to help you solve a problem.

Randy, Kay, and Jim each planted trees for Earth Day. Each person planted 5 trees. How many trees did they plant in all?

Understand

Circle what you need to find out.

How many people planted trees?

How many trees did they plant?

Plan

What information would you use to draw a picture?

_____ people who planted trees.

_____ trees planted by each person.

Solve

Draw a picture. Use the picture to write a multiplication sentence.

_____ × _____ = _____ trees

Look Back

How can you check your answer?

Guided Practice

Solve each problem.
Draw a picture to help you.

Remember:
- ► Understand
- ► Plan
- ► Solve
- ► Look Back

Remember to use the 4 steps.

1 Kip planted 2 rows of pine trees. Each row had 5 trees. How many trees did Kip plant?

Think: How many trees are in each row?

Draw or write to explain.

_____ trees

2 Keisha saved 4 stacks of newspapers. Each stack had 10 newspapers. How many newspapers did she save?

Think: What should I draw?

_____ newspapers

3 Lyn and Juan cleaned up litter by the road. Each collected 5 cans for recycling. How many cans did they collect?

Think: What should I draw?

_____ cans

4 The recycling truck collects 4 loads every day. How many loads does it collect in 3 days?

Think: How many loads are collected each day?

_____ loads

At Home Make up a multiplication problem for your child. Ask him or her to draw a picture to help solve the problem.

Name_____

Choose a Strategy

Solve.

Strategies

Draw a Picture
Use Models to Act It Out
Write a Number Sentence

① 4 children plant sunflowers.
Each child plants 5 sunflowers.
How many sunflowers do they plant?

_____ sunflowers

Draw or write to explain.

sunflower

② Kyla has 13 tulips.
Paul has 24 tulips.
How many tulips do they have?

_____ tulips

tulip

③ Ellie has 6 groups of roses.
Each group has 10 roses.
How many roses does she have?

_____ roses

rose

④ Don has 15 daisy plants. He
gives 4 plants to his friend. He
uses 7 in his garden. How many
daisy plants does he have now?

_____ daisy plants

daisy

Mixed Practice

Find each sum or difference.

1.   43
  −29
	2. 67
	  −31
		3. 52
		  − 6
			4. 13
			  +75
				5. 48
				  +39

6.   60
  −46
	7. 97
	  −25
		8. 40
		  +53
			9. 81
			  −47
				10. 29
				  +67

11.   73
  −53
	12. 48
	  + 8
		13. 74
		  −66
			14. 51
			  −36
				15. 38
				  +47

Multiply. Memorize Your Facts

16.   7
  ×0
	17. 6
	  ×2
		18. 0
		  ×3
			19. 5
			  ×4
				20. 9
				  ×1
					21. 2
					  ×8

Brain Teaser Mystery Number

Use the clues to find the mystery number.

- I am in the circle.
- I am not in the triangle.
- I am an even number.

What number am I? _____

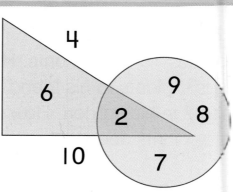

Internet Brain Teasers
Visit www.eduplace.com/kids/mhm
for more *Brain Teasers.*

Name _____

Check Your Understanding of Lessons 7–10

Find each product.

1.

$$\begin{array}{r} 2 \\ \times 4 \\ \hline \end{array}$$

4 × 2 = _____

2.

$$\begin{array}{r} 5 \\ \times 3 \\ \hline \end{array}$$

3 × 5 = _____

Multiply.

3. 8 × 0 = _____   4. 2 × 3 = _____   5. 10 × 4 = _____

6. $\begin{array}{r} 5 \\ \times 4 \\ \hline \end{array}$ 7. $\begin{array}{r} 2 \\ \times 0 \\ \hline 6 \end{array}$ 8. $\begin{array}{r} 1 \\ \times 8 \\ \hline \end{array}$ 9. $\begin{array}{r} 7 \\ \times 2 \\ \hline \end{array}$ 10. $\begin{array}{r} 2 \\ \times 6 \\ \hline \end{array}$ 11. $\begin{array}{r} 9 \\ \times 1 \\ \hline \end{array}$

12. $\begin{array}{r} 3 \\ \times 2 \\ \hline \end{array}$ 13. $\begin{array}{r} 5 \\ \times 6 \\ \hline \end{array}$ 14. $\begin{array}{r} 2 \\ \times 2 \\ \hline \end{array}$ 15. $\begin{array}{r} 5 \\ \times 2 \\ \hline \end{array}$ 16. $\begin{array}{r} 1 \\ \times 3 \\ \hline \end{array}$ 17. $\begin{array}{r} 0 \\ \times 6 \\ \hline \end{array}$

18. $\begin{array}{r} 4 \\ \times 1 \\ \hline \end{array}$ 19. $\begin{array}{r} 2 \\ \times 8 \\ \hline \end{array}$ 20. $\begin{array}{r} 6 \\ \times 0 \\ \hline \end{array}$ 21. $\begin{array}{r} 5 \\ \times 5 \\ \hline \end{array}$ 22. $\begin{array}{r} 0 \\ \times 4 \\ \hline \end{array}$ 23. $\begin{array}{r} 5 \\ \times 8 \\ \hline \end{array}$

Draw a picture to help solve the problem.

24. Jackie planted 2 rows of flowers. Each row had 6 flowers. How many flowers did Jackie plant?

_____ flowers

Draw or write to explain.

Name_____

Test Prep • Cumulative Review

Maintaining the Standards

Fill in the ○ for the correct answer. NH means Not Here.

1 Multiply.

$$5$$
$$\times 8$$

13   40   60   NH
○   ○   ○   ○

2 Mark the fraction of the shape that is shaded.

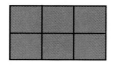

$\dfrac{1}{6}$ $\dfrac{1}{2}$ $\dfrac{3}{5}$ $\dfrac{6}{6}$
○   ○   ○   ○

3 Mark the shape that is used to make this shape.

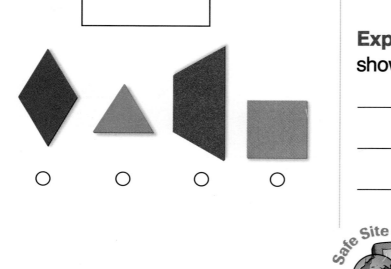

○   ○   ○   ○

4 Choose a sign to make the sentence true.

37 ◯ 73

>   <   =   ¢
○   ○   ○   ○

5 Subtract.

$$67$$
$$-28$$

52   49   38   NH
○   ○   ○   ○

6 Lily has 8 baskets. There is 1 bottle in each basket. How many bottles does she have in all?

$$8 \times 1 = \underline{\qquad}$$

Explain why this number sentence shows how many bottles Lily has.

_____

_____

_____

Copyright © Houghton Mifflin Company. All rights reserved.

Safe Site

Internet Test Prep
Visit www.eduplace.com/kids/mhm
for more *Test Prep Practice*.

Name _____

LESSON 11

Share Equally

Learn About It

You can share equally by making **equal groups.**

Review
Vocabulary
equal groups

There are 5 children who want to share 15 counters equally. How many counters does each child get?

Step 1 Start with 15 counters. Use 5 spaces on Workmat 1.

Step 2 Put a counter in each space to share.

Step 3 Keep sharing until all counters are gone.

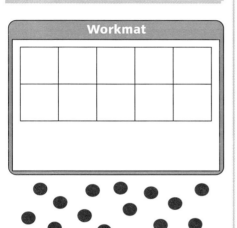

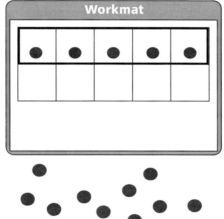

15 is 5 equal groups of 3.

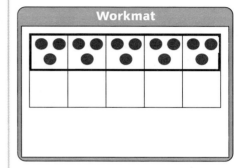

Each child gets 3.

Guided Practice

Use Workmat 1 with counters.

	Number of Counters	Number of Children	Number Each Child Gets
1.	8	2	4
2.	9	3	_____
3.	10	5	_____
4.	16	4	_____

Explain Your Thinking How could 4 people share 20 bottles of water equally?

Independent Practice

Use Workmat 1 with counters. Make equal groups in different ways.
Write how many in each group.

1.

Number of Counters	Number of Equal Groups	Number in Each Group
12	2	6
12	3	___
12	4	___
12	6	___

2.

Number of Counters	Number of Equal Groups	Number in Each Group
16	2	___
16	4	___
16	8	___

3.

Number of Counters	Number of Equal Groups	Number in Each Group
18	2	___
18	3	___
18	6	___
18	9	___

4.

Number of Counters	Number of Equal Groups	Number in Each Group
20	2	___
20	4	___
20	5	___
20	10	___

Problem Solving • Reasoning

Draw to show equal groups.

5. Three people share 12 apples
   equally. How many apples
   does each person get?

_____ apples

At Home Give your child 10 objects. Have him or her arrange them in two equal groups.

Standards
NS **3.0**, **3.2**, SDP **1.4**
MR **1.2**

LESSON 12 Equal Groups of 2

Learn About It

New
Vocabulary
divide

When you share equally, you **divide**.

Use 8 counters. Make equal groups of 2.
How many groups can you make?

Step 1 Start with 8 counters.	**Step 2** Subtract counters by groups of 2 until there are none left.	**Step 3** Write how many groups.
	• • • • • • • • **Think:** 8 − 2 − 2 − 2 − 2 = 0.	**divided by** 8 ÷ 2 = __4__ groups 8 divided by 2 equals 4.

Guided Practice

Use counters.

	Start with this many.	Number in each group	Divide. How many groups?
1.	4	2	4 ÷ 2 = __2__ groups
2.	6	2	6 ÷ 2 = ____ groups
3.	8	2	8 ÷ 2 = ____ groups
4.	10	2	10 ÷ 2 = ____ groups
5.	12	2	12 ÷ 2 = ____ groups

Explain Your Thinking Think about 8 + 8.
Think about 2 × 8. How are they the same?

Independent Practice

Circle equal groups of 2.
Divide. Write the number of groups.

1.

$14 \div 2 =$ __7__ groups.

2.

$18 \div 2 =$ _____ groups.

3.

$16 \div 2 =$ _____ groups.

4.

$20 \div 2 =$ _____ groups.

Problem Solving•Reasoning

Using Data

5. How many bags of litter were collected on Tuesday?

_____ bags

6. How many bags of litter were collected on Thursday and Friday?

_____ bags

7. **Write Your Own** Use the information from the pictograph to write a problem. Then solve.

Bags of Litter Collected

| Monday |
| Tuesday |
| Wednesday |
| Thursday |
| Friday |

Each 🛍 stands for 2 bags.

At Home Ask your child to divide 12 objects into equal groups of 2.

Equal Groups of 5

Learn About It

A **division sentence** tells how many equal groups there are.

> **New Vocabulary**
> division sentence

Use 15 counters. Make equal groups of 5.
How many groups can you make?

Step 1 Start with 15 counters.	**Step 2** Subtract counters by groups of 5 until there are none left.	**Step 3** Write a division sentence to show how many groups there are.
	(counter groups) **Think:** $15 - 5 - 5 - 5 = 0$.	$\underline{15} \div \underline{5} = \underline{3}$ division sentence There are 3 equal groups.

Guided Practice

Use counters. Then write the division sentence.

	Start with this many.	Number in each group	Divide. How many groups?
1.	10	5	$\underline{10} \div \underline{5} = \underline{2}$
2.	20	5	$\underline{} \div \underline{} = \underline{}$
3.	35	5	$\underline{} \div \underline{} = \underline{}$
4.	25	5	$\underline{} \div \underline{} = \underline{}$
5.	30	5	$\underline{} \div \underline{} = \underline{}$

Explain Your Thinking How can you use subtraction to find the number of groups you can make?

Independent Practice

Use counters. Then write the division sentence.

	Start with this many.	Number in each group	Divide. How many groups?
1.	15	5	_15_ ÷ _5_ = _3_
2.	40	5	____ ÷ ____ = ____
3.	5	5	____ ÷ ____ = ____
4.	10	5	____ ÷ ____ = ____
5.	30	5	____ ÷ ____ = ____
6.	50	5	____ ÷ ____ = ____
7.	45	5	____ ÷ ____ = ____
8.	25	5	____ ÷ ____ = ____

Problem Solving • Reasoning

9. Carla has 25 cans. She wants to share them equally among 5 people. Circle the picture that shows how she should divide.

At Home Tell your child that there are 20 objects in 4 equal groups. Ask him or her to write a division sentence that shows how many are in each group.

LESSON 14 Equal Groups With Remainders

New **Vocabulary**
remainder

Learn About It

When you divide, the number left over is called the **remainder**.

Use 9 counters to make 4 equal groups.
How many are in each group?

Step 1 Start with 9 counters.	**Step 2** Make 4 equal groups until all the counters are used.	**Step 3** There are 2 in each group. One counter is left over.

$$9 \div 4 = \underline{2} \text{ remainder } \underline{1}$$

number   number of   number in   left over
in all   groups   each group

Guided Practice

Use 10 counters and make equal groups.
Complete each division sentence. Write the remainder.

Think: Are any counters left over?

	Number of equal groups	Complete the division sentence.
1.	2	$\underline{10} \div \underline{2} = \underline{5}$ remainder $\underline{0}$
2.	3	____ ÷ ____ = ____ remainder ____
3.	4	____ ÷ ____ = ____ remainder ____
4.	5	____ ÷ ____ = ____ remainder ____
5.	10	____ ÷ ____ = ____ remainder ____

Explain Your Thinking Can 3 children share 14 snacks equally? How do you know?

Independent Practice

Use counters. Make equal groups.

Complete each division sentence. Write the remainder.

	Start with this many.	Number of equal groups	Complete the division sentence.
1.	12	5	$12 \div 5 = \underline{\;2\;}$ remainder $\underline{\;2\;}$
2.	12	6	$12 \div 6 = \underline{\quad}$ remainder $\underline{\quad}$
3.	12	7	$12 \div 7 = \underline{\quad}$ remainder $\underline{\quad}$
4.	12	8	$12 \div 8 = \underline{\quad}$ remainder $\underline{\quad}$

	Start with this many.	Number of equal groups	Complete the division sentence.
5.	9	2	$9 \div 2 = \underline{\quad}$ remainder $\underline{\quad}$
6.	9	3	$9 \div 3 = \underline{\quad}$ remainder $\underline{\quad}$
7.	9	5	$9 \div 5 = \underline{\quad}$ remainder $\underline{\quad}$
8.	9	6	$9 \div 6 = \underline{\quad}$ remainder $\underline{\quad}$

Problem Solving • Reasoning

Circle the division sentence that shows the answer to the problem.

9. There are 15 trash bags. Five people will share the bags equally to pick up litter. How many trash bags does each person get?

$$15 \div 3 = 5 \qquad 15 \div 5 = 3$$

$$5 + 5 = 20 \qquad 15 \div 5 = 10$$

Draw or write to explain.

At Home Ask your child to explain why there are remainders sometimes in division.

Name_____

LESSON
15

Problem Solving:
Choose the Operation

Standards
MR **1.0, 1.1, 3.0**

You may need to add, subtract, or multiply to solve a problem.

The Cole family collected bottles, cans, and newspapers to recycle. The table shows how many they collected.

Item	Number Collected
Cans	29
Bottles	17
Stacks of Newspaper	2

Sometimes you need to subtract to solve a problem.

How many more cans than bottles did the Cole family collect?

_____ ◯ _____ = _____ cans

Think:
I subtract to compare or find how many are left.

Sometimes you need to add to solve a problem.

How many cans and bottles did the Cole family collect altogether?

_____ ◯ _____ = _____ items

Think:
I add to find a total.

Sometimes you need to multiply to solve a problem.

The Coles collected 2 stacks of newspaper each week for 3 weeks. How many stacks did they collect?

_____ ◯ _____ = _____ stacks of newspaper

Think:
How many groups are there? Are the groups equal?

Guided Practice

Add, subtract, or multiply.

1 Jack collected 5 bins of cans on Monday and 4 bins on Tuesday. How many bins did he collect?

Think: Am I finding how many in all, or am I comparing?

Draw or write to explain.

_____ ◯ _____ = _____ bins

2 Ben recycled 2 stacks of newspapers. Each stack had 8 newspapers. How many newspapers did Ben recycle?

Think: How many groups are there? Are the groups equal?

_____ ◯ _____ = _____ newspapers

3 Mary has 10 bottles for recycling. 4 bottles are recycled. How many bottles does she still have?

Think: Am I finding how many in all or how many are left?

_____ ◯ _____ = _____ bottles

4 Sara collected 10 cans on Monday and 12 cans on Tuesday. How many cans did Sara collect?

Think: What do I want to find out?

_____ ◯ _____ = _____ cans

At Home Ask your child how he or she decided which operation to use in each problem.

Strategies

Draw a Picture
Use Models to Act It Out
Write a Number Sentence

Choose a Strategy

Solve.

1 Kenny made 8 small planters and 4 larger planters. He gave 5 to a friend. How many planters does he have?

Draw or write to explain.

_____ planters

planter

2 Jan used 3 jars to make snow globes. She used 2 bottles of glitter in each. How many bottles of glitter did she use?

_____ bottles of glitter

snow globes

3 Eric used cans and yarn to make 7 pencil holders. He gave 3 away. How many pencil holders does he have left?

_____ pencil holders

pencil holder

4 Nina made 2 birdfeeders. She put 6 stickers on each birdfeeder. How many stickers did she use?

_____ stickers

birdfeeder

Mixed Practice

Find each sum or difference.

1. 12 + 11 = 23

2. 47 − 5 = 42

3. 75 + 15 = 4̶0̶

4. 25 − 5 = 20

5. 32 + 10 = 42

6. 50 − 10 = 40

7. 35
   +16

   51

8. 42
   −26

   18

9. 74
   −55

   1

10. 53
   +37

   90

11. 24
   +65

   89

12. 20
   −14

   86

13. 82
   −45

   37

14. 28
   +36

   64

15. 93
   −71

   22

16. 54
   + 7

   61

Multiply.

17. 5 × 9 = 45

18. 2 × 7 = 14

19. 10 × 7 = 70

20. 8
   × 5

   40

21. 3
   × 2

   6

22. 5
   × 1

   5

23. 5
   × 6

   30

24. 4
   × 0

   0

Brain Teaser Pattern Puzzles

Part of each pattern is missing.
Draw the part of each pattern that is missing.

25.

26.

Safe Site

Internet Brain Teasers
Visit **www.eduplace.com/kids/mhm**
for more *Brain Teasers*.

Check Your Understanding of Lessons 11–15

Use Workmat 1 with counters.

	Show this many.	Make this many groups.	How many in each group?
1.	8	2	
2.	12	4	

Use counters. Make equal groups.
Complete each division sentence. Write the remainder.

	Start with this many.	Make this many groups.	Complete the division sentence.
3.	8	3	8 ÷ 3 = _2_ remainder _2_
4.	13	4	13 ÷ 4 = _3_ remainder _01_
5.	20	5	20 ÷ 5 = _4_ remainder _6_
6.	9	2	9 ÷ 2 = _4_ remainder _1_
7.	15	5	15 ÷ 5 = _3_ remainder _0_
8.	18	5	18 ÷ 5 = _3_ remainder _3_

9. Add, subtract, or multiply.

Tom planted 5 rows of trees.
There are 3 trees in each row.
How many trees did he plant?

_15_ trees

Draw or write to explain.

5 X 3 = 15

Name _____

Test Prep • Cumulative Review

Maintaining the Standards

Fill in the ○ for the correct answer. NH means Not Here.

① Multiply.
$$\begin{array}{r} 2 \\ \times\, 5 \\ \hline \end{array}$$

15	10	5	NH
○	○	○	○

② Mark the amount of money shown.

32¢	75¢	77¢	82¢
○	○	○	○

③ Mark the picture that shows equal groups of 2.

④ Find the sum.

$$2 + 8 + 6 = \blacksquare$$

12	14	17	NH
○	○	○	○

⑤ Mark the number ninety-three.

93	90	39	9
○	○	○	○

⑥ Subtract.
$$\begin{array}{r} 4\,4 \\ -\,1\,8 \\ \hline \end{array}$$

36	34	26	NH
○	○	○	○

⑦ Multiply.

$$4 \times 2 = \underline{\hspace{2cm}}$$

Explain how you know your answer is right.

_____

_____

_____

Copyright © Houghton Mifflin Company. All rights reserved.

Safe Site

Internet Test Prep
Visit **www.eduplace.com/kids/mhm**
for more *Test Prep Practice*.

Name _____

Chapter Review

Use the examples for Exercises 1–3.
Write a word to complete each sentence.

3
× 2
———
6

6 ÷ 2 = 3

1. The red sign means _____.

2. The green number is the _____.

3. The blue sign means _____.

Skip count to find how many in all.

4.

_____, _____, _____, _____, _____   _____ in all

Write an addition sentence and a multiplication
sentence for the picture. Then solve.

5.

____ + ____ + ____ = ____

____ × ____ = ____

Multiply.

6. $2 \times 4 =$ ____ $4 \times 2 =$ ____   7. $5 \times 6 =$ ____ $6 \times 5 =$ ____

8. $3 \times 10 =$ ____   9. $7 \times 2 =$ ____   10. $10 \times 6 =$ ____

11. $2 \times 9 =$ ____   12. $5 \times 8 =$ ____   13. $10 \times 4 =$ ____

Multiply.

14.	15.	16.	17.	18.	19.
0 × 2	8 × 2	3 × 5	5 × 5	3 × 1	4 × 5

20.	21.	22.	23.	24.	25.
2 × 5	1 × 7	8 × 0	5 × 9	4 × 1	9 × 2

Circle equal groups.
Write the number of groups.

26. groups of 2

12 is _____ groups of 2.

27. groups of 5

15 is _____ groups of 5.

Circle equal groups.
Complete the division sentence.

28. groups of 5

13 ÷ 5 = _____ remainder _____

29. groups of 2

9 ÷ 2 = _____ remainder _____

Draw a picture to help you solve the problem.
Then write the number sentence and solve.

30. Sarah has 3 boxes for recycling.
Each box has 10 bottles in it.
How many bottles does Sarah have?

_____ ◯ _____ = _____

Draw or write to explain.

Copyright © Houghton Mifflin Company. All rights reserved.

Chapter Test

Skip count to find how many in all.

1.

____, ____, ____, ____   ____ in all

Write an addition and multiplication
sentence for each picture. Then solve.

2.

____ + ____ + ____ + ____ = ____

____ × ____ = ____

3.

____ + ____ = ____

____ × ____ = ____

Multiply.

4. 10 × 8 = ____   8 × 10 = ____ | 5. 1 × 9 = ____   9 × 1 = ____

6. 2 × 2 = ____   7. 7 × 5 = ____   8. 10 × 2 = ____

9. 0 × 5 = ____   10. 9 × 1 = ____   11. 8 × 2 = ____

12. 5 × 10 = ____   13. 0 × 8 = ____   14. 1 × 10 = ____

15.	7	16.	1	17.	2	18.	7	19.	2	20.	5
	× 10		× 2		× 5		× 0		× 7		× 8

Circle equal groups.
Write the number of groups.

21.

10 is _____ groups of 5.

22.

8 is _____ groups of 2.

Circle equal groups.
Complete the division sentence.

23.

$7 \div 2 =$ _____ remainder _____

24.

$11 \div 5 =$ _____ remainder _____

Draw a picture to help you solve the problem.
Then write the number sentence and solve.

25. Ana has 6 piles of newspapers.
She puts 3 piles at the curb.
How many piles are left?

Draw or write to explain.

Write About It

Barb picks 2 baskets of apples. There
are 5 apples in each basket. How can
she use multiplication to find out how many
apples she picked?

_____

_____

_____

Copyright © Houghton Mifflin Company. All rights reserved.

Name _____

Multiplication Toss

Players 2–4

What You Need

2 number cubes
  one labeled 1, 2, 5, 1, 2, 5
  one labeled 0, 1, 2, 3, 4, 5

How to Play

① Take turns tossing the number cubes.

② Use the numbers to write a multiplication sentence.

③ After each turn, add the products. The first player to reach 75 wins.

Multiplication Sentence	Product	Total of Products
_____ × _____ = _____	product _____	total _____
_____ × _____ = _____	product _____	total _____
_____ × _____ = _____	product _____	total _____
_____ × _____ = _____	product _____	total _____
_____ × _____ = _____	product _____	total _____
_____ × _____ = _____	product _____	total _____
_____ × _____ = _____	product _____	total _____
_____ × _____ = _____	product _____	total _____

Enrichment

Properties of Multiplication

Color to show each exercise.
Write the missing number to make the sentence true.

1.

   5×2 = $2 \times$ 5

2.

   1×5 = $5 \times$ ___

3.

   4×2 = ___ $\times 4$

4.

   2×3 = ___ $\times 2$

Write the missing number to make the sentence true.
Write each product.

5. $10 \times 7 = 7 \times$ ____

   The product is ____.

6. $5 \times 6 =$ ____ $\times 5$

   The product is ____.

7. $2 \times$ ____ $= 1 \times 2$

   The product is ____.

8. ____ $\times 3 = 3 \times 5$

   The product is ____.

9. $5 \times 4 = 4 \times$ ____

   The product is ____.

10. $10 \times$ ____ $= 4 \times 10$

    The product is ____.

11. $1 \times 10 =$ ____ $\times 1$

    The product is ____.

12. ____ $\times 6 = 6 \times 5$

    The product is ____.

Copyright © Houghton Mifflin Company. All rights reserved.

CHAPTER 9

Measurement

Accessing Prior Knowledge

This story will help you review

- nonstandard units of length and height
- nonstandard units of weight

Who's the Greatest?

A Read-Aloud Story

written by Rob Arego

illustrated by Lyn Martin

A Math Storybook for

_____

"There's no doubt about it," boasted Giraffe.
"At 20 feet tall, I'm the tallest," he laughed.
Gorilla looked up, eyes wide as could be.
"To be as tall as you, I'd need _____ of me."

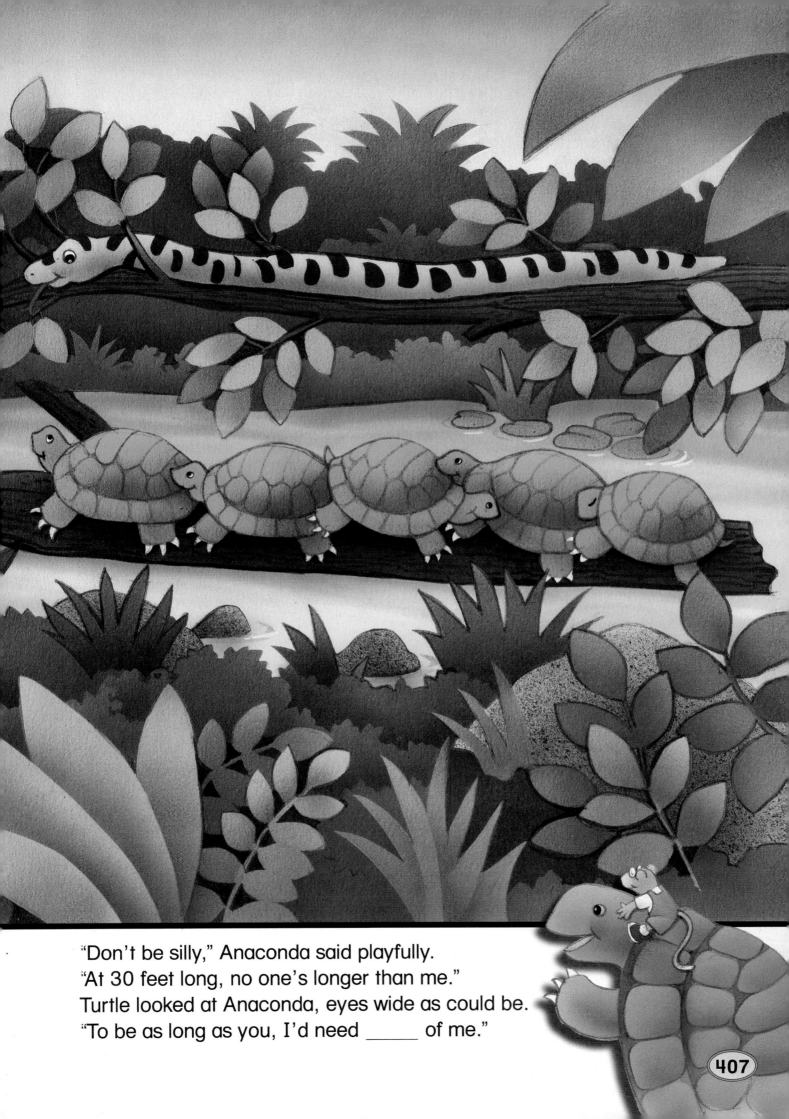

"Don't be silly," Anaconda said playfully.
"At 30 feet long, no one's longer than me."
Turtle looked at Anaconda, eyes wide as could be.
"To be as long as you, I'd need _____ of me."

407

"How funny," said Elephant, grinning with glee.
"I weigh 2 tons! Who could weigh more than me?"
Rhino looked at Elephant, eyes wide as could be.
"To weigh as much as you, I'd need _____ of me."

"There's really no question," said Condor, "you see."
"My wingspan's 9 feet. No one's wider than me."
Parrot looked at Condor, eyes wide as could be.
"To be as wide as you, I'd need _____ of me."

Mouse smiled at the animals, large and small.
"Each of you is greatest—wide, short, or tall."
"How can that be?" they all wanted to know.
"I'll tell you," said Mouse, "just how it is so."

"The earth's filled with creatures both large and small.
You'll find size and weight do not matter at all.
Now stop all that bragging about your size.
Knowing each one is special makes all of us wise."

Family Letter

Vocabulary

degrees Fahrenheit (°F) The customary unit used to measure temperature.

kilogram (kg) A metric unit used to measure mass.

liter (L) A metric unit used to measure liquid.

perimeter The distance around a plane shape.

pound (lb) A customary unit used to measure weight.

Dear Family,

During the next few weeks, our math class will be learning about measurement.

You can expect to see work that provides practice with estimating and measuring length, weight, mass, and capacity. There will also be work that provides practice in reading a thermometer.

As we learn about measuring length and about standard units, you may wish to point out to your child everyday items that are about the same length as the standard units. This will help your child remember the lengths of various units.

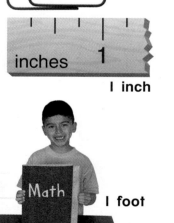

1 inch

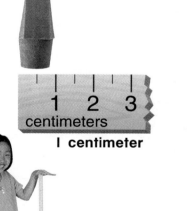

1 centimeter

1 foot

1 meter

Sincerely,

Your child's teacher

Name _____

Nonstandard Units

Learn About It

You can use units such as cubes to measure length.

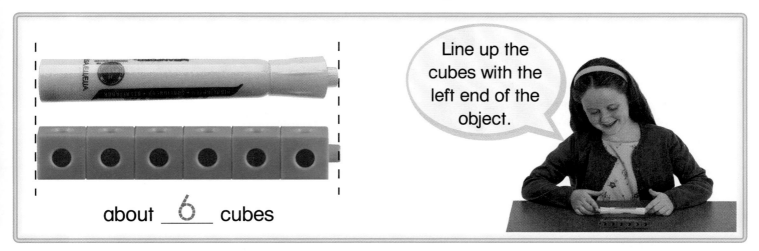

about __6__ cubes

Line up the cubes with the left end of the object.

Guided Practice

Measure the objects below.

	Find the object.	Use this to measure.	Estimate.	Measure.
1.		▣	about ____ ▣	about ____ ▣
2.		⬭	about ____ ⬭	about ____ ⬭
3.		▣	about ____ ▣	about ____ ▣
4.		⬭	about ____ ⬭	about ____ ⬭
5.		▣	about ____ ▣	about ____ ▣

Explain Your Thinking What could you use as a unit to measure the length of your classroom? Tell why.

Independent Practice

Use the unit shown.
Estimate. Then measure.

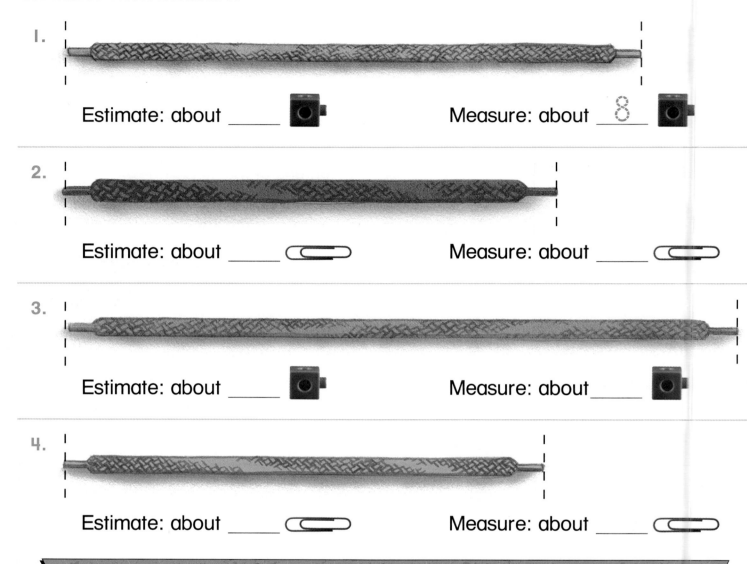

1. 

Estimate: about _____  Measure: about 8 

2. 

Estimate: about _____  Measure: about _____ 

3. 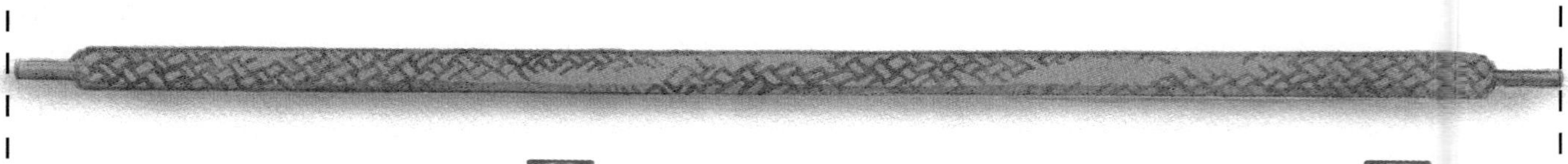

Estimate: about _____  Measure: about _____ 

4. 

Estimate: about _____  Measure: about _____ 

Problem Solving • Reasoning

Number Sense

5. Millie estimates the length of a desk to be 3 pencils long. Max estimates it to be 13 pencils long. Whose estimate is the closest?

____

6. **Write About It** Explain how you know whose estimate was the closest.

At Home Ask your child to use a crayon or paper clip to measure the length of an object such as a book.

Name_____

Standards
MR **1.2, 2.0**
MG **1.0, 1.2**

Compare Nonstandard Units

Learn About It

You can use different units to measure the same object.

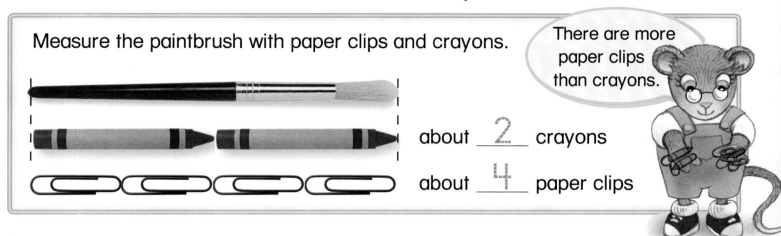

Measure the paintbrush with paper clips and crayons.

There are more paper clips than crayons.

about ___2___ crayons

about ___4___ paper clips

Guided Practice

Measure each object with the units shown.

Find objects like these.	Circle the unit that you would use more of.	Then measure.
1.		about _____ ⊂⊃ about _____ ▪
2.		about _____ ▪ about _____ ▬
3.		about _____ ⊂⊃ about _____ ▬

Explain Your Thinking   Would you need more paper clips or more crayons to measure the length of your book? Tell why.

Independent Practice

Measure with cubes.
Then measure with paper clips.
Circle the unit you use more of.

1.

   about __6__    about __4__ ⌒⌐

2.

   about _____   about _____ ⌒⌐

3.

   about _____   about _____ ⌒⌐

4.

   about _____   about _____ ⌒⌐

Problem Solving • Reasoning

5. The children measure the length of their classroom by taking steps.

   | Jenna: 21 steps |
   | Billy: 23 steps |
   | Tim: 24 steps |

   Think:
   What happens when you have a longer step?

   Who takes the longest step?

   _____

At Home Ask your child to use a pencil and then paper clips to measure the length of a table. Talk about why more paper clips are used.

Name _____

Perimeter

New Vocabulary
perimeter

Learn About It

The distance around a plane shape is its **perimeter**.

Find the perimeter of the shape in centimeters.

Measure each side. Then add to find the perimeter.

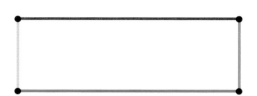

___6___ + ___2___ + ___6___ + ___2___ = __16__ cm

The perimeter is 16 centimeters.

Guided Practice

Use a ruler. Measure each side in centimeters.
Write the measure. Add to find the perimeter.

1.

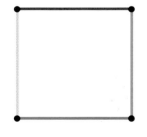

___3___ + _____ + _____ + _____ = _____ cm

2.

_____ + _____ + _____ = _____ cm

Explain Your Thinking How many sides of a square do you need to measure to find the perimeter? Tell why.

Independent Practice

Use a ruler. Measure each side in centimeters.
Write each measure. Add to find the perimeter.

1.

   __5__ + ____ + ____ + ____ = ____ cm

2.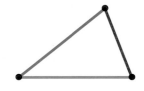

   ____ + ____ + ____ = ____ cm

3.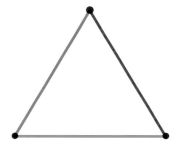

   ____ + ____ + ____ + ____ = ____ cm

4.

   ____ + ____ + ____ = ____ cm

Problem Solving•Reasoning

5. Sarah wants to put a fence around her garden. How much fencing does she need?

   _____ meters

   6 meters

   3 meters   3 meters

   6 meters

6. **Write About It** Explain how you found how much fencing she will need.

At Home Use a ruler to help your child measure and find the distance around objects in your home, such as a book or small table.

Name_____

LESSON 6
Problem Solving: Guess and Check

Standards
MG **1.0, 1.1**
MR **1.2, 2.1, 2.2, 3.0**

You can find the **area** of a shape by covering it with square units.

How many square units are needed to cover this shape?

I square unit

Understand

Circle what you need to find out.

the measure around the shape

the number of square units that cover the shape

Plan

Guess how many square units are needed.

To check, measure by covering the shape with square units.

Guess: _____ square units

Solve

Use square units to cover the shape. Count how many.

Check: _____ square units

Look Back

Was your guess close? Explain why or why not.

Guided Practice

How many square units will cover each shape?
Guess. Then measure to check.

I square unit

Remember:
► Understand
► Plan
► Solve
► Look Back

1

Think:
How can the size of the square unit help me make a guess?

Guess: _____ square units

Check: __8__ square units

2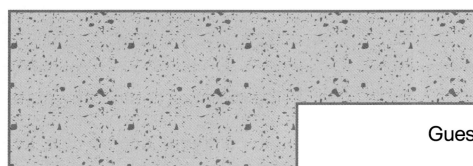

Think:
How can I make a guess that is close?

Guess: _____ square units

Check: _____ square units

3

Guess: _____ square units   Check: _____ square units

4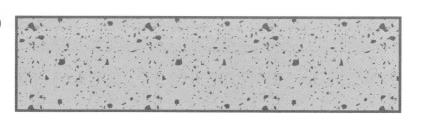

Guess: _____ square units

Check: _____ square units

At Home Cut several 1-inch paper squares like the orange square above.
Ask your child to measure small objects at home using the square units.

Name_____

Choose a Strategy

Solve.

① Kevin is making a tile pattern using 1-inch square tiles. How many tiles does he need to cover the shape below?

1-inch square

Guess: _____ tiles

Check: _____ tiles

tile

② Mark needs 4 pieces of ribbon to make a picture. Each piece needs to be 4 inches long. How much ribbon does Mark need?

_____ in. of ribbon

Draw or write to explain.

ribbon

③ Tanya has 75 beads. She uses 45 of them to make a necklace. How many beads does she have left?

_____ beads

necklace

④ Joey painted 16 racecars. He wants to put them in rows of 4 to dry. How many rows will he have?

_____ rows

racecar

Mixed Practice

Add or subtract.

1. 7 + 6 = ____
2. 30 − 10 = ____
3. 65 + 30 = ____

4.
```
  37
+ 12
```
44

5.
```
  86¢
− 41¢
```
47

6.
```
  72
− 52
```
20

7.
```
  58
+ 23
```
81

8.
```
  60
+ 15
```
75

9.
```
  70
− 13
```
63

10.
```
  24
−  6
```

11.
```
  48¢
+ 39¢
```

12.
```
  93
− 25
```

13.
```
  52
+ 39
```

Multiply. **Memorize Your Facts**

14.
```
  0
× 3
```
0

15.
```
  8
× 0
```
0

16.
```
  7
× 1
```
7

17.
```
  5
× 5
```

18.
```
  7
× 5
```

19.
```
  6
× 2
```

20.
```
  2
× 8
```

21.
```
  3
× 5
```

22.
```
  5
× 4
```

23.
```
  5
× 8
```

24.
```
  9
× 2
```

25.
```
  2
× 5
```

Brain Teaser Mystery Page Number

Cody is reading a book. He is
on a page that is between 30 and 45.
The sum of the two digits equals 10.
What page is Cody reading?

page ____

Internet Brain Teasers
Visit **www.eduplace.com/kids/mhm**
for more *Brain Teasers.*

Safe Site

Check Your Understanding of Lessons 1-6

1. Use the unit shown. Estimate. Then measure.

Estimate: about _____   Measure: about _____

2. Measure with  and .

about _____ 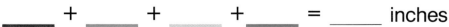   about _____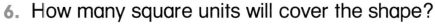

3. Estimate. Then use a ruler to measure to the nearest inch.

Estimate: about _____ in.

Measure: about _____ in.

4. How tall is the real object? Circle the better estimate.

22 cm tall

22 m tall

Use the shape for Exercises 5 and 6.

5. Measure each side in inches. Add to find the total.

____ + ____ + ____ +____ = _____ inches

6. How many square units will cover the shape?

_____ square units

1 square unit

Test Prep • Cumulative Review

Maintaining the Standards

Fill in the ○ for the correct answer. NH means Not Here.

1 Mark the number that will make the number sentence true.

$$4 + 9 = \blacksquare + 5$$

13	10	8	6
○	○	○	○

2 Use your centimeter ruler to find how long the paper clip is. Mark how many centimeters long.

1	4	6	7
○	○	○	○

3 Multiply. $3 \times 10 = \blacksquare$

30	13	10	NH
○	○	○	○

4 Subtract.

$$\begin{array}{r} 7\,1 \\ -\,1\,5 \\ \hline \end{array}$$

66	63	55	NH
○	○	○	○

5 Mark the unit you would use more of to measure a pencil.

○

○

○

○

6 About how tall is the desk? Circle the better estimate.

3 inches tall

1 foot tall

3 feet tall

Explain why the estimate you chose is correct.

_____

_____

_____

_____

Copyright © Houghton Mifflin Company. All rights reserved.

Safe Site

Internet Test Prep
Visit www.eduplace.com/kids/mhm
for more *Test Prep Practice.*

LESSON 7 Pounds

New
Vocabulary
pound (lb)

Learn About It

You can measure weight in **pounds.**

less than 1 pound   1 pound   more than 1 pound

Guided Practice

1. Circle the objects that weigh more than 1 pound.

2. Circle the objects that weigh less than 1 pound.

Explain Your Thinking Which weighs more, a pound of feathers or a pound of rocks? Tell why.

Independent Practice

Does each object weigh more than or less than 1 pound?
Circle the better estimate.

1.

more than 1 pound

(less than 1 pound)

2.

more than 1 pound

less than 1 pound

3.

more than 1 pound

less than 1 pound

4.

more than 1 pound

less than 1 pound

5.

more than 1 pound

less than 1 pound

6.

more than 1 pound

less than 1 pound

7.

more than 1 pound

less than 1 pound

8.

more than 1 pound

less than 1 pound

9.

more than 1 pound

less than 1 pound

Problem Solving•Reasoning

10. Circle the object that weighs the most.

four hundred thirty

At Home Give your child 2 cans or boxes of food. Have him or her find the weight of each container.

Name

LESSON 8 Kilograms

Learn About It

You can use **kilograms** to measure.

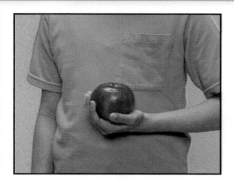

less than 1 kilogram

1 kilogram

more than 1 kilogram

Guided Practice

1. Circle the objects that are more than 1 kilogram.

2. Circle the objects that are less than 1 kilogram.

Explain Your Thinking Does a large object always weigh more than a small object?

Independent Practice

Is each object more than or less than 1 kilogram?
Circle the better estimate.

1.

   (more)   less

2.

   more   less

3.

   more   less

4.

   more   less

5.

   more   less

6.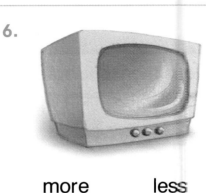

   more   less

7.

   more   less

8.

   more   less

9.

   more   less

Problem Solving • Reasoning

10. Draw the shapes on the scale so that the same number of kilograms are on each side.

    1 kg   2 kg   3 kg   4 kg

 At Home Show your child a spoon, a pen, and a chair and ask him or her to tell you which is more than 1 kilogram.

Cups, Pints, and Quarts

LESSON 9

New
Vocabulary

cup (c)
pint (pt)
quart (qt)

Learn About It

You can use **cups**, **pints**, and **quarts** to measure how much a container can hold.

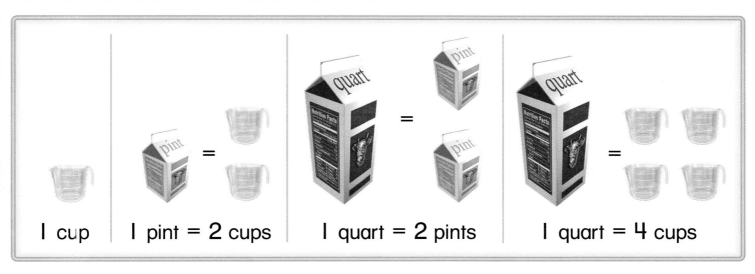

| 1 cup | 1 pint = 2 cups | 1 quart = 2 pints | 1 quart = 4 cups |

Guided Practice

Circle the number of containers you can fill.

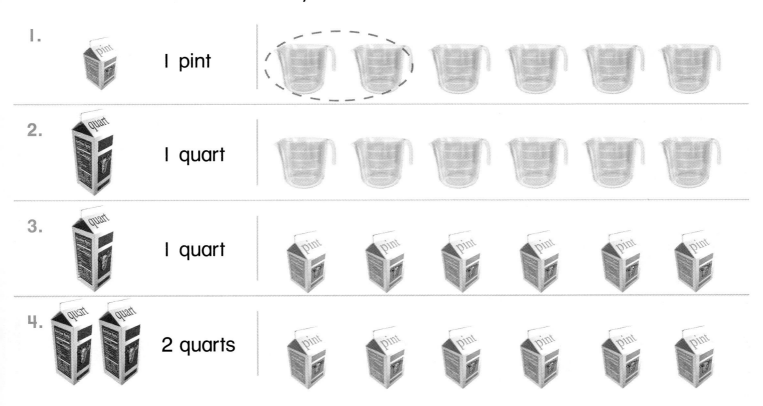

1. 1 pint
2. 1 quart
3. 1 quart
4. 2 quarts

Explain Your Thinking If 4 cups fill one quart, how many cups would be needed to fill 2 quarts?

Independent Practice

Write how many cups, pints, or quarts.

Remember:

2 cups = 1 pint

2 pints = 1 quart

4 cups = 1 quart

1. 4 = __2__

2. 2 = _____

3. 3 = _____

4. 4 = _____

5. 6 = _____

6. 1 = _____

7. _____ = 2

8. _____ = 12

9. 2 = _____

10. 2 = _____

Problem Solving • Reasoning

Using Vocabulary

11. The children bring juice to school.

   Alex brings 2 **quarts**.

   Su Lin brings 2 **pints**.

   Mark brings 6 **cups**.

Who brought the most? _____

Who brought the least? _____

Draw or write to explain.

At Home Using a measuring cup, have your child experiment and decide which is greatest and which is least: 1 pint, 1 quart, or 1 cup.

LESSON 10 Liters

New Vocabulary
liter (L)

Learn About It

You can use **liters** to measure how much a container can hold.

less than 1 liter

1 liter

more than 1 liter

Guided Practice

Is the amount each container holds more than, less than, or the same as 1 liter? Circle the best estimate.

1.

more

less

(same as)

2.

more

less

same as

3.

more

less

same as

4.

more

less

same as

5.

more

less

same as

6.

more

less

same as

Explain Your Thinking Does a large fish tank hold about 2 liters or about 20 liters?

Independent Practice

Put an X on the containers that hold **less than** 1 liter.
Circle the containers that hold **more than** 1 liter.

Quick ✓ Check

Check Your Understanding of Lessons 7–10

Does the object weigh more than or less than 1 pound?
Circle the better estimate.

1. 	2. 	3.
more than 1 pound	more than 1 pound	more than 1 pound
less than 1 pound	less than 1 pound	less than 1 pound

Is the object more than or less than 1 kilogram?
Circle the better estimate.

4. 	5.	6. 
more than 1 kilogram	more than 1 kilogram	more than 1 kilogram
less than 1 kilogram	less than 1 kilogram	less than 1 kilogram

Write the correct answers.

7.   4 = _____

8.   _____ = 16

Is the amount each holds more than, less than,
or the same as 1 liter? Circle the best estimate.

9. 	10. 	11. 
more	more	more
same as	same as	same as
less	less	less

Name _____

Test Prep • Cumulative Review

Maintaining the Standards

Fill in the ○ for the correct answer. NH means Not Here.

1 Subtract.

$$63$$
$$-8$$

58	54	51	NH
○	○	○	○

Use the tally to answer Questions 2 and 3.

Favorite Fruits	
Fruit	**Number of Children**
Apples	IIII
Grapes	IIII III
Bananas	II

2 How many children chose apples?

2	4	5	8
○	○	○	○

3 How many more children chose grapes than bananas?

8	6	5	2
○	○	○	○

4 Mark the object that would weigh more than 1 pound.

○	○	○	○

5 Multiply. $5 \times 5 = \blacksquare$

25	10	5	NH
○	○	○	○

6

15¢   16¢   10¢   12¢

James buys 2 rocks. He spends 31¢. What is the price of each rock that he buys?

_____ , _____

Explain how you found the answer.

_____

_____

_____

Copyright © Houghton Mifflin Company. All rights reserved.

Safe Site

Internet Test Prep
Visit **www.eduplace.com/kids/mhm**
for more *Test Prep Practice.*

LESSON 11 Temperature

Learn About It

You can measure **temperature** in **degrees Fahrenheit (°F)**.

New
Vocabulary

temperature
degrees Fahrenheit (°F)

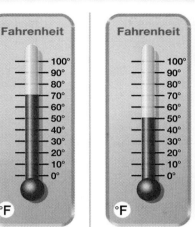

70°F

70 degrees Fahrenheit

50°F

50 degrees Fahrenheit

Guided Practice

Write each temperature.

1.

_90_ °F

2.
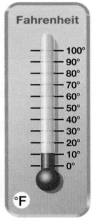

_____ °F

Explain Your Thinking Why is it helpful to know the temperature?

Independent Practice

Write each temperature.

1.
   Fahrenheit
   $\underline{40}$ °F

2.
   Fahrenheit
   _____ °F

3.
   Fahrenheit
   _____ °F

4.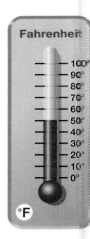
   Fahrenheit
   _____ °F

5.
   Fahrenheit
   _____ °F

6.
   Fahrenheit
   _____ °F

7.
   Fahrenheit
   _____ °F

8.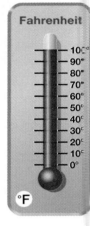
   Fahrenheit
   _____ °F

Problem Solving • Reasoning

Using Data

9. Use the table to answer the question.

Monday's Temperatures	
Time of Day	**Temperature**
Morning	50° F
Night	30° F

How many degrees did the
temperature change from morning to night? _____

At Home With your child, listen to the radio, watch TV, or read the newspaper to find out what the temperature will be tomorrow. Discuss if it will be hot or cold.

Name_____

Measurement Units and Tools

Learn About It

You can use different units and tools for different measurements.

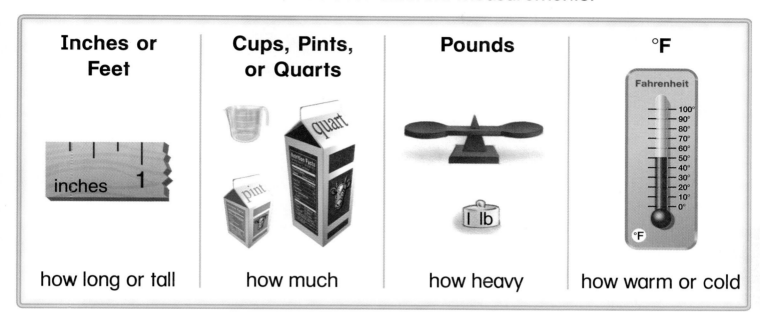

Inches or Feet	Cups, Pints, or Quarts	Pounds	°F
how long or tall	how much	how heavy	how warm or cold

Guided Practice

Circle the correct unit of measure.

1. How heavy are the books?

    cups

    inches

    (pounds)

    °F

2. How tall is the giraffe?

    pints

    feet

    pounds

    °F

3. How much milk is in the bottle?

    quarts

    inches

    pounds

    °F

4. What is the temperature?

    cups

    feet

    pounds

    °F

Explain Your Thinking Which units would you use to find the length of a piece of string? Tell why.

Independent Practice

Circle the correct tool to measure each object.

1. How much water is in the bucket?

2. How tall are you?

3. What is the temperature?

4. How heavy is the apple?

Problem Solving • Reasoning

Write About It

5. Tell how you would use each of the tools
   and what you could measure with it.

At Home Ask your child if he or she would use a scale, a ruler, or a thermometer to find how heavy a book is.

Copyright © Houghton Mifflin Company. All rights reserved.

Name _____

Problem Solving: Use Measurement

You can measure the length
of a path that is not straight.

Sometimes you can use a ruler to measure.

Measure each part of the path to the nearest inch.
Then add the parts.

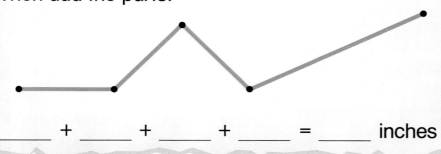

_____ + _____ + _____ + _____ = _____ inches

Sometimes it helps to use a string and a ruler to measure.

Put a string along the path.
Then measure the string with a ruler.

_____ inches

Guided Practice

How long is the path?
Use a ruler to measure.
Use a string if you need to.

1

Think:
Can I use a ruler to measure each part of the path?

_____ + _____ + _____ = _____ in.

2

Think:
Can I use a ruler to measure each part of the path?

_____ + _____ + _____ = _____ in.

3

Think:
Why should I measure first with a string?

_____ in.

4

Think:
Why should I measure first with a string?

_____ in.

444 four hundred forty-four

At Home Have your child use a ruler, or string and a ruler, to measure objects that are less than 12 inches in length.

Name _____

Choose a Strategy

Solve.

Strategies

Draw a Picture
Guess and Check
Write a Number Sentence

1 This path shows how far a
grasshopper hopped in one jump.
What is the length of the jump?   _____ inches

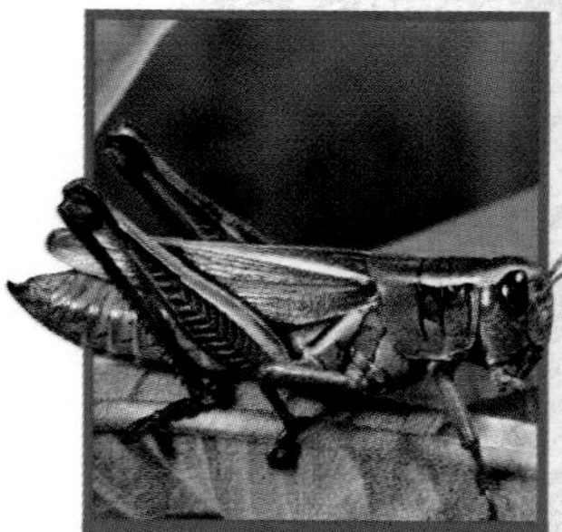

grasshopper

2 A butterfly has 4 wings.
How many wings are on
3 butterflies?

_____ wings

butterfly

3 A toad jumps 6 inches in
3 jumps of equal length. What
is the length of each jump?

_____ inches

toad

4 A beetle has 6 legs. How
many legs are on 2 beetles?

_____ legs

beetle

Name

Mixed Practice

Find each sum or difference.

1. $\begin{array}{r} 34 \\ +42 \\ \hline \end{array}$	2. $\begin{array}{r} 42 \\ -26 \\ \hline \end{array}$	3. $\begin{array}{r} 63 \\ -17 \\ \hline \end{array}$	4. $\begin{array}{r} 58 \\ +\ 9 \\ \hline \end{array}$	5. $\begin{array}{r} 81 \\ +12 \\ \hline \end{array}$
6. $\begin{array}{r} 90 \\ -67 \\ \hline \end{array}$	7. $\begin{array}{r} 58 \\ +23 \\ \hline \end{array}$	8. $\begin{array}{r} 37 \\ -\ 8 \\ \hline \end{array}$	9. $\begin{array}{r} 65 \\ -49 \\ \hline \end{array}$	10. $\begin{array}{r} 82 \\ -74 \\ \hline \end{array}$

Multiply.  Memorize Your Facts

11. $5 \times 3 =$ ____   12. $2 \times 4 =$ ____   13. $4 \times 10 =$ ____

14. $\begin{array}{r} 5 \\ \times 6 \\ \hline \end{array}$	15. $\begin{array}{r} 7 \\ \times 2 \\ \hline \end{array}$	16. $\begin{array}{r} 9 \\ \times 0 \\ \hline \end{array}$	17. $\begin{array}{r} 8 \\ \times 5 \\ \hline \end{array}$	18. $\begin{array}{r} 5 \\ \times 1 \\ \hline \end{array}$	19. $\begin{array}{r} 6 \\ \times 5 \\ \hline \end{array}$
20. $\begin{array}{r} 2 \\ \times 4 \\ \hline \end{array}$	21. $\begin{array}{r} 8 \\ \times 2 \\ \hline \end{array}$	22. $\begin{array}{r} 2 \\ \times 1 \\ \hline \end{array}$	23. $\begin{array}{r} 0 \\ \times 5 \\ \hline \end{array}$	24. $\begin{array}{r} 7 \\ \times 5 \\ \hline \end{array}$	25. $\begin{array}{r} 9 \\ \times 2 \\ \hline \end{array}$

 Brain Teaser A Juicy Problem

How can you make these pitchers have the same amount of juice?

Pour _____ cups from Pitcher A into Pitcher B.

Each pitcher now has _____ cups.

 cup

Pitcher A   Pitcher B

8 cups   4 cups

Internet Brain Teasers
Visit **www.eduplace.com/kids/mhm**
for more *Brain Teasers*.

Safe Site

Copyright © Houghton Mifflin Company. All rights reserved.

Quick ✓ Check

Check Your Understanding of Lessons 11–13

Write each temperature.

1.

Fahrenheit
— 100°
— 90°
— 80°
— 70°
— 60°
— 50°
— 40°
— 30°
— 20°
— 10°
— 0°
°F

_____ °F

2.

Fahrenheit
— 100°
— 90°
— 80°
— 70°
— 60°
— 50°
— 40°
— 30°
— 20°
— 10°
— 0°
°F

_____ °F

3.

Fahrenheit
— 100°
— 90°
— 80°
— 70°
— 60°
— 50°
— 40°
— 30°
— 20°
— 10°
— 0°
°F

_____ °F

4.

Fahrenheit
— 100°
— 90°
— 80°
— 70°
— 60°
— 50°
— 40°
— 30°
— 20°
— 10°
— 0°
°F

_____ °F

Circle the unit you would use to measure.

5. How heavy is a kitten?

    cup   pound

6. How tall is a tree?

    feet   pounds

7. How much water does a bottle hold?

    liters   kilograms

8. What is the temperature?

    °F   pounds

Circle the correct tool to measure each object.

9. How heavy is the package?

10. How cold is it?

11. How long is the path?
Use a ruler to measure its length in inches.

_____ + _____ + _____ + _____ = _____ inches

Name _____

Test Prep • Cumulative Review

Maintaining the Standards

Fill in the ○ for the correct answer. NH means Not Here.

1 Choose a sign to make the sentence true.

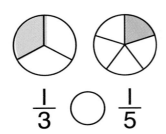

$$\frac{1}{3} \bigcirc \frac{1}{5}$$

>	<	=	¢
○	○	○	○

---

2 Mark the unit you could use to measure the length of your math book.

○ quarts   ○ cups

○ inches   ○ pounds

---

3 Mark the best estimate for the length of the ribbon.

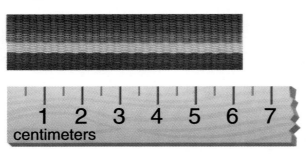

4 cm	5 cm	6 cm	7 cm
○	○	○	○

---

4 Multiply. $\begin{array}{r} 7 \\ \times\, 2 \\ \hline \end{array}$

18	14	9	NH
○	○	○	○

---

5 Add.   34 + 47 = ■

64	81	84	NH
○	○	○	○

---

6 Subtract. $\begin{array}{r} 98 \\ -\, 89 \\ \hline \end{array}$

13	11	9	NH
○	○	○	○

---

7 A rabbit hops 8 feet in 4 equal hops.

Explain why each hop cannot be 4 feet long.

_____

_____

Copyright © Houghton Mifflin Company. All rights reserved.

Safe Site

Internet Test Prep
Visit **www.eduplace.com/kids/mhm**
for more *Test Prep Practice*.

Name _____

Chapter Review

Which unit of measure would you use?

| pound |
| inch |
| degrees Fahrenheit (°F) |
| quart |

1. How long is it? _____

2. How heavy is it? _____

3. How much can it hold? _____

4. How hot is it? _____

5. Measure with .
   Then measure with ⌒.
   Circle the unit you use more of.

about _____

about _____ ⌒

How tall is the real object?
Circle the better estimate.

6.

about 12 inches

about 12 feet

7.

2 cm tall

2 m tall

8. Use a ruler to measure each side in inches.
   Add to find the total.

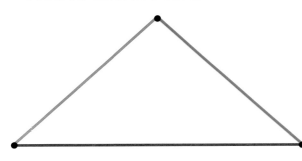

_____ + _____ + _____ = _____ inches

Circle the better estimate.

9. Is it more or less than 1 pound?

more than 1 pound

less than 1 pound

10. Is it more or less than 1 kilogram?

more than 1 kilogram

less than 1 kilogram

Circle the number of containers you can fill.

11.

1 quart

12. Circle the one that holds more than 1 liter.

13. Write the temperature.

_____ °F

14. Keli is covering this shape with 1-inch-square tiles. How many tiles does she need?

Guess: _____ tiles

Check: _____ tiles

15. A grasshopper jumps a total of 16 inches in 2 equal jumps. How long is each jump?

_____ inches

Draw or write to explain.

Copyright © Houghton Mifflin Company. All rights reserved.

Name _____

Chapter Test

1. Measure with .
   Then measure with .
   Circle the unit you use more of.

   about _____

   about _____

How long or tall is the real object?
Circle the better estimate.

2.    about 2 inches

   about 2 feet

3.    about 20 cm

   about 20 m

How much would the real object measure?
Circle the better estimate.

4.

   more than 1 pound

   less than 1 pound

5.

   more than 1 kilogram

   less than 1 kilogram

6. Circle the containers you can fill.

7. Circle the object that holds more than 1 liter.

8. Write the temperature.

_____ °F

---

9. How many 1-inch-square tiles
are needed to cover the blue shape?

1-inch square

Guess: _____ tiles

Check: _____ tiles

---

10. What is the distance around this shape?
Use an inch ruler to measure.

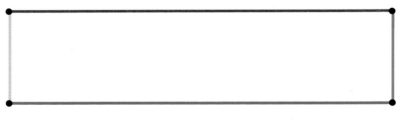

_____ + _____ + _____ + _____ = _____ inches

Write About It

Molly wants to find the distance
around this shape. She knows that
each side is the same length.

Explain how Molly can find the
distance around the shape.

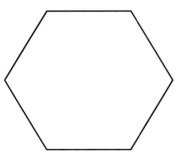

_____

_____

Copyright © Houghton Mifflin Company. All rights reserved.

Measurement Hunt

Players
Teams of
2, 3, or 4

What You Need

• ruler to measure in inches

inches   1   2

How to Play

① Work in a team.

② Look for objects that you think measure 3 inches, 6 inches, 9 inches, and 12 inches. Measure the objects.

③ Draw or write about one object for each length.

④ The first team to find an object for each length wins.

3 inches

6 inches

9 inches

12 inches

Enrichment

Nearest Half-Inch

Measure each object to the nearest half inch.
Circle your answer.

1.

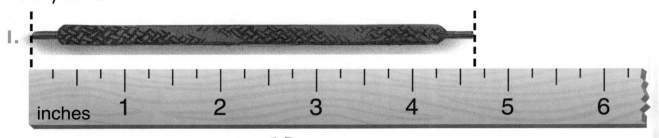

4 in. $4\frac{1}{2}$ in.   5 in. $5\frac{1}{2}$ in.

2.

5 in. $5\frac{1}{2}$ in.   6 in. $6\frac{1}{2}$ in.

3.

$2\frac{1}{2}$ in.   3 in. $3\frac{1}{2}$ in.   4 in.

4.

$1\frac{1}{2}$ in.   2 in. $2\frac{1}{2}$ in.   3 in.

5.

5 in. $5\frac{1}{2}$ in.   6 in. $6\frac{1}{2}$ in.

6.   1 in. $1\frac{1}{2}$ in.   2 in. $2\frac{1}{2}$ in.

Copyright © Houghton Mifflin Company. All rights reserved.

Time and Calendar

Accessing Prior Knowledge

This story will help you review
- Telling time to the hour

The Tortoise and the Hare Race Again

A Read-Aloud Story

written by Laura Black
illustrated by Greg Scheetz

A Math Storybook for

_____

The race is beginning.
Here are the rules.
Bike over the mountain
and swim through the pool.
Then put on your helmet,
your kneepads, and skates.
Skate to the finish line
and you'll win the race!

What time is it ? _____ : _____

Copyright © Houghton Mifflin Company. All rights reserved.

Tortoise must speed up!
An hour has passed.
While Hare races forward,
poor Tortoise is last.

What time is it? ____:____

457

It has been two hours
since this race began.
Tortoise climbs to the top,
while Hare rests in the sand.

What time is it? _____:_____

Copyright © Houghton Mifflin Company. All rights reserved.

458

Another hour has passed.
Hare puts on his gear.
Tortoise is still swimming—
he's not even near.

What time is it? _____ : _____

Hare sees the finish line
from his spot by the tree.
With so little time left,
he thinks he's home free!

What time is it? _____:_____

Copyright © Houghton Mifflin Company. All rights reserved.

Tortoise crosses the finish line
with time to spare.
Slow and steady won the race—
will someone wake up Hare?

What time is it? _____:_____

Family Letter

Dear Family,

During the next few weeks, our math class will be learning about time and calendars.

You can expect to see work that provides practice reading and writing time. There will also be work that provides practice reading and using calendars and schedules.

As we learn about time and calendars, you may wish to use the following samples as a guide.

Vocabulary

calendar A table that shows the days, weeks and months of a year.

half-hour A period of time equal to 30 minutes.

hour A unit of time equal to 60 minutes.

minute A unit of time equal to 60 seconds.

quarter-hour A period of time equal to 15 minutes.

second A unit of time; there are 60 seconds in one minute.

Telling Time

| 10 o'clock | 15 minutes after 10 | 30 minutes after 10 | 45 minutes after 10 |
| 10:00 | 10:15 | 10:30 | 10:45 |

Using a Schedule

Cory's After-School Schedule	
Snack	3:30 – 4:00
Homework	4:00 – 6:00
Dinner	6:00 – 6:30

Sincerely,

Your child's teacher

LESSON 1

What Is a Minute?

New Vocabulary
seconds
minute

Learn About It

There are 60 **seconds** in one **minute**.

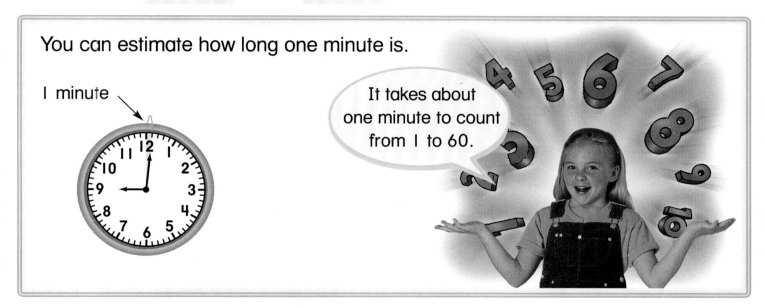

You can estimate how long one minute is.

I minute

It takes about one minute to count from I to 60.

Guided Practice

How many can you do in one minute?
Estimate. Then count.

	Activity	Estimate how many you can do.	Count how many you can do.
1.	Touch your toes.		
2.	Jump up and down.		
3.	Write your name.		
4.	Hop on one foot.		
5.	Say the alphabet.		
6.	Count to 25.		

Explain Your Thinking What do you do that
takes about one minute?

Independent Practice

Will the activity take more than or less than one minute?
Circle your answer.

1. Read a book.

(more)

less

2. Paint a picture.

more

less

3. Find 3 + 4.

more

less

4. Play a board game.

more

less

5. Eat dinner.

more

less

6. Throw a ball.

more

less

Problem Solving•Reasoning

Write About It

7. Draw a picture to show something you do that takes **less** than one minute.

8. Draw another picture to show something you do that takes **more** than one minute.

At Home Have your child tell you things that he or she does every day that take more than and less than one minute.

Copyright © Houghton Mifflin Company. All rights reserved

Standards
MG **1.4**, MR **3.0**

LESSON 2 Time to the Hour

New Vocabulary

hour

Learn About It

There are 60 minutes in one **hour**.

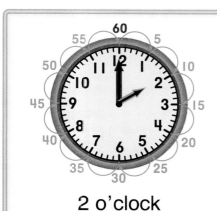

minute hand

hour hand

2 o'clock

2 : 00

In one hour the minute hand moves all the way around a clock.

Guided Practice

Write each time.

1.

8:00

2. _____ : _____

3. _____ : _____

4. _____ : _____

5.  _____ : _____

6.  _____ : _____

7.  _____ : _____

8.  _____ : _____

Explain Your Thinking Where is the minute hand on the hour?

Independent Practice

Write each time.

1.

10:00

2.

___ : ___

3.

___ : ___

4.

___ : ___

5.

___ : ___

6.

___ : ___

7.

___ : ___

8.

___ : ___

9.

___ : ___

10.

___ : ___

11.

___ : ___

12.

___ : ___

Problem Solving • Reasoning

13. Write each time. Then label the clocks 1–4 from the earliest to the latest time shown.

11:00

___

___ : ___

___

___ : ___

___

___ : ___

___

At Home Have your child use a clock with hands to show you where the minute hand is on the hour.

	Standards
	MG **1.4**

LESSON 3 Time to the Half-Hour

Learn About It

There are 30 minutes in a **half-hour**.

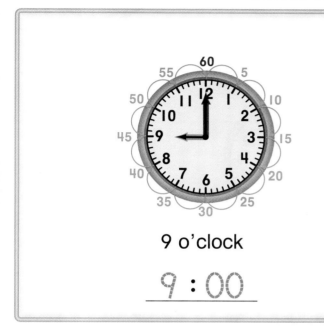

9 o'clock

$9 : 00$

30 minutes after 9

hour → $9 : 30$ ← minutes after the hour

In a half-hour the minute hand moves halfway around a clock.

Guided Practice

Write each time.

1. $3:30$

2.  $\quad : \quad$

3.  $\quad : \quad$

4. $\quad : \quad$

5.  $\quad : \quad$

6. $\quad : \quad$

7.  $\quad : \quad$

8.  $\quad : \quad$

Explain Your Thinking Where is the hour hand on the half-hour?

Independent Practice

Write each time.

1.

   2:30

2.

   ___:___

3.

   ___:___

4.

   ___:___

5.

   ___:___

6.

   ___:___

7.

   ___:___

8.

   ___:___

9.

   ___:___

10.

    ___:___

11.

    ___:___

12.

    ___:___

Problem Solving • Reasoning

13. The soccer team practices for 30 minutes. Then they play a game for a half-hour. How long does soccer last?

    _____ minutes

    Draw or write to explain.

14. What is another way to write this amount of time?

    _____ hour

At Home Have your child use a clock with hands to show you where the hour hand is on the half-hour.

Copyright © Houghton Mifflin Company. All rights reserved.

Standards
MG **1.4**, SDP **2.1**

 LESSON 4

Time to Five Minutes

Learn About It

Use what you know about counting by 5s to tell time to 5 minutes.

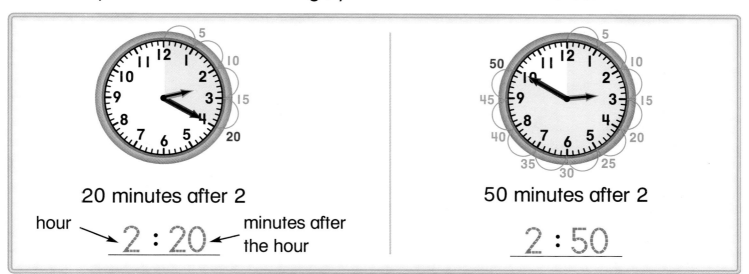

20 minutes after 2

hour ⟶ 2 : 20 ⟵ minutes after the hour

50 minutes after 2

2 : 50

Guided Practice

Write each time.

1. 5 : 35

2. ___ : ___

3. ___ : ___

4. ___ : ___

Draw the minute hand to show each time.

5.

4:50

6.

2:25

7.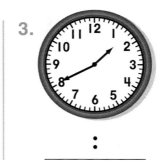

9:45

8.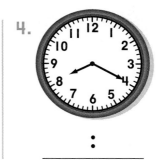

6:05

Explain Your Thinking Why can you count by 5s to find the minutes after the hour?

Independent Practice

Write each time.

1.

   4 : 55

2.

   ___ : ___

3.

   ___ : ___

4.

   ___ : ___

5.

   ___ : ___

6.

   ___ : ___

7.

   ___ : ___

8.

   ___ : ___

Draw the minute hand to show each time.

9.

   2:45

10.

    9:00

11.

    3:30

12.

    6:10

Problem Solving • Reasoning

Patterns

Extend the pattern. Write the times that most likely come next.

13. **6:00** **6:05** **6:10** ___:___ ___:___

14. **1:30** **1:35** **1:40** ___:___ ___:___

15. **Write Your Own** Create your own clock pattern. Ask a friend to extend it.

At Home Have your child use the exercises on this page to show you how he or she counts by 5s to tell the time.

Copyright © Houghton Mifflin Company. All rights reserved.

Time to 15 Minutes

LESSON 5

New
Vocabulary
quarter-hour

Learn About It

There are 15 minutes in a **quarter-hour**.

4:00

15 minutes after 4

4:15

30 minutes after 4

4:30

45 minutes after 4

4:45

Guided Practice

Write each time.

In a quarter-hour the minute hand moves around one quarter of a clock.

1.

2:00

2.

:

3.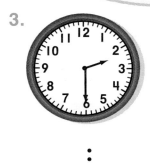

:

4. :

Draw the minute hand to show each time.

5.

10:15

6.

10:30

7.

10:45

8.

11:00

Explain Your Thinking How many quarter-hours are in 1 hour?

Independent Practice

Write each time.

1.

9:15

2.

____:____

3.

____:____

4.

____:____

5.

____:____

6.

____:____

7.

____:____

8.

____:____

Draw the minute hand to show each time.

9.

8:00

10.

7:30

11.

10:15

12.

12:45

Problem Solving·Reasoning

Using Vocabulary

Write the word that completes each sentence.

13. There are 60 minutes in an _____.

14. There are 15 minutes in a _____.

15. There are 30 minutes in a _____.

| quarter-hour |
| half-hour |
| hour |

At Home Discuss with your child the things that he or she does everyday that take about 15 minutes, like making lunch.

LESSON 6 Elapsed Time

Learn About It

A clock can help you find how much time has passed.

Game Starts
11:00 A.M.

Game Ends
2:00 P.M.

A.M. is used for the hours between 12 midnight and 12 noon.

P.M. is used for the hours between 12 noon and 12 midnight.

How long does the game last? ___3___ hours

Guided Practice

Write each time. Then write how much time has passed.

1.
Start

End

__10:00__ A.M. __1:00__ P.M.

___3___ hours passed

2.
Start

End

_____ : _____ P.M. _____ : _____ P.M.

_____ hours passed

3.
Start

End

_____ : _____ A.M. _____ : _____ A.M.

_____ hours passed

4.
Start

End

_____ : _____ P.M. _____ : _____ P.M.

_____ hour passed

Explain Your Thinking How would you find out how much time has passed from 8:00 to 11:00?

Independent Practice

Write the times.
Find out how much time has passed.

	Activity	Start	End	How much time passed?
1.		8:00 A.M.	9:00 A.M.	_____ hour passed
2.		_____ : _____ A.M.	_____ : _____ A.M.	_____ hours passed
3.		_____ : _____ A.M.	_____ : _____ P.M.	_____ hours passed
4.		_____ : _____ A.M.	_____ : _____ P.M.	_____ hours passed
5.		_____ : _____ P.M.	_____ : _____ P.M.	_____ hour passed
6.		_____ : _____ P.M.	_____ : _____ P.M.	_____ hours passed

At Home Have your child write the times, to the nearest hour, he or she eats dinner and goes to sleep. Discuss how many hours pass between those times.

Name _____

Standards
MG 1.5
MR 1.1, 1.2, 2.2

LESSON 7 Problem Solving: Use Models to Act It Out

You can use a clock to help you solve problems.

A boat race starts at 1:00.
It lasts 1 hour and 30 minutes.
What time does the race end?

Understand

Circle what you need to find out.

How long does the race last?

What time does the race end?

Plan

Use a clock to act out the problem.

What time does the race start? _____ : _____

How long does the race last? _____ hour _____ minutes

How will you use the clock to show how much time has passed?

Solve

Start at this time.

_____ : _____

How long does the race last?

_____ hour _____ minutes

What time does it end?

_____ : _____

Look Back

Did you answer the question?
Explain how you know your answer is correct.

Guided Practice

Use a clock to solve each problem.
Draw the hands for the end time.
Then write the time.

Remember:
► Understand
► Plan
► Solve
► Look Back

Remember to use these 4 steps.

1 Linda goes swimming at 1:00.
She swims for 2 hours and 30
minutes. What time does she finish?

Think:
Start at 1:00. Count on
2 hours and 30 minutes.

Start   End

3:30

2 Paul starts his run at 5:30.
He runs for 45 minutes. What
time does he finish?

Think:
Start at 5:30. Count on
45 minutes.

Start   End

____:____

3 The baseball game begins
at 3:00. It lasts for 2 hours and
30 minutes. What time does the
game end?

Think:
What time does the game
begin? How long does it last?

Start   End

____:____

4 Gwen begins soccer practice
at 10:30. It lasts for 1 hour
and 30 minutes. She gets home
30 minutes after practice ends.
What time does Gwen get home?

Think:
What should I do first?

Start   End

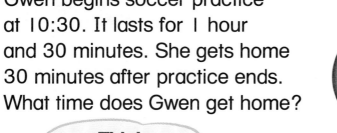

____:____

At Home Help your child find how much time passes, to the nearest hour,
while he or she is in school.

Name_____

Choose a Strategy

Solve.

Strategies

Use Models to Act It Out
Draw a Picture
Write a Number Sentence

1 The sailboat show starts at 8:00. It lasts 3 hours and 30 minutes. What time does it end?

Start   End

_____:_____

sailboat

2 The raft race starts at 2:00. It lasts for 2 hours. What time does it end?

Start   End

_____:_____

raft

3 There are 5 canoes. There are 3 children in each canoe. How many children are there in all?

Draw or write to explain.

_____ children

canoe

4 There are 12 children in line for paddleboats. 4 children go in the first boat. 3 children go in the second boat. How many children are still in line?

_____ children

paddleboat

Name _____

Mixed Practice

Find each sum or difference.

| 1. 47
+26 | 2. 50
−38 | 3. 89
−63 | 4. 53
+17 | 5. 36
+38 |

| 6. 73
−43 | 7. 61
−53 | 8. 49
+28 | 9. 91
−34 | 10. 57
+29 |

| 11. 78¢
−22¢ | 12. 10¢
+75¢ | 13. 90¢
−45¢ | 14. 82¢
−54¢ | 15. 61¢
+32¢ |

Multiply.  **Memorize Your Facts**

| 16. 5
× 3 | 17. 8
× 2 | 18. 5
× 4 | 19. 1
× 2 | 20. 5
× 0 | 21. 2
× 5 |

 Brain Teaser Mystery Time

This time is between 5:00 and 6:00. You say this time when you count by 5s to tell time. All three digits are the same.
What time is it?

_____ : _____

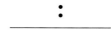 **Safe Site**

Internet Brain Teasers
Visit **www.eduplace.com/kids/mꓱm**
for more *Brain Teasers*.

Quick ✓ Check

Check Your Understanding of Lessons 1–7

Will the activity take more than or less than one minute?
Circle your answer.

1. Lock a door.

more

less

2. Walk a dog.

more

less

Write each time.

Draw the minute hand.

3.

___ : ___

4.

___ : ___

5.

```
3:25
```

6.

```
4:45
```

Write each time. Then write how much time has passed.

7.

___ : ___

___ : ___

_____ hours passed

8.

___ : ___

___ : ___

_____ hours passed

9. Ann goes for a walk at 5:00.
She walks for 30 minutes.
Draw the clock hands to show
what time Ann finishes her walk.

Test Prep • Cumulative Review

Maintaining the Standards

Fill in the ○ for the correct answer. NH means Not Here.

1 What time does the clock show?

  2:00   2:30   2:40   6:10
   ○   ○   ○   ○

2 Add.
$$\begin{array}{r} 50 \\ +30 \\ \hline \end{array}$$

  20   60   80   NH
  ○   ○   ○   ○

3 Mark the fraction of circles that are blue.

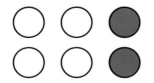

  $\frac{2}{3}$ $\frac{1}{2}$ $\frac{2}{6}$ $\frac{1}{6}$

  ○   ○   ○   ○

4 Lin buys a ball for 65¢. She pays with 3 quarters. What change does she get?

  1¢   5¢   10¢   25¢
  ○   ○   ○   ○

5 Mark the unit of measurement that would be used to measure your height.

○ pounds   ○ feet

○ kilograms   ○ cups

6

The clock shows 3:00.
Explain how you can tell.

_____

_____

_____

_____

Copyright © Houghton Mifflin Company. All rights reserved.

Safe Site

Internet Test Prep
Visit **www.eduplace.com/kids/mhm**
for more *Test Prep Practice*.

Standards
MG **1.4**, MR **2.0**

LESSON 8 Calendar

Learn About It

A **calendar** shows the days, weeks, and months in a year.

New
Vocabulary
calendar

April

Sunday	Monday	Tuesday	Wednesday	Thursday	Friday	Saturday
	1	2	3	4	5	6
7	8	9	10	11	12	13
14	15	16	17	18	19	20
21	22	23	24	25	26	27
28	29	30				

Guided Practice

Use the calendar to answer each question.

This month has 30 days.

1. How many days are in one week? _____7_____

2. What day of the week is April 5? _____

3. What is the date of the first Sunday in this month? _____

4. What is the date of the third Tuesday in this month? _____

5. How many Saturdays are in this month? _____

6. On what day of the week will the next month begin? _____

Explain Your Thinking When do you use a calender?

Independent Practice

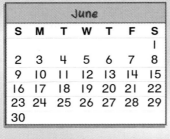

January

S	M	T	W	T	F	S
		1	2	3	4	5
6	7	8	9	10	11	12
13	14	15	16	17	18	19
20	21	22	23	24	25	26
27	28	29	30	31		

February

S	M	T	W	T	F	S
					1	2
3	4	5	6	7	8	9
10	11	12	13	14	15	16
17	18	19	20	21	22	23
24	25	26	27	28		

March

S	M	T	W	T	F	S
					1	2
3	4	5	6	7	8	9
10	11	12	13	14	15	16
17	18	19	20	21	22	23
24	25	26	27	28	29	30
31						

April

S	M	T	W	T	F	S
	1	2	3	4	5	6
7	8	9	10	11	12	13
14	15	16	17	18	19	20
21	22	23	24	25	26	27
28	29	30				

May

S	M	T	W	T	F	S
			1	2	3	4
5	6	7	8	9	10	11
12	13	14	15	16	17	18
19	20	21	22	23	24	25
26	27	28	29	30	31	

June

S	M	T	W	T	F	S
						1
2	3	4	5	6	7	8
9	10	11	12	13	14	15
16	17	18	19	20	21	22
23	24	25	26	27	28	29
30						

July

S	M	T	W	T	F	S
	1	2	3	4	5	6
7	8	9	10	11	12	13
14	15	16	17	18	19	20
21	22	23	24	25	26	27
28	29	30	31			

August

S	M	T	W	T	F	S
					1	2	3
4	5	6	7	8	9	10
11	12	13	14	15	16	17
18	19	20	21	22	23	24
25	26	27	28	29	30	31

September

S	M	T	W	T	F	S
1	2	3	4	5	6	7
8	9	10	11	12	13	14
15	16	17	18	19	20	21
22	23	24	25	26	27	28
29	30					

October

S	M	T	W	T	F	S
		1	2	3	4	5
6	7	8	9	10	11	12
13	14	15	16	17	18	19
20	21	22	23	24	25	26
27	28	29	30	31		

November

S	M	T	W	T	F	S
					1	2
3	4	5	6	7	8	9
10	11	12	13	14	15	16
17	18	19	20	21	22	23
24	25	26	27	28	29	30

December

S	M	T	W	T	F	S
1	2	3	4	5	6	7
8	9	10	11	12	13	14
15	16	17	18	19	20	21
22	23	24	25	26	27	28
29	30	31				

Use the calendar to answer each question.

1. How many months are in one year? __12__

2. Which is the twelfth month of the year? _____

3. Which is the sixth month of the year? _____

4. What date follows March 31? _____

5. What is the date one week after October 4? _____

Problem Solving • Reasoning

Write About It

6. How many months have 30 days? _____   How many months have 31 days? _____

   Write the names of the months for each.

At Home Have your child use the calendar on this page to find his or her birthday. Ask which month comes before and which month comes after.

LESSON 9 Hours, Days, Weeks, Months

Learn About It

Time is measured in different ways.

Which is longer, 2 weeks or 10 days?

Sunday	Monday	Tuesday	Wednesday	Thursday	Friday	Saturday
1	2	3	4	5	6	7
8	9	10	11	12	13	14

Think: 1 week = 7 days.
2 weeks = 14 days.

2 weeks is longer than 10 days.

Time
24 hours = 1 day
7 days = 1 week
52 weeks = 1 year
12 months = 1 year

Guided Practice

Circle which is longer.

1. (30 hours) or 1 day   2. 8 days or 1 week

3. 1 year or 6 months   4. 45 weeks or 1 year

5. 5 days or 1 week   6. 12 months or 60 weeks

Circle which is shorter.

7. (1 week) or 10 days   8. 15 hours or 1 day

9. 2 days or 24 hours   10. 1 year or 57 weeks

11. 10 days or 3 weeks   12. 48 weeks or 12 months

Explain Your Thinking Is 2 weeks longer than 15 days?
Explain how you know.

Independent Practice

Circle the best estimate for each activity.

1. Skating

days

< hours >

2. Spending the summer

days

months

3. Riding a bike

hours

months

4. Camping

days

hours

5. Playing a baseball game

months

hours

6. Growing a garden

weeks

hours

Problem Solving•Reasoning

Logical Thinking

7. I am greater than the number of days in a week. I am less than the number of hours in a day. What number am I? _____

6

30

18

8. **Write Your Own** Write a riddle using information about hours, days, weeks, or months. Ask a friend to solve it.

At Home Have your child explain to you which is longer, 10 days or 2 weeks. Have him or her use a calendar to help.

Name _____

Problem Solving: Use a Schedule

Sometimes you can use a schedule to solve a problem.

You can use a clock to help you solve a problem.

How long does soccer practice last?

Start | End

: _____   : _____

Practice lasts _____ hour _____ minutes.

PARK ACTIVITIES

3:30 – 4:00 Arts and Crafts
4:00 – 5:30 Soccer Practice
5:30 – 6:00 Story Time

Use the start time and the end time to find how long the activity lasts.

You can use reasoning to help you solve a problem.

Margie leaves for arts and crafts at 3:00. She arrives on time. How long does it take her to get there?

What time does Margie leave? _____ : _____

What time does arts and crafts begin? _____ : _____

How long does it take Margie to get there? _____ minutes

Use the time Margie leaves and the time she arrives to find how long it takes her to get there.

Guided Practice

Solve. Use the schedule and
a clock to help you.

FIELD DAY SCHEDULE

TIME	EVENT
9:00–9:30	Flag Ceremony
9:30–10:30	Track Games
10:30–11:00	Beanbag Toss
11:00–11:30	Kickball

1 How long do the track
games last?

_____ hour

> **Think:**
> What time do the
> track games
> begin and end?

Draw or write to explain.

2 Grace leaves for the
flag ceremony at 8:30.
She arrives on time.
How long did it take
her to get there?

_____ minutes

> **Think:**
> What time does
> the ceremony begin?

3 How long does the
beanbag toss last?

_____ minutes

> **Think:**
> What time does it
> begin and end?

4 Juan leaves after
kickball. He gets home
at 12:00. How long does
it take him to get home?

_____ minutes

> **Think:**
> What time does
> kickball end?

486 four hundred eighty-six

At Home Have your child tell you what time you should leave if you
have to be somewhere at 3:00 and it takes 30 minutes to get there.

Name ____________________

Choose a Strategy

Strategies

Use Models to Act It Out
Write a Number Sentence
Draw a Picture

Solve.

AFTER-SCHOOL ACTIVITIES

ACTIVITY	TIME
Computer Club	3:00–4:00
Swimming Club	3:30–4:30
Gym Club	3:30–5:00
Game Club	3:30–4:00

1. How long does Computer Club last?

   _____ hour

Draw or write to explain.

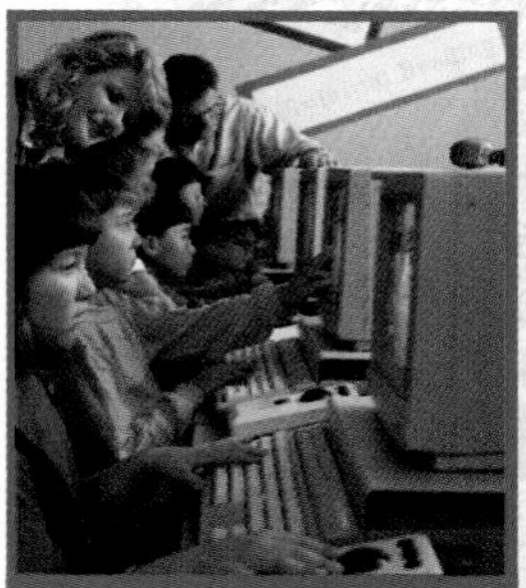

computer

2. There are 20 second-graders in Gym Club. There are also 15 third-graders. How many children are in Gym Club?

   _____ children

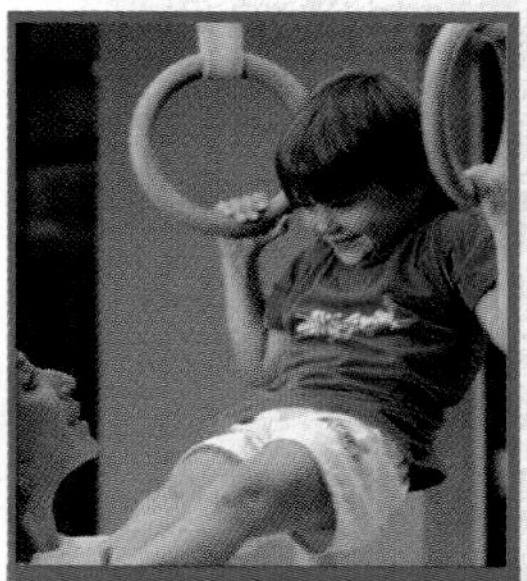

gym

3. How long does Swimming Club last?

   _____ hour

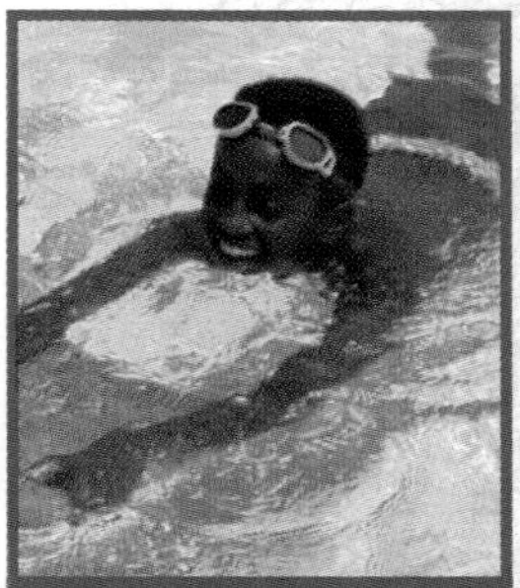

swimming

4. There are 3 teams playing games. Each team has 5 children. How many children are playing games?

   _____ children

games

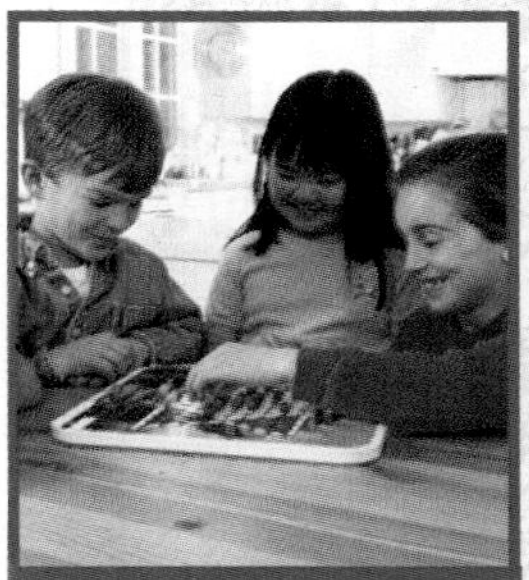

Name _____

Mixed Practice

Find each sum or difference.

1. 95
   −34

2. 16
   +72

3. 63
   −48

4. 51
   +27

5. 45
   +45

6. 82
   −36

7. 45
   −15

8. 12
   +64

9. 39
   −18

10. 40
   +15

11. 60
   −45

12. 31
   +29

13. 77
   −49

14. 90
   −30

15. 37
   +58

Multiply. **Memorize Your Facts**

16. 2
   × 3

17. 5
   × 6

18. 5
   × 8

19. 3
   × 5

20. 4
   × 2

21. 2
   × 9

 Brain Teaser Birthday Puzzle

Matt's birthday is on June 30. What day of the week is Matt's birthday? Use the July calendar to help you.
Hint: June has 30 days.

_____

July						
S	M	T	W	T	F	S
						1
2	3	4	5	6	7	8
9	10	11	12	13	14	15
16	17	18	19	20	21	22
23	24	25	26	27	28	29
30	31					

Safe Site

Internet Brain Teasers
Visit www.eduplace.com/kids/mhm
for more *Brain Teasers.*

Name

Quick ✓ Check

Check Your Understanding of Lessons 8–10

June						
S	M	T	W	T	F	S
						1
2	3	4	5	6	7	8
9	10	11	12	13	14	15
16	17	18	19	20	21	22
23	24	25	26	27	28	29
30						

July						
S	M	T	W	T	F	S
	1	2	3	4	5	6
7	8	9	10	11	12	13
14	15	16	17	18	19	20
21	22	23	24	25	26	27
28	29	30	31			

August						
S	M	T	W	T	F	S
					1	2	3
4	5	6	7	8	9	10
11	12	13	14	15	16	17
18	19	20	21	22	23	24
25	26	27	28	29	30	31

September						
S	M	T	W	T	F	S
1	2	3	4	5	6	7
8	9	10	11	12	13	14
15	16	17	18	19	20	21
22	23	24	25	26	27	28
29	30					

Use these calendars to answer each question.

1. Which months have 30 days? _____

2. How many days are in 2 weeks? _____

3. What is the date one week before August 30? _____

4. How many Fridays are in July? _____

5. Circle which is longer.

   3 weeks   or   1 month

6. Circle which is shorter.

   35 days   or   2 months

Use the schedule to answer each question.

7. What show starts at 3:30?

   _____

8. How long does Cow Winners last?

   _____ minutes

9. What time does the Sheep Show end?

   ____:____

10. It takes Tanya 1 hour to get to the fair. What time should she leave to get to the Horse Show?

    ____:____

Farm Fair	
Horse Show	10:00–11:00
Cow Winners	2:30–3:00
Best Pigs	3:30–4:00
Sheep Show	5:00–6:30

four hundred eighty-nine **489**

Name_____

Test Prep • Cumulative Review
Maintaining the Standards

Fill in the ○ for the correct answer. NH means Not Here.

1 Mark the number fifty-three.

53   50   35   3
○   ○   ○   ○

---

2 Choose the sign to make the sentence true.

1 week ◯ 10 days

$ >   =   <
○   ○   ○   ○

---

3 Mark how much time has passed.

Start   End

○ 1 hour
○ 2 hours
○ 3 hours
○ 4 hours

4 Mark the shape that is not a rectangle.

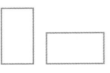

○   ○   ○   ○

---

5 Subtract.   5 8
                   − 3 9

18   29   97   NH
○   ○   ○   ○

---

6 Solve.

2 + 2 + 2 + 2 = _____

2 × 4 = _____

Explain how the number sentences are the same.

_____

_____

_____

Copyright © Houghton Mifflin Company. All rights reserved.

Safe Site

Internet Test Prep
Visit **www.eduplace.com/kids/mhm**
for more *Test Prep Practice*.

Chapter Review

Name_____

Write the word that completes each sentence.

| minute |
| quarter-hour |
| half-hour |
| hour |

1. 60 minutes is the same as an _____.

2. 15 minutes is the same as a _____.

3. 30 minutes is the same as a _____.

4. 60 seconds is the same as a _____.

Write each time.

5.

: _____

6.

: _____

7.

: _____

8.

: _____

9.

: _____

10.

: _____

11.

: _____

12.

: _____

Draw the hands for the end time.

Start   End

13. The football game begins at 2:00. It lasts 2 hours. What time does the game end?

: _____

Draw the minute hand to show each time.

14.

6:45

15.

12:25

16.

5:10

17.

3:40

Write each time. Then write how much time has passed.

18.

Start    End

:_____   :_____

_____ hours passed

19.

Start   End

:_____   :_____

_____ hours passed

Use the calendar to answer each question.

20. What day of the week is June 3? _____

21. What is the date of the first Friday? _____

22. How many days are in one week? _____

June						
S	M	T	W	T	F	S
						1
2	3	4	5	6	7	8
9	10	11	12	13	14	15
16	17	18	19	20	21	22
23	24	25	26	27	28	29
30						

Use the schedule to answer each question.

23. How long does Cory's snack last?

_____ minutes

24. Cory goes to bed 2 hours after dinner ends. What time does she go to bed?

:_____

Cory's After-School Schedule	
Snack	3:30 – 4:00
Homework	4:00 – 6:00
Dinner	6:00 – 6:30

Copyright © Houghton Mifflin Company. All rights reserved.

Name _____

Chapter Test

Write each time.

1.

____ : ____

2.

____ : ____

3.

____ : ____

4.

____ : ____

5.

____ : ____

6.

____ : ____

7.

____ : ____

8.

____ : ____

Draw the minute hand to show each time.

9.

`5:50`

10.

`11:35`

11.

`7:55`

12.

`4:15`

Draw the hands to show the end time.

Start   End

13. Lee starts to jog at 5:00.
She jogs for 30 minutes. What
time does she finish?

____ : ____

Write each time. Then write how much time has passed.

14.
Start  End

_____ : _____   _____ : _____

_____ hours passed

15.
Start  End

_____ : _____   _____ : _____

_____ hour passed

Use the calendar to answer each question.

February						
S	M	T	W	T	F	S
					1	2
3	4	5	6	7	8	9
10	11	12	13	14	15	16
17	18	19	20	21	22	23
24	25	26	27	28		

16. How many days are in February? _____

17. What day of the week is February 9? _____

18. What is the date of the third Friday? _____

Use the schedule to answer each question.

Craft Day	
Basket Weaving	9:00 – 10:00
Paper Making	10:30 – 11:30
Clay Play	11:30 – 12:00

19. How long does Paper Making last?

_____ hour

20. Amy goes home after Clay Play ends.
It takes her 30 minutes to get home.
What time will she get home?

_____ : _____

 Write About It

Billy wants to leave his house in 30
minutes. What time should he leave?

_____ : _____

Explain how you found the time.

_____

Copyright © Houghton Mifflin Company. All rights reserved.

Play Through the Day

Players 2

What You Need

counter for each player ● ○

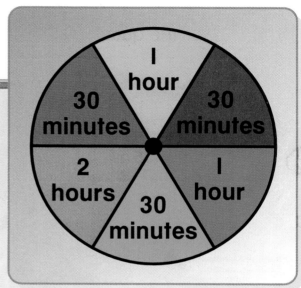

How to Play

① Put counters on **START TIME**.

② Take turns spinning the spinner. Move forward that amount of time.

③ The first player to reach 4:00 wins.

START TIME 7:30

END

Name _____

Enrichment

Travel Time

Use the picture and a clock to help
you answer the questions.

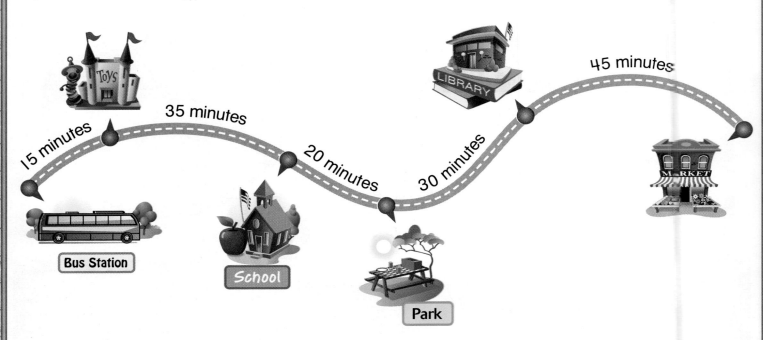

1. A bus leaves the station at 2:00.
    It goes to the toy store. What
    time does it get there?

    ____ : ____

2. A bus arrives at the park at 3:15.
    What time did it leave the school?

    ____ : ____

3. A bus leaves the station at
    10:05. It goes to the school.
    What time does it get there?

    ____ : ____

4. A bus leaves the library at
    11:35. It goes to the market.
    What time does it get there?

    ____ : ____

5. A bus arrives at the park at
    2:30. What time did it leave
    the school?

    ____ : ____

6. A bus leaves the park at 4:00.
    It goes to the market. What time
    does it get there?

    ____ : ____

Copyright © Houghton Mifflin Company. All rights reserved.

CHAPTER 11

Numbers and Patterns to 1,000

Accessing Prior Knowledge

This story will help you review

- Counting tens and ones

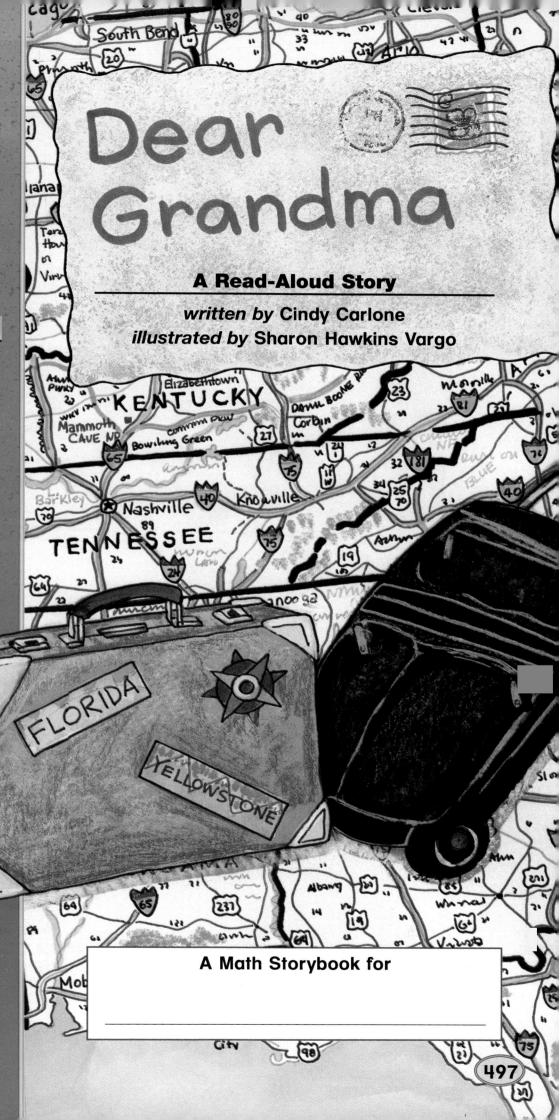

Dear Grandma

A Read-Aloud Story

written by Cindy Carlone
illustrated by Sharon Hawkins Vargo

A Math Storybook for

_____

Dear Grandma,

Here we come. We're on our way to visit you. Today we drove through a national park. I saw the biggest tree in the world! It was 36 feet wide at the trunk. It took me a while to walk all the way around it.

Love,
Joey

How many tens and ones are in 36?

_____tens _____ones

Dear Grandma,

Today I was 94 yards below sea level, but I wasn't underwater. I was in Death Valley, California, and boy, was it hot there!

Love,
Joey

How many tens and ones are in 94?

_____tens _____ones

Dear Grandma,

Today I saw dinosaur footprints at a place called Dinosaur Ridge, Colorado. They were gigantic! One footprint was 24 inches long. I'm glad dinosaurs are not around anymore.

Love,
Joey

How many tens and ones are in 24?

_____ tens _____ ones

Dear Grandma,

In St. Louis, I got a ride to the top of the
Gateway Arch. The arch is 75 feet taller
than the Washington Monument which I saw
last year! Some people call the arch the
Gateway to the West.

Love,
Joey

How many tens and ones are in 75?

_____ tens _____ ones

Dear Grandma,

I went inside the biggest cave ever! It was hot outside, but only 54 degrees inside the cave. The tour guide told us that the temperature stays the same in the cave all year long. I should have brought my sweatshirt!

Love,
Joey

How many tens and ones are in 54?

_____tens _____ones

Dear Grandma,

Hooray! We're finally in Florida at an alligator farm. The biggest alligator was 84 inches long! I can't wait to see you tomorrow and give you a great-big hug.

Love,
Joey

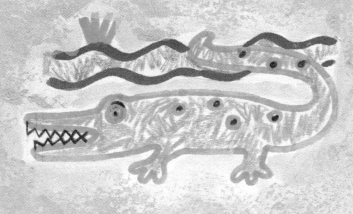

How many tens and ones are in 84?

_____tens _____ones

Family Letter

Vocabulary

decimal point The dot used to separate dollars and cents.

digit Any of the symbols used to write numbers.

hundred A group of 10 tens.

greater than (>) A symbol used to compare two numbers.

less than (<) A symbol used to compare two numbers.

regroup To rename a number by trading 10 ones for 1 ten or 10 tens for 1 hundred.

Dear Family,

During the next few weeks, our math class will be learning about place value to 1,000.

You can expect to see work that provides practice with reading, writing, comparing, and ordering numbers through 1,000. You will also see work that provides practice writing dollars and cents.

As we learn about place value you may wish to use the following as a guide.

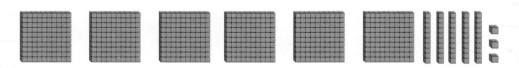

Hundreds	Tens	Ones
6	5	3

Sincerely,

Your child's teacher

Standards
NS **1.1, 1.2**
MR **1.2, 2.1**

Count by 100s

New
Vocabulary
hundreds

Learn About It

You count by **hundreds**.

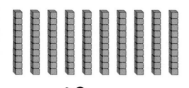

10 tens   =   1 hundred

____1____ hundred   100

I can count by hundreds. 100, 200, …

Guided Practice

Count the hundreds. Write the numbers.

1.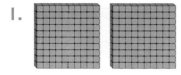

___2___ hundreds   200

2.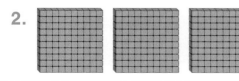

_____ hundreds   _____

3.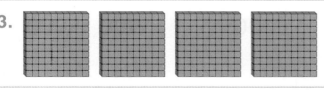

_____ hundreds   _____

4.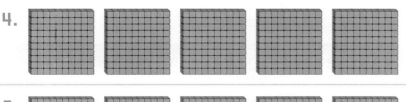

_____ hundreds   _____

5.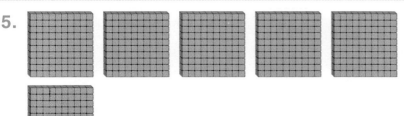

_____ hundreds   _____

Explain Your Thinking What pattern do you see in the numbers you have written?

Independent Practice

Count the hundreds. Write the numbers.

1.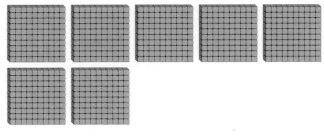

   ___7___ hundreds   700

2.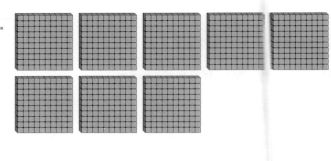

   _____ hundreds   _____

3.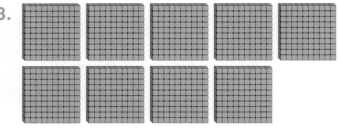

   _____ hundreds   _____

4.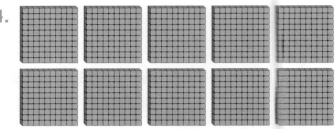

   _____ hundreds   1,000

Write the missing numbers.

5. 100, 200, _____, 400, _____, _____, 700, _____, 900, 1,000

6. 1,000, 900, _____, _____, 600, 500, _____, _____, 200, _____

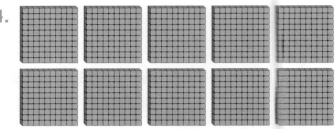
Problem Solving • Reasoning

Write About It

7. How is 30 different from 300?
   Draw a picture to show each number.

Draw or write to explain.

At Home Ask your child to tell you how many hundreds are in numbers such as 300 (3), 500 (5), and 800 (8).

Name _____

LESSON 2 Hundreds, Tens, Ones

Learn About It

You can show a number as hundreds, tens, and ones.

Show 134.

Workmat		
Hundreds	**Tens**	**Ones**

Hundreds	Tens	Ones
1	3	4

134

one hundred thirty-four

1 hundred = 100
3 tens = 30
4 ones = 4
100 + 30 + 4 = 134

Guided Practice

Use Workmat 4 with blocks.
Show the numbers. Write how many.

1. Show 6 ⬛, 4 ▭, and 7 ▫.

Hundreds	Tens	Ones
6	4	7

647

2. Show 3 ⬛, 5 ▭, and 2 ▫.

Hundreds	Tens	Ones

____

3. Show 2 ⬛, 2 ▭, and 5 ▫.

Hundreds	Tens	Ones

____

4. Show 5 ⬛, 7 ▭, and 6 ▫.

Hundreds	Tens	Ones

____

Explain Your Thinking Explain why 3 does not have the same value in the numbers 163 and 361.

Independent Practice

Use Workmat 4 with blocks.

Show this many.	Write how many hundreds, tens, and ones.			Write the number.
1.	Hundreds 2	Tens 4	Ones 2	242 two hundred forty-two
2.	Hundreds	Tens	Ones	_____ three hundred seventy-five
3.	Hundreds	Tens	Ones	_____ one hundred thirty-nine
4.	Hundreds	Tens	Ones	_____ six hundred twenty-seven

Write the missing numbers.

5. 210, 211, _____, 213, 214, _____, 216, _____, _____, 219, _____

6. 460, _____, 462, 463, _____, _____, 466, 467, _____, 469, _____

Problem Solving•Reasoning

Number Sense

Circle the best answer.

7. I go to school about __?__ days each year.

    2   20   200

8. My class has about __?__ children.

    2   20   200

Draw or write to explain.

At Home Help your child collect one hundred objects such as buttons or beans, and count them in groups of 10.

LESSON 3 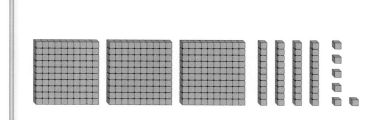 Numbers Through 500

Learn About It

You can write the hundreds, tens, and ones in a three-digit number.

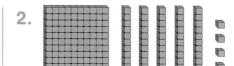

Hundreds	Tens	Ones
3	4	6

346

three hundred forty-six

Guided Practice

Write how many.

1.

Hundreds	Tens	Ones
2	4	3

243

two hundred forty-three

2.

Hundreds	Tens	Ones

_____

one hundred fifty-four

3.

Hundreds	Tens	Ones

_____

three hundred seven

4.

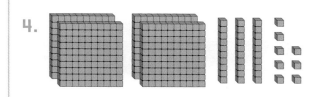

Hundreds	Tens	Ones

_____

four hundred thirty-eight

Explain Your Thinking How is 408 different from 48?

Independent Practice

Decide how many hundreds, tens, and ones there are.
Write the number.

1. 4 ones   3 hundreds   6 tens

   <u>364</u>

2. 2 hundreds   4 tens   9 ones

   _____

3. 3 hundreds   1 one   3 tens

   _____

4. 3 ones   0 tens   4 hundreds

   _____

5. 9 ones   1 hundred   4 tens

   _____

6. 4 hundreds   2 ones   8 tens

   _____

7. 3 tens   0 ones   2 hundreds

   _____

8. 9 tens   6 ones   1 hundred

   _____

Write the missing numbers.

9. 365, 366, _____, _____, 369, _____, 371, 372, _____, _____, 375

10. 279, _____, _____, 282, _____, _____, 285, 286, _____, 288, _____

Problem Solving • Reasoning

Patterns

11. How many 🔲 in 5? _____

    How many 🔲 in 50? _____

    How many 🔲 in 500? _____

12. How many 🔲 in 3? _____

    How many 🔲 in 30? _____

    How many 🔲 in 300? _____

510   five hundred ten

LESSON 4

Numbers Through 1,000

Standards
NS **1.1, 1.2**
SDP **1.4**

Learn About It

Find the hundreds, tens, and ones in each number.

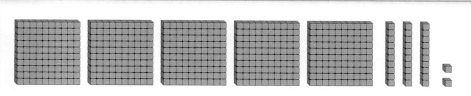

532
five hundred thirty-two

There are 5 hundreds 3 tens 2 ones.

Guided Practice

Write how many.

1.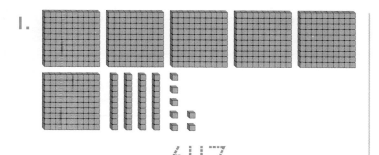

647
six hundred forty-seven

2.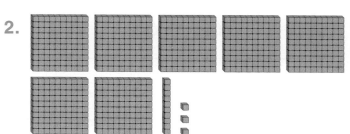

seven hundred thirteen

3.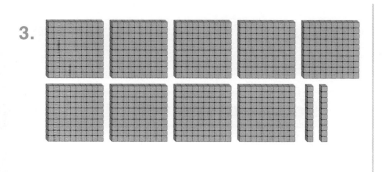

_____
nine hundred twenty

4.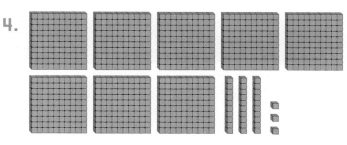

_____
eight hundred thirty-three

Explain Your Thinking Tell how you would show the number 906 with hundreds, tens, and ones blocks.

Independent Practice

1. Write the missing numbers.

901	902	903	904			907	908		910
	912	913		915	916			919	
921			924				928		930
	932			935		937	938		
941				945	946			949	
951			954		956		958		
	962	963				967			970
	973	974		976				979	980
981	982			985			988		
	992		994		996				1,000

Problem Solving•Reasoning

Using Data

2. How many people were at the fair on Friday and Saturday?

_____ people

People at the Fair	
Friday	♀ ♀
Saturday	♀ ♀ ♀ ♀
Sunday	♀ ♀ ♀

Each ♀ stands for 100 people.

At Home Write a number between 700 and 900. Have your child tell how many hundreds, tens, and ones are in the number.

LESSON 5 Identify Place Value

Learn About It

To find the value of a **digit**, first find the value of the place it is in.

> Review
> **Vocabulary**
> **digit**

Hundreds	Tens	Ones
2	5	7

200 + 50 + 7

2 5 7

Guided Practice

Circle the value of each red digit.

1. **597**

   900   (90)   9

2. **429**

   400   40   4

3. **915**

   500   50   5

4. **849**

   800   80   8

5. **962**

   600   60   6

6. **781**

   800   80   8

7. **294**

   400   40   4

8. **352**

   300   30   3

9. **527**

   200   20   2

Explain Your Thinking Explain why the digit 9 has different values in Exercises 1, 2, and 3.

Independent Practice

Write each number.

1.

Hundreds	Tens	Ones
2	4	8

200 + 40 + 8

_248_

2.

Hundreds	Tens	Ones
1	2	3

100 + 20 + 3

___

3. 900 + 90 + 1

___

4. 60 + 8 + 300

___

5. 300 + 4

___

6. 1 + 20 + 300

___

7. 500 + 70

___

8. 200 + 4 + 80

___

9. 6 + 800

___

10. 7 + 60

___

11. 3 + 10 + 400

___

Problem Solving•Reasoning

Logical Thinking

Use the clues to help find David's number.

12. • 2 is in the hundreds place.
 • The ones digit is 2 greater than the hundreds digit.
 • The tens digit is double the ones digit.

___ ___ ___
hundreds tens ones

13. **Write Your Own** Write your own number clues for a three-digit number. Share your clues with a friend.

At Home Write a three-digit number, such as 465 or 891. Have your child tell you the value of the digit in the tens place.

Copyright © Houghton Mifflin Company. All rights reserved.

Regroup Tens as Hundreds

Learn About It

Review
Vocabulary
regroup

You can **regroup** 10 tens as 1 hundred.

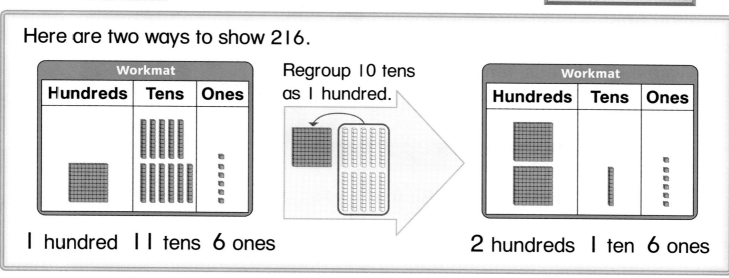

Here are two ways to show 216.

1 hundred 11 tens 6 ones

Regroup 10 tens as 1 hundred.

2 hundreds 1 ten 6 ones

Guided Practice

Use Workmat 4 with ▦ , ▭▭▭ , and ▪.

	Show this many.	Regroup 10 tens as 1 hundred.
1.	2 hundreds 16 tens 5 ones	_3_ hundreds _6_ tens _5_ ones
2.	8 hundreds 18 tens 1 one	____ hundreds ____ tens ____ one
3.	4 hundreds 17 tens 3 ones	____ hundreds ____ tens ____ ones
4.	3 hundreds 13 tens 9 ones	____ hundreds ____ tens ____ ones
5.	5 hundreds 12 tens 4 ones	____ hundreds ____ tens ____ ones
6.	6 hundreds 15 tens 0 ones	____ hundreds ____ tens ____ ones

Explain Your Thinking Explain why you can regroup
1 hundred 15 tens as 2 hundreds 5 tens.

Independent Practice

Use Workmat 4 with ▦ and ▭▭ .

1. Spin the spinner two times. Write both numbers. Find the sum. Take that many tens.

2. Regroup 10 tens as 1 hundred when you can.

3. Write the hundreds, tens, and ones you have. Write the number.

First Spin	Second Spin	Sum
____	____	____

Hundreds	Tens	Ones

____

First Spin	Second Spin	Sum
____	____	____

Hundreds	Tens	Ones

____

First Spin	Second Spin	Sum
____	____	____

Hundreds	Tens	Ones

____

First Spin	Second Spin	Sum
____	____	____

Hundreds	Tens	Ones

____

First Spin	Second Spin	Sum
____	____	____

Hundreds	Tens	Ones

____

First Spin	Second Spin	Sum
____	____	____

Hundreds	Tens	Ones

____

At Home Choose one number in an exercise above. Ask your child what the new number would be if there were 9 more tens.

Name_____

LESSON 7

Problem Solving: Make a Table

Standards
MR **1.0, 1.1, 2.0, 2.2**
SDP **2.1, 2.2**

Sometimes you can make a table to help solve a problem.

Toby's family went on a rafting trip. They drove for 5 days. Each day they drove 100 miles. How far did they drive?

Understand

Circle what you need to find out.

How far did Toby's family drive in one day?

How far did Toby's family drive in 5 days?

Plan

You can make a table.
What information would you want in your table?

_____ miles each day

_____ days

Solve

Make the table. Continue counting the miles for 5 days.

Days	1	2	3	4	5
Miles	100	200	300		

How far did Toby's family drive?   _____ miles

Look Back

How did the table help you find the answer?

Guided Practice

Solve. Complete the table.

1 Toby's family is ready to go rafting.
There are 20 people in each raft.
How many people are in 4 rafts?

Raft	1	2		
People	20	40		

Think:
How many people
are in each raft?

_____ people

---

2 The rafting company serves 100 apples each day.
How many apples do they need for 6 days?

Day	1					
Apples	100					

Think:
How many days
am I counting?

_____ apples

---

3 Each tent on the rafting trip holds 6 people.
How many tents are needed for 30 people?

Tent	1				
People	6				

Think:
What do I need
to find out?

_____ tents

---

4 There are 10 paddles in each raft.
How many paddles are in 4 rafts?

Raft	1			
Paddles	10			

Think:
How many paddles
are in each raft?

_____ paddles

518 five hundred eighteen

At Home Ask your child to explain how he or she completed
the tables to help solve the problems.

Copyright © Houghton Mifflin Company. All rights reserved.

Name_____

Choose a Strategy

Solve.

Strategies

Make a Table
Guess and Check
Write a Number Sentence

① Tara saw 71 newts. 36 were tan. How many newts were not tan?

Draw or write to explain.

_____ newts

newt

② There are 5 eagle's nests along the river. There are 2 eagles in each nest. How many eagles are along the river?

Nest	1	2			
Eagles	2				

_____ eagles

eagle

③ Luis spent 96¢ in all. 59¢ was spent for deer food. Circle what else he bought to feed the deer.

47¢   37¢

deer

④ There are 16 beaver paw prints by the river. If each beaver makes 4 prints, how many beavers walked by the river?

_____ beavers

beaver

Name _____

Mixed Practice

Add or subtract.

1. $16 - 7 =$ _____

2. $8 + 4 =$ _____

3. $13 - 6 =$ _____

4. _____ $= 9 + 5$

5. $15 - 5 =$ _____

6. $7 +$ _____ $= 12$

7. $11 - 9 =$ _____

8. $7 +$ _____ $= 14$

9. $10 + 9 =$ _____

10.
$$\begin{array}{r} 73 \\ +9 \\ \hline \end{array}$$

11.
$$\begin{array}{r} 59 \\ -26 \\ \hline \end{array}$$

12.
$$\begin{array}{r} 61 \\ -35 \\ \hline \end{array}$$

13.
$$\begin{array}{r} 48 \\ +30 \\ \hline \end{array}$$

14.
$$\begin{array}{r} 85 \\ -28 \\ \hline \end{array}$$

15.
$$\begin{array}{r} 45 \\ -37 \\ \hline \end{array}$$

16.
$$\begin{array}{r} 83 \\ -64 \\ \hline \end{array}$$

17.
$$\begin{array}{r} 16 \\ +78 \\ \hline \end{array}$$

18.
$$\begin{array}{r} 70 \\ -8 \\ \hline \end{array}$$

19.
$$\begin{array}{r} 27 \\ +65 \\ \hline \end{array}$$

20.
$$\begin{array}{r} 92 \\ -38 \\ \hline \end{array}$$

21.
$$\begin{array}{r} 80 \\ -46 \\ \hline \end{array}$$

22.
$$\begin{array}{r} 63 \\ +20 \\ \hline \end{array}$$

23.
$$\begin{array}{r} 21 \\ -14 \\ \hline \end{array}$$

24.
$$\begin{array}{r} 53 \\ +27 \\ \hline \end{array}$$

 Brain Teaser How Many Books?

How many books did each read?

Kay read this number of books: 13 tens 6 ones.   Kay _____

Matt read this number of books: 1 hundred 18 ones.   Matt _____

Rosa read this number of books: 12 tens 19 ones.   Rosa _____

Internet Brain Teasers
Visit **www.eduplace.com/kids/mhm**
for more *Brain Teasers.*

Safe Site

Quick ✓ Check

Check Your Understanding of Lessons 1–7

Write how many.

1. 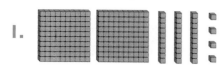 _____

2. _____

3. _____

Use Workmat 4 with ▨ , ▬▬ , and ▪ .

4.

Show this many.	Write how many hundreds, tens, and ones.			Write the number.
	Hundreds	Tens	Ones	
				_____

5.

Show this many.	Regroup 10 tens as 1 hundred.
6 hundreds 11 tens 4 ones	____ hundreds ____ ten ____ ones

Circle the value of the red digit.

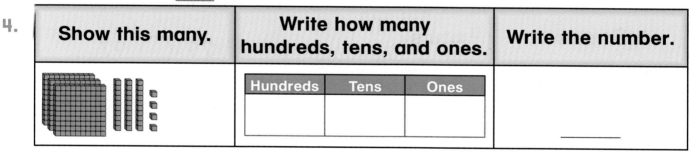

6. **263**

7. **948**

8. **725**

600	60	6	800	80	8	700	70	7

Solve. Complete the table.

9. A small raft holds 4 people.
   How many people are in 4 rafts?

Rafts	1	2		
People	4	8		

Test Prep • Cumulative Review

Maintaining the Standards

Fill in the ○ for the correct answer. NH means Not Here.

1 Mark the number three hundred sixty-eight.

68	300	368	386
○	○	○	○

2 A movie begins at 1:00. It ends at 3:00. How long does it last?

○ 1 hour   ○ 2 hours

○ 3 hours   ○ 4 hours

3 Subtract.
$$
\begin{array}{r} 6\,0 \\ -2\,5 \\ \hline \end{array}
$$

45	40	36	NH
○	○	○	○

4 Multiply.

$$1 \times 5 = \blacksquare$$

1	5	6	NH
○	○	○	○

5 Mark the value of the underlined digit.

2<u>8</u>4

200	800	80	40
○	○	○	○

6 Choose a sign to make the sentence true.

79 ◯ 97

>	<	=	¢
○	○	○	○

7 Tyler showed 149 this way.

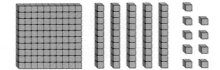

Explain what Tyler did wrong. What blocks should he use?

_____

_____

_____

Copyright © Houghton Mifflin Company. All rights reserved.

Safe Site

Internet Test Prep
Visit **www.eduplace.com/kids/mhm** for more *Test Prep Practice*.

Different Ways to Show Numbers

Learn About It

You can show a number in different ways.

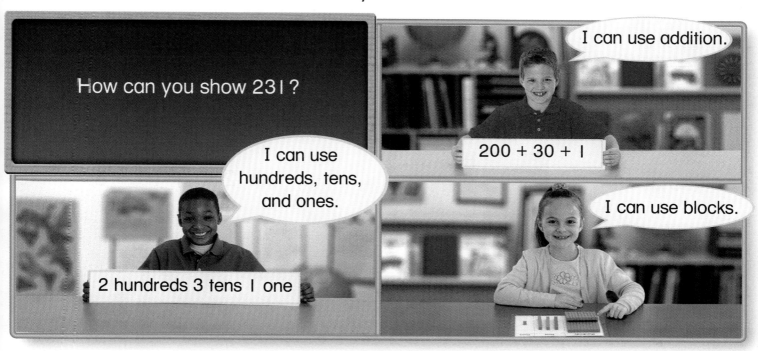

How can you show 231?

I can use hundreds, tens, and ones.

2 hundreds 3 tens 1 one

I can use addition.

200 + 30 + 1

I can use blocks.

Guided Practice

Circle another way to show each number.

1. **342**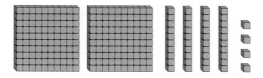

3 hundreds 4 tens 2 ones

2. **415** 400 + 10 + 5

3. **246** 200 + 40 + 6

4. **153** 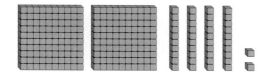 5 hundreds 1 ten 3 ones

Explain Your Thinking What are two other ways to show 196?

Independent Practice

Circle another way to show each number.

1. **442**

$$400 + 40 + 2$$

2. **323**   3 hundreds 2 tens 3 ones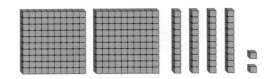

3. **205** $$200 + 10 + 5$$

4. **117**   1 hundred 7 tens 7 ones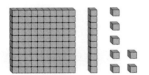

5. **640** $$600 + 40$$ 6 hundreds 0 tens 4 ones

6. **754** $$700 + 50 + 4$$ 7 hundreds 4 tens 5 ones

Problem Solving • Reasoning

7. Luis has three sheets with 10 stars each.
   He has two sheets with 100 stars each.
   He has one sheet with 6 stars.
   How many stars does he have?

   _____ stars

   Draw or write to explain.

At Home Choose a number between 300 and 400. Ask your child how many hundreds, tens, and ones are in the number.

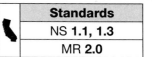

LESSON **9**

Compare Three-Digit Numbers

Learn About It

You can show that numbers are **greater than** by using >
or **less than** by using <.

Review
Vocabulary

**greater than
less than**

First compare hundreds.

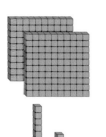

213 is **greater than** 124.

213 > 124

If the hundreds are the same,
compare the tens.

124 is **less than** 135.

124 < 135

If hundreds and
tens are the same,
compare ones.

Guided Practice

Compare. Write **greater** or **less**.
Write **>** or **<** in the ◯.

1. 523 is __less__ than 621.

   523 ◁ 621

2. 983 is _____ than 973.

   983 ◯ 973

3. 777 is _____ than 771.

   777 ◯ 771

4. 431 is _____ than 441.

   431 ◯ 441

Explain Your Thinking Did you need to compare
tens in Exercise 1? Tell why or why not.

Independent Practice

Compare the numbers.
Write >, <, or = in the ◯.

Remember:
> greater than
< less than
= equals

1. 425 ⊘ 503

2. 343 ◯ 351

3. 852 ◯ 851

4. 416 ◯ 372

5. 476 ◯ 476

6. 255 ◯ 401

7. 785 ◯ 779

8. 625 ◯ 498

9. 20 ◯ 220

10. 803 ◯ 803

11. 236 ◯ 240

12. 491 ◯ 472

13. 465 ◯ 507

14. 365 ◯ 374

15. 247 ◯ 198

16. 531 ◯ 508

17. 964 ◯ 968

18. 713 ◯ 713

19. 921 ◯ 912

20. 354 ◯ 352

Problem Solving • Reasoning

Write About It

21. Patty drove 834 miles from San Diego to Denver. Marco drove 844 miles from Los Angeles to Denver. Who drove farther?

_____

22. Explain how you compared the numbers.

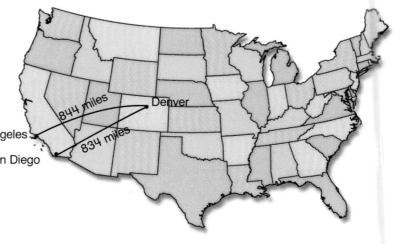

844 miles
Denver
Los Angeles
834 miles
San Diego

Copyright © Houghton Mifflin Company. All rights reserved.

At Home Ask your child to explain what numbers he or she compared in Exercises 4–6.

Before, After, Between

Learn About It

A number line can help you find a number that is just before, just after, or between two numbers.

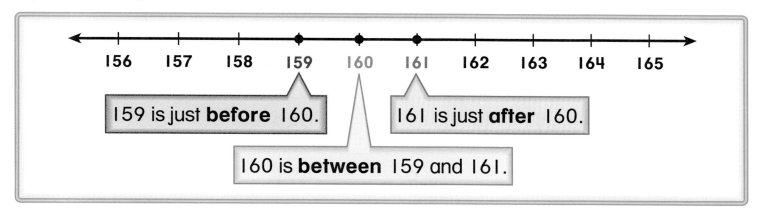

156 157 158 159 160 161 162 163 164 165

159 is just **before** 160.

161 is just **after** 160.

160 is **between** 159 and 161.

Guided Practice

Use the number line. Write each number.

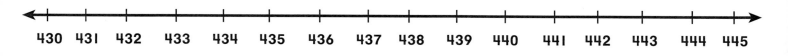

430 431 432 433 434 435 436 437 438 439 440 441 442 443 444 445

	Before	Between	After
1.	430, 431	432, 433, 434	435, 436
2.	_____, 436	437, _____, 439	440, _____
3.	_____, 440	441, _____, 443	444, _____
4.	_____, 438	439, _____, 441	442, _____
5.	_____, 442	435, _____, 437	431, _____
6.	_____, 441	430, _____, 432	437, _____

Explain Your Thinking How would you find which number comes just before 250?

Independent Practice

Write each number.

	Before	Between	After
1.	686, 687	689, 690, 691	695, 696
2.	_____, 340	360, _____, 362	379, _____
3.	_____, 700	719, _____, 721	799, _____
4.	_____, 200	251, _____, 253	299, _____
5.	_____, 550	569, _____, 571	590, _____

Write the missing numbers.

6. 753, _____, _____, 756, 757, 758, _____, 760, _____, 762, _____

7. 96, 97, _____, 99, _____, 101, _____, _____, 104, 105, _____

8. 594, 595, _____, _____, _____, 599, _____, 601, 602, _____, 604

9. 895, _____, _____, 898, 899, _____, _____, 902, 903, _____, _____

10. 697, 698, _____, _____, _____, 702, 703, _____, _____, 706, _____

Problem Solving • Reasoning

Using Vocabulary

11. Match the words to the right sign.

greater than	equal to	less than
=	<	>

Copyright © Houghton Mifflin Company. All rights reserved.

 At Home Name a three-digit number. Ask your child to name the numbers that come before and after the number.

LESSON 11 Order Three-Digit Numbers

Learn About It

Understanding place value can help you order numbers from **least** to **greatest** .

Review Vocabulary

least
greatest

Order the numbers from least to greatest.

212	159	215

Compare the hundreds.
Compare the tens.
Compare the ones.

159, 212, 215

212 and 215 each have 2 hundreds and 1 ten. I need to compare the ones.

Guided Practice

Order the numbers from **least** to **greatest**.

1. 530, 175, 525   175, 525, 530

2. 791, 719, 305   _____, _____, _____

3. 267, 262, 226   _____, _____, _____

Order the numbers from **greatest** to **least**.

4. 451, 328, 382   451, 382, 328

5. 763, 869, 789   _____, _____, _____

6. 327, 237, 732   _____, _____, _____

Explain Your Thinking How does place value help you to order numbers?

Independent Practice

Order the numbers from **least** to **greatest**.

1. 199, 154, 291, 192   154, 192, 199, 291

2. 430, 434, 345, 344   ——, ——, ——, ——

3. 795, 800, 759, 805   ——, ——, ——, ——

4. 674, 681, 671, 680   ——, ——, ——, ——

5. 341, 314, 317, 374   ——, ——, ——, ——

Order the numbers from **greatest** to **least**.

6. 175, 180, 158, 178   180, 178, 175, 158

7. 922, 892, 927, 828   ——, ——, ——, ——

8. 723, 774, 747, 727   ——, ——, ——, ——

9. 605, 506, 650, 560   ——, ——, ——, ——

10. 509, 590, 501, 500   ——, ——, ——, ——

Problem Solving • Reasoning

11. Look at the picture. Numbers have fallen off three of the mailboxes. Put the numbers in order.

——— ——— ———

12. **Write About It** Write how you would put the numbers 241, 263, and 214 in order.

Copyright © Houghton Mifflin Company. All rights reserved.

530 five hundred thirty

At Home Write 3 three-digit numbers, such as 415, 411, and 381. Have your child put the numbers in order from least to greatest.

Standards
NS **5.0, 5.1, 5.2**
MR **2.0**

LESSON 12 Count Dollars and Cents

Review Vocabulary
dollar sign
decimal point

Learn About It

Use a **dollar sign** and **decimal point** to show money.

First count the dollars, and then count the coins.

$1.00, $2.00, $2.05, $2.06, $2.07 $2.07
total

Guided Practice

Write the total value of the bills and coins.

1.
   $3.51
   total

2.
   $___.___
   total

3.
   Think: There are no dollar bills in this amount.
   $___.___
   total

Explain Your Thinking Explain why you count the dollar bills first and then the coins.

Independent Practice

Write the total value of the bills and coins.

1.

$3.71
total

2.  $.
total

3.

$.
total

4.

$.
total

Problem Solving • Reasoning

Circle the correct way to show each amount.

5.  $2.06 $2.60 $2.16

6.  $.06 $.60 $6.00

 **At Home** Ask your child to show you how he or she counted the money on this page.

Copyright © Houghton Mifflin Company. All rights reserved.

Name_____

Problem Solving: Using Money

Standards	
NS **5.0, 5.1**	
MR **1.0, 1.1**	

You can count bills and coins
to find out if there is enough money.

$1.10

sticker

pen

$1.50

**If you have enough money,
decide which bills and coins to use.**

Eric has this amount.

 $ _____ . _____

Can he buy a sticker? Write **yes** or **no**. _____
Circle the bills and coins he could use.

**If you do not have enough money, decide
which bills and coins are needed.**

Mia has this amount.

 $ _____ . _____

Can she buy the pen? Write **yes** or **no**. _____
Draw the coins that she needs.

Guided Practice

$1.70

$2.50

$2.10

Write how much money.
Decide if there is enough money.
Write **yes** or **no**.

1 Mike has this amount.

$ 1.75

Does he have enough
to buy the game? _____
Circle the bills and coins he could use.

Think:
Is there
enough
money?

2 Rea has this amount.

$. _____

Does she have enough
to buy the flag? _____
Draw the coins she needs.

Think: How
much money
does she need?

Draw the coins.

3 Katie has this amount.

$. _____

Does she have enough
to buy the book? _____
Draw the coins she needs.

Think: How
much money
does she need?

Draw the coins.

At Home Ask your child to count the money in each exercise and explain how
he or she solved the problem.

Copyright © Houghton Mifflin Company. All rights reserved.

Name_____

Choose a Strategy

Solve each problem.

1 Toy dinosaurs cost 12¢ each.
Ellie wants to buy 6 dinosaurs.
How much money does she need?

Dinosaur	1					
Cost	12¢					

$ __ . ____

dinosaur

---

2 Tony bought a whistle for 65¢
and a sticker for 20¢.
How much did he spend?

Draw or write to explain.

_____ ¢

whistle

---

3 Write the total value of the bills and coins.

$ __ . ____

Is there enough to buy
a toy boat that costs $2.70?

Write **yes** or **no**. _____

boat

---

4 There are 8 bags of gems.
Each bag has 10 gems in it.
How many gems are there?

_____ gems

gems

Name _____

Mixed Practice

Write the missing numbers.

1. 4 + ____ = 8 + 2   2. 6 + 9 = 7 + ____   3. 9 + ____ = 8 + 5

4. 17 − ____ = 8   5. 14 − ____ = 6   6. 9 + ____ = 16

Find each sum or difference.

7. 49
   +36

8. 54
   −27

9. 71
   −13

10. 62
    +28

11. 53
    + 4

12. 86
    −39

13. 97
    −58

14. 14
    +43

15. 30
    −24

16. 40
    +51

17. 72
    −45

18. 24
    +16

19. 41
    − 9

20. 85
    + 6

21. 32
    −16

 Brain Teaser

Chris forgot Pam's house number. He knows it has three digits and the sum of the digits is 7. The hundreds digit is one more than the tens digit. The ones digit is 0. What is the number?

Copyright © Houghton Mifflin Company. All rights reserved.

 Safe Site

Internet Brain Teasers
Visit **www.eduplace.com/kids/mhm**
for more *Brain Teasers.*

Quick ✔ Check

Check Your Understanding of Lessons 8–13

Circle another way to show the number.

1. | 637 | | 600 + 70 + 3 | | 6 hundreds 3 tens 7 ones |

Compare the numbers. Write **>**, **<**, or **=** in the ◯.

2. 428 ◯ 482   3. 302 ◯ 203   4. 787 ◯ 787

Write the number.

	Before	Between	After
5.	_____, 524	529, _____, 531	537, _____
6.	_____, 910	914, _____, 916	919, _____

Order the numbers from **greatest** to **least**.

7. 246, 264, 244, 263   _____, _____, _____, _____

8. This is Tim's money.
   Write the total value of the bills and coins.

  $ ___ . _____

   total

Does Tim have enough to buy
a puzzle that costs $2.61?

Write **yes** or **no**. _____

Name ____________________

Test Prep • Cumulative Review

Maintaining the Standards

Fill in the ○ for the correct answer. NH means Not Here.

1 About how many clips long is the ribbon?

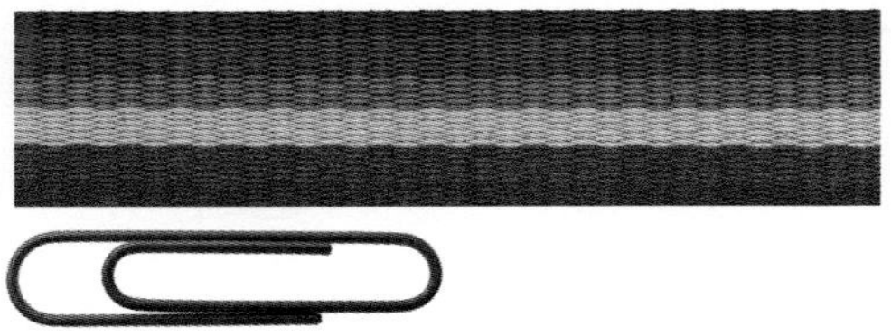

1	2	3	4
○	○	○	○

2 Mark the next number if the numbers are least to greatest.

248, 249, 250, ____

240	250	251	252
○	○	○	○

3 Mark the amount of money shown.

$1.50	$1.35	$1.20	$0.35
○	○	○	○

4 Mark the time on the clock.

9:20	5:15	4:45	3:45
○	○	○	○

5 Subtract. 80 − 50 = ■

80	30	3	NH
○	○	○	○

6 4 cars are going to the park. There are 5 people in each car. Complete the table to find how many people are going to the park.

Car	1	2		
People	5			

Explain how the table helps you find the answer.

____

____

Safe Site

Internet Test Prep
Visit **www.eduplace.com/kids/mhm** for more *Test Prep Practice.*

Copyright © Houghton Mifflin Company. All rights reserved.

Chapter Review

Name_____

Write the letter that matches the red symbol.

1. < _____   2. > _____

3. $1.00 _____   4. $1.00 _____

| A. decimal point |
| B. dollar sign |
| C. greater than |
| D. less than |

5. In the number 752, which **digit** is in the **hundreds** place? _____

6. Circle the number that is the **greatest**.   451   223   168

Count the hundreds. Write the number.

7. _____ hundreds

Write the missing numbers.

8. 100, 200, 300 _____, 500, 600, _____, 800, _____, 1,000

Write how many.

9.

Hundreds	Tens	Ones

_____

10.

Hundreds	Tens	Ones

_____

Circle the value of the red digit.

11. | 619 |

100 10 1

12. | 905 |

500 50 5

13. | 356 |

300 50 6

Circle another way to show the number.

14.

322

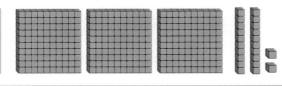

3 hundreds 4 tens 2 ones

15.

165

1 hundred 6 tens 15 ones

100 + 60 + 5

Compare the numbers. Write >, <, or =.

16. 236 ◯ 136 **17.** 490 ◯ 495 **18.** 621 ◯ 621

19. 480 ◯ 590 **20.** 912 ◯ 912 **21.** 750 ◯ 745

Order the numbers from **least** to **greatest**.

22. 426, 424, 425, 427 _____, _____, _____, _____

23. 902, 900, 905, 910 _____, _____, _____, _____

Solve each problem.

24. Ken has this amount.

$ ___ . ___

Can he buy a game that costs $1.75?

Write **yes** or **no**. _____

Draw or write to explain.

25. There are 20 boats at each dock.
How many boats are at 4 docks? _____ boats

Docks	1			
Boats	20			

Draw or write to explain.

Copyright © Houghton Mifflin Company. All rights reserved.

Name _____

Chapter Test

Count the hundreds, tens, and ones.

Write how many.

1.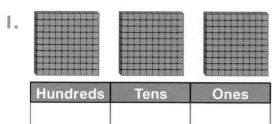

Hundreds	Tens	Ones

_____

2.

Hundreds	Tens	Ones

_____

Circle the value of the red digit.

3. | 482 |

800 80 8

4. | 905 |

900 90 9

5. | 281 |

100 10 1

6. Write the missing numbers.

100, 200, _____, _____, 500, _____, 700, _____, _____, 1,000

Circle another way to show the number.

7. 312   3 hundreds 2 tens 1 one

8. 475   4 hundreds 5 tens 5 ones   400 + 70 + 5

Compare. Write >, <, or =.

9. 236 ◯ 136   10. 467 ◯ 476   11. 960 ◯ 906

12. 677 ◯ 677   13. 710 ◯ 730   14. 561 ◯ 165

Order the numbers from **least** to **greatest**.

15. 562, 560, 563, 561   _____ , _____ , _____ , _____

16. 895, 855, 805, 875   _____ , _____ , _____ , _____

Order the numbers from **greatest** to **least**.

17. 674, 676, 677, 675   _____ , _____ , _____ , _____

18. 453, 444, 450, 440   _____ , _____ , _____ , _____

19. Write the total value of the bills and coins.

  $ _____ . _____

Is there enough to buy a book that costs $1.60?

Write **yes** or **no**. _____

Draw or write to explain.

20. There are 5 children sitting at each table.
How many children are at 8 tables?

Tables	1							
Children	5							

_____ children

 Write About It

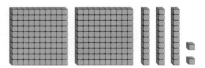   200 + 30 + 2   232

Explain how these 3 ways show the same number.

_____

_____

Copyright © Houghton Mifflin Company. All rights reserved.

Go for the Greatest!

What You Need

- 3 number cubes
- paper and pencil

How to Play

① Label the paper **Player 1** and **Player 2**.

② Take turns tossing the 3 number cubes. Use the numbers to make a three-digit number. Record the number.

③ Compare the numbers. Circle the greater number.

④ The player with the greater number gets 1 point. The first player to get 5 points wins.

Standards
NS 6.0

Enrichment

Round to the Nearest Hundred

400   410   420   430   440   450   460   470   480   490   500

430 is closer to 400 than 500, so 430 rounds to 400.

480 is closer to 500 than 400, so 480 rounds to 500.

Use the number line.
Round each number to the nearest hundred.

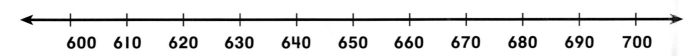

600   610   620   630   640   650   660   670   680   690   700

1. 690 rounds to _700_

2. 640 rounds to _____

3. 610 rounds to _____

4. 670 rounds to _____

5. 660 rounds to _____

6. 620 rounds to _____

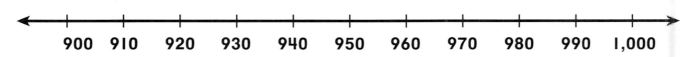

900   910   920   930   940   950   960   970   980   990   1,000

7. 930 rounds to _____

8. 990 rounds to _____

9. 970 rounds to _____

10. 920 rounds to _____

11. 910 rounds to _____

12. 980 rounds to _____

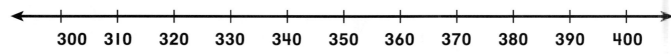

300   310   320   330   340   350   360   370   380   390   400

13. 360 rounds to _____

14. 390 rounds to _____

15. 340 rounds to _____

16. 380 rounds to _____

Copyright © Houghton Mifflin Company. All rights reserved.

Adding and Subtracting Three-Digit Numbers

The Queen's Key

A Read-Aloud Story

written by **Malcom Higgins**
illustrated by **Tuko Fujisaki**

Accessing Prior Knowledge

This story will help you review
- Adding one-digit numbers
- Adding two-digit numbers

A Math Storybook for

_____

One morning, Bee's niece
made a telephone call.
She said, "Please, Aunt Bee.
Can you help me at all?

"When I was at your house,
I forgot the queen's key.
It opens the chest
of royal honey, you see."

Bee found the key
and got into her car.
After an hour,
she thought she'd gone far.

She drove 50 miles,
then 7 miles more,
before her car broke down
in front of Ant's door.

How many miles did Aunt Bee drive?
_____ miles

Bee said to Ant,
"Can you help me?
I promised my niece
I'd deliver this key."

Ant took the key
and got into his boat.
He picked up an oar
and soon was afloat.

He rowed 40 miles,
then 12 miles more.
But his boat sprang a leak
near Spider's front door.

How many miles did Ant row?
_____ miles

Ant said to Spider,
"Can you please help me?
I promised Bee
that I'd deliver this key."

Spider strapped on his skates
and with key in hand,
he skated as fast as he could
through the land.

He'd gone 60 miles,
then 10 miles more,
when his skate lost a wheel
just at Ladybug's door.

How many miles did Spider skate?
_____ miles

Spider said to Ladybug,
"Can you help me?
I promised Ant
that I'd deliver this key."

"I'll hop in my plane,"
Ladybug began,
"and I'll fly just as fast
as a ladybug can."

She flew 70 miles,
then 25 more.
She landed her plane
at the castle's front door.

How many miles did Ladybug fly?
_____ miles

Copyright © Houghton Mifflin Company. All rights reserved.

When Bee's niece got the key
from her friend Ladybug,
she shouted for joy
and gave her a hug!

"You've traveled so far
and in such a short time!
I'd like to repay you
for being so kind.

"These gifts are for all
who carried the key.
Please give them my thanks.
I'm a most grateful bee!"

ROYAL HONEY

Family Letter

Dear Family,

During the next few weeks, our math class will be learning about adding and subtracting three-digit numbers with and without regrouping.

You can expect to see work that provides practice with adding and subtracting three-digit numbers. There will also be work that provides practice using money.

As we learn about three-digit addition and subtraction, you may wish to use the following sample as a guide.

Vocabulary

decimal point The point used to separate dollars and cents.

dollar sign The sign ($) used to indicate dollars.

estimate An approximate amount, rather than an exact amount.

hundred A group of 10 tens.

regroup To rename a number by trading ones, tens, and hundreds.

Addition With Regrouping

$$
\begin{array}{r}
\boxed{1} \\
4\ 5\ 2 \\
+\ 1\ 3\ 9 \\
\hline
5\ 9\ 1
\end{array}
$$

To add, regroup 10 ones as 1 ten.

Subtraction With Regrouping

$$
\begin{array}{r}
\boxed{7}\ \boxed{12} \\
5\ 8\ 2 \\
-\ 2\ 5\ 9 \\
\hline
3\ 2\ 3
\end{array}
$$

To subtract, regroup 1 ten as 10 ones.

Sincerely,

Your child's teacher

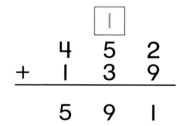

Standards
NS **2.3**, AF **1.3**
SDP **2.2**

LESSON 1
Mental Math: Add Hundreds

Review Vocabulary

hundreds

Learn About It

To add **hundreds,** think of an addition fact.

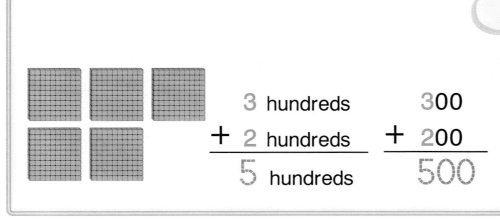

$3 + 2 = 5$

3 hundreds	300
+ 2 hundreds	+ 200
5 hundreds	500

Guided Practice

Add. Look for a pattern.

1.
```
   4      40      400
  +3     +30     +300
   7      70      700
```

2.
```
   2      20      200
  +6     +60     +600
```

3.
```
   5      50      500
  +2     +20     +200
```

4.
```
   3      30      300
  +3     +30     +300
```

5.
```
   4      40      400
  +5     +50     +500
```

6.
```
   2      20      200
  +7     +70     +700
```

7.
```
   1      10      100
  +2     +20     +200
```

8.
```
   2      20      200
  +2     +20     +200
```

Explain Your Thinking How does $6 + 3 = 9$ help you solve $600 + 300$?

Independent Practice

Add. Look for a pattern.

1.
```
   3      30      300
  +5     +50     +500
   8      80      800
```

2.
```
   4      40      400
  +4     +40     +400
```

3.
```
   3      30      300
  +1     +10     +100
```

4.
```
   2      20      200
  +5     +50     +500
```

5.
```
   3      30      300
  +6     +60     +600
```

6.
```
   1      10      100
  +5     +50     +500
```

7.
```
  600     200
 +200    +600
```

8.
```
  400     300
 +300    +400
```

9.
```
  200     700
 +700    +200
```

10.
```
  300     200
 +200    +300
```

Problem Solving · Reasoning

Algebra Readiness · Functions

Follow each rule.

11.

Add 100	
200	
300	
400	
500	

12.

Add 300	
100	
200	
300	
400	

13.

Add 500	
100	
200	
300	
400	

At Home Ask your child to tell you how knowing 3 + 2 = 5 helps him or her solve 300 + 200.

Copyright © Houghton Mifflin Company. All rights reserved.

Name _____

Standards
NS **2.2**, AF **1.0**
MR **1.2**

Regroup Ones

Learn About It

If there are 10 or more ones, **regroup** 10 ones as 1 ten.

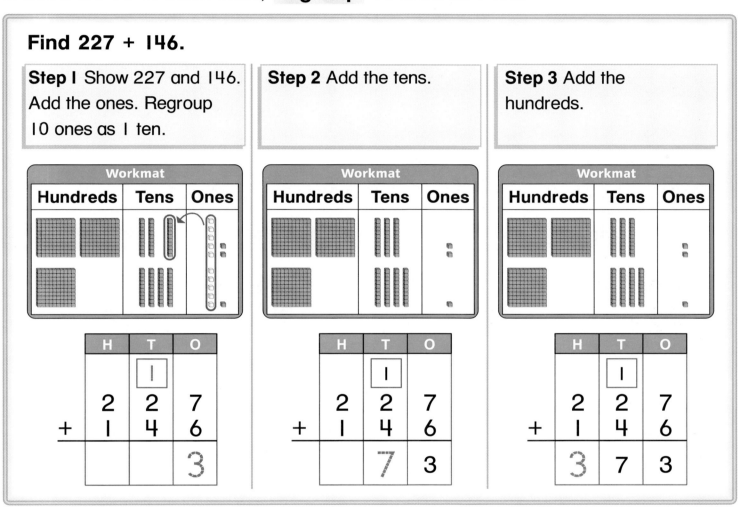

Find 227 + 146.

Step 1 Show 227 and 146. Add the ones. Regroup 10 ones as 1 ten.

Step 2 Add the tens.

Step 3 Add the hundreds.

Guided Practice

Use Workmat 4 with 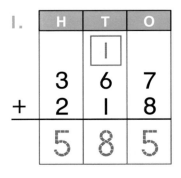, ▭▭▭▭▭▭, and ▫. Add.

Think: Do I need to regroup?

Explain Your Thinking How does knowing that 15 ones is the same as 1 ten 5 ones help you add?

Independent Practice

Use Workmat 4 with ▦ , ▭▭▭▭▭▭ , and ▪. Add.

1.

H	T	O
	[1]	
6	1	7
+	4	5
6	6	2

2.

H	T	O
	[ ]	
1	4	3
+ 5	2	4

3.

H	T	O
	[ ]	
3	5	8
+ 5	2	6

4.

	[ ]	
1	2	3
+ 3	5	9

5.

	[ ]	
3	1	8
+	3	5

6.

	[ ]	
5	4	2
+ 2	5	6

7.
```
  237
+ 428
  665
```

8.
```
  468
+   7
```

9.
```
  736
+ 142
```

10.
```
  305
+ 327
```

11.
```
  223
+ 619
```

12.
```
  570
+  29
```

13.
```
  189
+ 307
```

14.
```
  472
+ 516
```

Problem Solving • Reasoning

Use Workmat 4 with ▦ , ▭▭▭▭▭▭ , and ▪ to solve.

15. Liz has 147 stamps from Mexico and 49 stamps from Japan. How many does she have in all?

_____ stamps

Draw or write to explain.

At Home Ask your child to circle the exercises on this page in which he or she regrouped the ones and then explain why regrouping was necessary.

Name _____

Regroup Tens

Learn About It

If there are 10 or more tens, regroup 10 tens as 1 hundred.

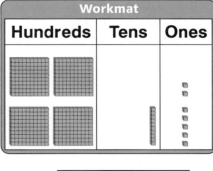

Find 152 + 265.

Step 1 Show 152 and 265. Add the ones.

Step 2 Add the tens. Regroup 10 tens as 1 hundred.

Step 3 Add the hundreds.

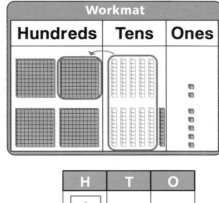

H	T	O
	1	5	2
+	2	6	5
			7

H	T	O
1			
	1	5	2
+	2	6	5
		1	7

H	T	O
1			
	1	5	2
+	2	6	5
	4	1	7

Guided Practice

Use Workmat 4 with ▨ , ▭▭▭ , and ▪ . Add.

1.

H	T	O
1		
4	6	2
+ 4	6	7
9	2	9

Think: Do I need to regroup?

2.

H	T	O
2	5	3
+	7	5

3.

H	T	O
1	3	8
+ 4	1	4

Explain Your Thinking How do you know if you need to regroup tens as 1 hundred?

Independent Practice

Add. Use Workmat 4 with , ⬛⬛⬛⬛⬛ , and 🔴 if you want.

1.
```
    1  8  3
 +  5  2  6
 ─────────
    7  0  9
```

2.
```
 3  5  7
 +     1  4
 ──────────
 3  7  1
```

3.
```
    4  3  1
 +  2  9  4
```

4.
```
   325
 +  66
```

5.
```
   252
 +176
```

6.
```
   647
 +128
```

7.
```
   584
 +   3
```

8.
```
   410
 +294
```

9.
```
   335
 +156
```

10.
```
   136
 +792
```

11.
```
   936
 +  48
```

12.
```
   762
 +    7
```

13.
```
   624
 +159
```

14.
```
   342
 +364
```

15.
```
   653
 +293
```

Problem Solving • Reasoning

Write About It

16. A ticket for a boat ride costs $1.25.
Both children can buy a ticket. Explain why.

Kerry's Money

Ryan's Money

At Home Your child is learning how to regroup 10 tens as 1 hundred. Have your child explain how he or she did the exercises on this page.

Check Your Understanding of Lessons 1–3

Add. Look for a pattern.

1.
```
    6        60        600
  + 3      + 30      + 300
```

2.
```
    1        10        100
  + 5      + 50      + 500
```

3.
```
  400       500
+ 500     + 400
```

4.
```
  300       200
+ 200     + 300
```

Add.

5.
```
      4 | 1 | 6
  +   3 | 2 | 6
```

6.
```
      3 | 3 | 6
  +     | 7 | 1
```

7.
```
      2 | 6 | 6
  +   2 | 2 | 5
```

8.
```
  136
+ 604
```

9.
```
  785
+ 162
```

10.
```
  511
+  48
```

11.
```
  819
+ 131
```

12.
```
  474
+  82
```

13.
```
  261
+ 317
```

14.
```
  360
+ 297
```

15.
```
  853
+   8
```

16.
```
  255
+ 112
```

17.
```
  582
+  37
```

18.
```
  646
+ 327
```

19.
```
  135
+   9
```

Test Prep • Cumulative Review
Maintaining the Standards

Fill in the ○ for the correct answer. NH means Not Here.

Use the tally chart to answer Questions 1 and 2.

Bugs Seen	
Bug	**Number**
Spider	|||
Bee	||
Fly	||||| ||
Ant	||||| |||||

1 Mark how many ants were seen.

12   10   5   2
○   ○   ○   ○

2 Mark how many more ants were seen than bees.

12   10   8   2
○   ○   ○   ○

3 Mark which shape would most likely come next.

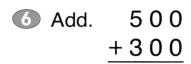 ?

○   ○   ○   ○

4 Add.   3 1 7
           + 2 7 5

42   182   592   NH
○   ○   ○   ○

5 Mark the amount of money shown.

○ $1.25   ○ $1.46
○ 46¢   ○ $1.21

6 Add.   5 0 0
           + 3 0 0

Explain what fact you used to help you add.

_____

_____

_____

Copyright © Houghton Mifflin Company. All rights reserved.

Safe Site

Internet Test Prep
Visit **www.eduplace.com/kids/mhm**
for more *Test Prep Practice*.

Mental Math: Subtract Hundreds

Standards
NS **2.3**, AF **1.3**
SDP **2.2**

Review Vocabulary
hundreds

Learn About It

To subtract **hundreds,** think of a subtraction fact.

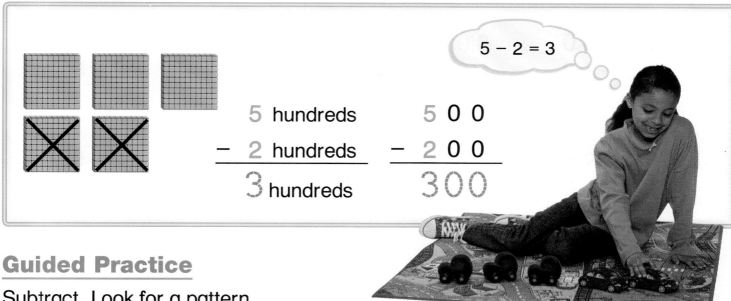

$5 - 2 = 3$

5 hundreds	5 0 0
− 2 hundreds	− 2 0 0
3 hundreds	3 0 0

Guided Practice

Subtract. Look for a pattern.

1.
7	7 0	7 0 0
−2	−2 0	−2 0 0
5	5 0	5 0 0

2.
9	9 0	9 0 0
−6	−6 0	−6 0 0

3.
8	8 0	8 0 0
−3	−3 0	−3 0 0

4.
6	6 0	6 0 0
−3	−3 0	−3 0 0

5.
9	9 0	9 0 0
−5	−5 0	−5 0 0

6.
6	6 0	6 0 0
−4	−4 0	−4 0 0

7.
5	5 0	5 0 0
−4	−4 0	−4 0 0

8.
3	3 0	3 0 0
−1	−1 0	−1 0 0

Explain Your Thinking How does $6 - 2 = 4$ help you solve $600 - 200$?

Independent Practice

Subtract. Look for a pattern.

1.
9	90	900
−1	−10	−100
8	80	800

2.
6	60	600
−4	−40	−400

3.
8	80	800
−5	−50	−500

4.
7	70	700
−2	−20	−200

5.
9	90	900
−6	−60	−600

6.
5	50	500
−3	−30	−300

7.
300	300
−100	−200

8.
700	700
−400	−300

9.
600	600
−200	−400

10.
400	400
−100	−300

Problem Solving • Reasoning

Using Data

11. How many more rooms does the Market Hotel have than the Castle Hotel?

    _____ more rooms

Hotel Name	Number of Rooms
Castle Hotel	300
Sandy Hotel	700
Market Hotel	500

12. **Write Your Own** Use data from the table to write a subtraction problem.

Copyright © Houghton Mifflin Company. All rights reserved.

At Home Ask your child to tell you how knowing 6 − 4 = 2 helps him or her solve 600 − 400.

Regroup Tens

Learn About It

If there are not enough ones to subtract,
regroup 1 ten as 10 ones.

Find 253 − 137.

Step 1 Regroup 1 ten as 10 ones. Subtract the ones.

Workmat		
Hundreds	**Tens**	**Ones**

H	T	O
	4	13
2	5̸	3̸
− 1	3	7
		6

Step 2 Subtract the tens.

Workmat		
Hundreds	**Tens**	**Ones**

H	T	O
	4	13
2	5̸	3̸
− 1	3	7
		6

Step 3 Subtract the hundreds.

Workmat		
Hundreds	**Tens**	**Ones**

H	T	O
	4	13
2	5̸	3̸
− 1	3	7
	1	6

Guided Practice

Use Workmat 4 with , ⬛⬛⬛⬛⬛⬛⬛⬛, and ▪. Subtract.

1.

H	T	O
	6	12
5	7̸	2̸
− 2	1	8
3	5	4

Think:
Do I need to regroup?

2.

H	T	O
6	9	4
− 3	8	9

3.

H	T	O
3	6	8
− 3	2	6

Explain Your Thinking Why do you need to regroup in Exercise 2?

Independent Practice

Use Workmat 4 with , ⬛⬛⬛⬛⬛⬛⬛, and ▪. Subtract.

1.

H	T	O
	8	13
3	9̸	3̸
− 1	6	5
2	2	8

2.

H	T	O
	☐	☐
5	7	5
− 5	1	6

3.

H	T	O
	☐	☐
4	8	7
−	3	2

4.

	☐	☐
5	6	0
− 2	2	8

5.

	☐	☐
1	9	3
−	4	6

6.

	☐	☐
3	8	8
−	7	9

7.
$$572 \\ -\ 35$$
⁶ ¹²
537

8.
$$226 \\ -\ \ \ 9$$

9.
$$952 \\ -\ 517$$

10.
$$629 \\ -\ 108$$

11.
$$159 \\ -\ 107$$

12.
$$370 \\ -\ 221$$

13.
$$438 \\ -\ 329$$

14.
$$899 \\ -\ 632$$

Problem Solving·Reasoning

Visual Thinking

15. Ant and Grasshopper are climbing the hill. They have 75 more feet to go before they reach the top. How far have they climbed already?

_____ feet

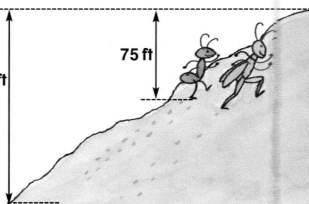

891 ft   75 ft

At Home Have your child circle the exercises in which he or she regrouped tens, and then explain why regrouping was necessary.

Copyright © Houghton Mifflin Company. All rights reserved.

Regroup Hundreds

Learn About It

If there are not enough tens to subtract, regroup 1 hundred as 10 tens.

Find 336 − 172.

Step 1 Show 336. Subtract the ones.	**Step 2** Regroup 1 hundred as 10 tens. Subtract the tens.	**Step 3** Subtract the hundreds.

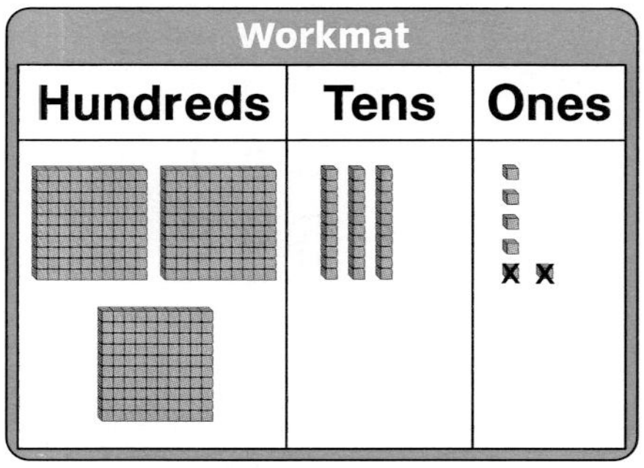

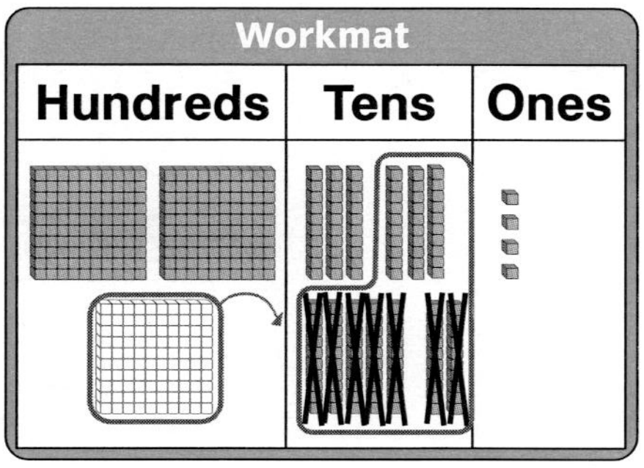

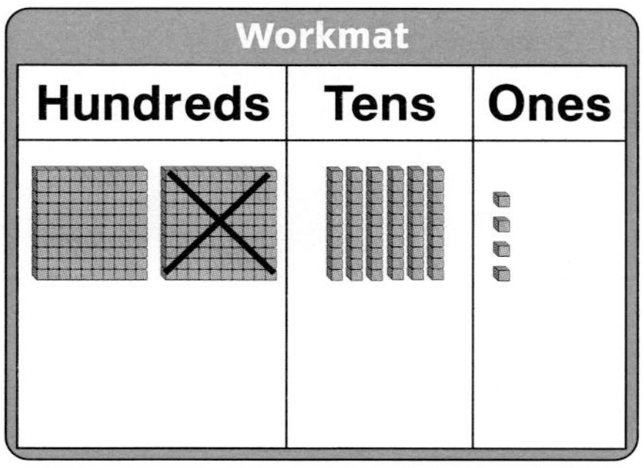

Workmat		
Hundreds	**Tens**	**Ones**
<image blocks>		

H	T	O
3	3	6
− 1	7	2
		4

Workmat		
Hundreds	**Tens**	**Ones**

H	T	O
2	13	
3̸	3̸	6
− 1	7	2
	6	4

Workmat		
Hundreds	**Tens**	**Ones**

H	T	O
2	13	
3̸	3̸	6
− 1	7	2
1	6	4

Guided Practice

Use Workmat 4 with 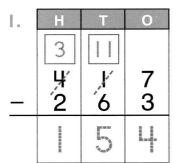 , ⬛⬛⬛⬛⬛, and ◾. Subtract.

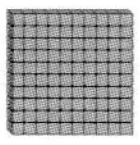

1.

H	T	O
3	11	
4̸	1̸	7
− 2	6	3
1	5	4

Think: Do I need to regroup?

2.

H	T	O
8	2	6
−	9	3

3.

H	T	O
6	9	2
− 3	7	8

Explain Your Thinking When do you need to regroup 1 hundred as 10 tens?

Independent Practice

Subtract. Use Workmat 4 with 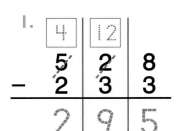 , ⬜⬜⬜⬜⬜⬜ , and ▪ if you want.

1.
$$\begin{array}{r} {\scriptstyle 4}\ {\scriptstyle 12} \\ 5\ \cancel{2}\ 8 \\ -\ 2\ 3\ 3 \\ \hline 2\ 9\ 5 \end{array}$$

2.
$$\begin{array}{r} {\scriptstyle 6}\ {\scriptstyle 13} \\ 5\ \cancel{7}\ \cancel{3} \\ -\ 2\ 5\ 7 \\ \hline 3\ 1\ 6 \end{array}$$

3.
$$\begin{array}{r} \square\ \square \\ 9\ 4\ 3 \\ -\ 4\ 7\ 1 \\ \hline \end{array}$$

4.
$$\begin{array}{r} 9\ 1\ 7 \\ -\ 7\ 3\ 6 \\ \hline \end{array}$$

5.
$$\begin{array}{r} 3\ 8\ 0 \\ -\ 1\ 7\ 7 \\ \hline \end{array}$$

6.
$$\begin{array}{r} 4\ 7\ 9 \\ -\ \ \ 9\ 9 \\ \hline \end{array}$$

7.
$$\begin{array}{r} 7\ 0\ 8 \\ -\ \ \ 6\ 4 \\ \hline \end{array}$$

8.
$$\begin{array}{r} 6\ 3\ 4 \\ -\ 4\ 7\ 1 \\ \hline \end{array}$$

9.
$$\begin{array}{r} 2\ 8\ 9 \\ -\ 1\ 9\ 9 \\ \hline \end{array}$$

10.
$$\begin{array}{r} 5\ 1\ 5 \\ -\ 2\ 7\ 3 \\ \hline \end{array}$$

11.
$$\begin{array}{r} 8\ 6\ 1 \\ -\ 5\ 4\ 8 \\ \hline \end{array}$$

12.
$$\begin{array}{r} 1\ 7\ 4 \\ -\ \ \ 3\ 9 \\ \hline \end{array}$$

13.
$$\begin{array}{r} 4\ 1\ 8 \\ -\ 1\ 9\ 3 \\ \hline \end{array}$$

14.
$$\begin{array}{r} 7\ 9\ 7 \\ -\ \ \ \ \ 9 \\ \hline \end{array}$$

15.
$$\begin{array}{r} 9\ 8\ 1 \\ -\ 6\ 9\ 0 \\ \hline \end{array}$$

16.
$$\begin{array}{r} 3\ 5\ 2 \\ -\ 1\ 4\ 9 \\ \hline \end{array}$$

17.
$$\begin{array}{r} 5\ 4\ 3 \\ -\ 3\ 1\ 7 \\ \hline \end{array}$$

18.
$$\begin{array}{r} 6\ 0\ 7 \\ -\ 4\ 2\ 6 \\ \hline \end{array}$$

19.
$$\begin{array}{r} 1\ 9\ 3 \\ -\ \ \ 7\ 9 \\ \hline \end{array}$$

Problem Solving•Reasoning

Using Vocabulary

20. After you **regrouped**, you had 3 hundreds, 14 tens, and 5 ones. What number did you start with?

_____

Draw or write to explain.

At Home Your child is learning how to regroup 1 hundred as 10 tens. Have your child explain how he or she did the exercises on this page.

Copyright © Houghton Mifflin Company. All rights reserved.

Name _____

 LESSON 7

Problem Solving: Choose the Operation

Standards
AF **1.2**, MR **1.1, 2.1**

Learn About It

To decide whether to add or subtract, think about whether you are putting numbers together or finding out how many more.

Cara drove to Washington, D.C. She drove 280 miles on Friday and 145 miles on Saturday.

Add when you are putting numbers together.

How many miles did Cara drive on both days?

Circle the number sentence you would use.

280 + 145 = 425 miles   280 − 145 = 135 miles

Explain how you know you chose the correct operation.

Think: How do I know when I need to add?

Subtract when you need to find how many more.

How many more miles did Cara drive on Friday than on Saturday?

Circle the number sentence you would use.

280 + 145 = 425 miles   280 − 145 = 135 miles

Explain how you know you chose the correct operation.

Think: How do I know when I need to subtract?

Guided Practice

Circle the number sentence you would use.
Then solve.

1. Mark drove to New York. He drove 410 miles on the first day and 325 miles the next day. How far did he drive?

   410 − 325 = ■

   (410 + 325 = ■)

   735 miles

   > **Think:** I need to find how far he drove in all.

   Draw or write to explain.

2. The Grand Canyon had 527 visitors on Friday and 473 visitors on Monday. How many more visitors were there on Friday?

   527 − 473 = ■

   527 + 473 = ■

   _____ visitors

   > **Think:** I need to compare two numbers.

3. 254 beach passes were sold in May. 175 beach passes were sold in June. How many passes were sold in all?

   254 − 175 = ■

   254 + 175 = ■

   _____ passes

   > **Think:** I need to find how many passes were sold in all.

At Home Ask your child to write a problem about traveling using the numbers 525 and 180. Then solve the problem together.

Name _____

Choose a Strategy

Solve.

1. There are 100 people in each tour group at the Capitol. How many people are in 4 groups?

   _____ people

   Draw or write to explain.

   Capitol

2. At the Washington Monument, Mandy climbed 627 steps. Then she climbed 270 more steps to the top. How many steps did she climb in all?

   _____ steps

   Washington Monument

3. The store in the Air and Space Museum sold 325 planet T-shirts and 250 rocket T-shirts. How many T-shirts did it sell in all?

   _____ T-shirts

   Air and Space Museum

4. Maggie arrived at the Lincoln Memorial at 1:30. She stayed for 2 hours. What time did she leave?

   _____ : _____

   Lincoln Memorial

Mixed Practice

Add or subtract.

1. $5 + 2 + 8 =$ _____

2. $7 + 9 + 4 =$ _____

3. _____ $= 10 + 7$

4. $7 + 8 =$ _____

5. _____ $= 4 + 5$

6.
$$\begin{array}{r} 82 \\ +14 \\ \hline \end{array}$$

7.
$$\begin{array}{r} 75 \\ -58 \\ \hline \end{array}$$

8.
$$\begin{array}{r} 52 \\ +47 \\ \hline \end{array}$$

9.
$$\begin{array}{r} 90 \\ -61 \\ \hline \end{array}$$

10.
$$\begin{array}{r} 57 \\ +24 \\ \hline \end{array}$$

11.
$$\begin{array}{r} 200 \\ +500 \\ \hline \end{array}$$

12.
$$\begin{array}{r} 123 \\ +382 \\ \hline \end{array}$$

13.
$$\begin{array}{r} 509 \\ +275 \\ \hline \end{array}$$

14.
$$\begin{array}{r} 785 \\ + 90 \\ \hline \end{array}$$

15.
$$\begin{array}{r} 900 \\ -700 \\ \hline \end{array}$$

16.
$$\begin{array}{r} 850 \\ -318 \\ \hline \end{array}$$

17.
$$\begin{array}{r} 547 \\ - 63 \\ \hline \end{array}$$

18.
$$\begin{array}{r} 341 \\ -151 \\ \hline \end{array}$$

Brain Teaser Egyptian Numbers

The Egyptians used these symbols for numbers. How much is each symbol worth?

I = _____   ∩ = _____

℮ = _____

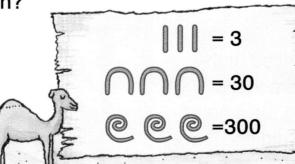

||| = 3

∩∩∩ = 30

℮ ℮ ℮ =300

Safe Site

Internet Brain Teasers
Visit www.eduplace.com/kids/mhm
for more *Brain Teasers*.

Name _____

Check Your Understanding of Lessons 4–7

Subtract. Look for a pattern.

1.
```
   8      80      800
 − 6    − 60    − 600
```

2.
```
   9      90      900
 − 4    − 40    − 400
```

3.
```
  600     600
− 200   − 400
```

4.
```
  700     700
− 500   − 200
```

Subtract.

5.
```
□ □
4 6 1
− 2 3 9
```

6.
```
□ □
7 3 7
−   9 6
```

7.
```
□ □
2 5 4
− 1 4 5
```

8.
```
  428
− 183
```

9.
```
  264
−  57
```

10.
```
  995
− 574
```

11.
```
  584
− 369
```

Circle the number sentence you would use. Then solve.

12. Tony drove to Dallas. He drove 235 miles in the morning and 150 miles in the afternoon. How far did Tony drive?

   235 − 150 = ▪

   235 + 150 = ▪   _____ miles

Draw or write to explain.

Test Prep • Cumulative Review

Maintaining the Standards

Fill in the ○ for the correct answer. NH means Not Here.

① Subtract.
$$\begin{array}{r} 600 \\ -200 \\ \hline \end{array}$$

800   600   500   NH
○   ○   ○   ○

② Mark the time shown on the clock.

5:30   6:15   7:40   2:05
○   ○   ○   ○

③ Mark the fraction of the shape that is blue.

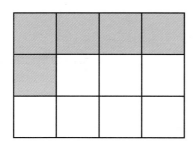

$\dfrac{3}{12}$ $\dfrac{7}{12}$ $\dfrac{1}{2}$ $\dfrac{5}{12}$
○   ○   ○   ○

④ Add.
$$\begin{array}{r} 432 \\ +194 \\ \hline \end{array}$$

238   526   626   NH
○   ○   ○   ○

⑤ Mark the number that belongs in the box.

$$6 + 8 = 9 + \blacksquare$$

4   5   6   7
○   ○   ○   ○

⑥ 345 children and 219 adults visited the zoo. How many people visited the zoo? Circle the number sentence you would use.

$$345 - 219 = 126$$

$$345 + 219 = 564$$

Explain how you decided which number sentence is correct.

_____

_____

Copyright © Houghton Mifflin Company. All rights reserved.

Safe Site

Internet Test Prep
Visit www.eduplace.com/kids/mhm
for more *Test Prep Practice*.

Standards
NS 2.2

LESSON 8 Horizontal Addition and Subtraction

Learn About It

Rewrite the numbers to help you add or subtract.

Find 346 + 235.

Rewrite the numbers. Add.

```
    1
  3 | 4 | 6
+ 2 | 3 | 5
  5 | 8 | 1
```

Find 549 − 367.

Rewrite the numbers. Subtract.

```
    4 | 14
  5 | 4 | 9
− 3 | 6 | 7
  1 | 8 | 2
```

Guided Practice

Add or subtract.

Watch the signs.

1. 428 + 162

```
    4 | 1 2 | 8
  +   | 6 | 2
    5 | 9 | 0
```

2. 654 − 82

3. 327 − 174

4. 229 + 456

5. 596 − 139

6. 723 + 246

Explain Your Thinking Why is it helpful to rewrite the numbers in these exercises?

Independent Practice

Add or subtract. To solve the riddle,
write the letter that matches each answer on the line below.

364 + 64	454 – 182	237 + 312	843 – 500
364 + 64 428	– ____	+ ____	– ____
K	**A**	**U**	**T**

745 – 182	408 + 263	473 – 58	986 – 249
– ____	+ ____	– ____	– ____
S	**R**	**E**	**A**

392 – 243	647 + 125	256 + 336
– ____	+ ____	+ ____
H	**H**	**N**

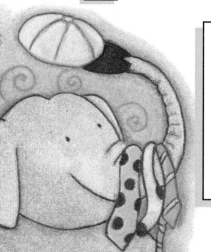

Why is an elephant
always ready to travel?

____ ____ ____ ____ ____ ____
149 415   772 272 563

____ ____ ____ ____ ____ K !
737   243 671 549 592 428

At Home Have your child show you how to rewrite a horizontal exercise.
Have him or her explain to you why it is helpful to rewrite the exercise.

Standards
NS **2.1, 2.2**

Algebra Readiness:
Check Subtraction

Learn About It

You can add to check subtraction.

- Start with the difference, 186.

- Add the number you subtracted, 162.

- The sum should equal the number you subtracted from.

Subtract.

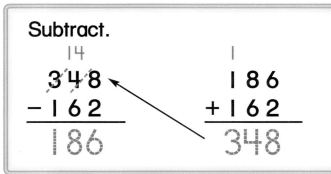

```
    14
  3 4 8          1 8 6
- 1 6 2        + 1 6 2
  1 8 6          3 4 8
```

Guided Practice

Subtract. Check by adding.

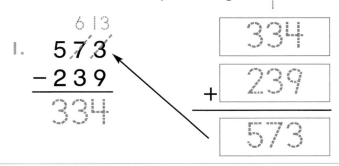

```
    6 13
1.  5 7 3
  - 2 3 9
    3 3 4
```

+
```
  3 3 4
  2 3 9
  5 7 3
```

2.
```
  8 1 8
- 5 4 7
```
+

3.
```
  5 3 9
- 1 4 6
```
+

4.
```
  4 5 5
-   3 7
```
+

5.
```
  2 6 1
- 1 3 4
```
+

6.
```
  6 1 7
- 4 3 6
```
+

Explain Your Thinking What does it mean if the sum does not equal the number you subtracted from?

Independent Practice

Subtract. Check by adding.

1.
$$
\begin{array}{r}
6\,|2 \\
37\cancel{2} \\
-109 \\
\hline
263
\end{array}
\qquad
\begin{array}{r}
263 \\
+109 \\
\hline
372
\end{array}
$$

2.
$$
\begin{array}{r}
484 \\
-26 \\
\hline
\end{array}
\qquad +\rule{2cm}{0.4pt}
$$

3.
$$
\begin{array}{r}
652 \\
-161 \\
\hline
\end{array}
\qquad +\rule{2cm}{0.4pt}
$$

4.
$$
\begin{array}{r}
777 \\
-269 \\
\hline
\end{array}
\qquad +\rule{2cm}{0.4pt}
$$

5.
$$
\begin{array}{r}
428 \\
-238 \\
\hline
\end{array}
\qquad +\rule{2cm}{0.4pt}
$$

6.
$$
\begin{array}{r}
691 \\
-345 \\
\hline
\end{array}
\qquad +\rule{2cm}{0.4pt}
$$

7.
$$
\begin{array}{r}
639 \\
-293 \\
\hline
\end{array}
\qquad +\rule{2cm}{0.4pt}
$$

8.
$$
\begin{array}{r}
932 \\
-704 \\
\hline
\end{array}
\qquad +\rule{2cm}{0.4pt}
$$

Problem Solving • Reasoning

Number Sense

Use these digits: | 2 | 3 | 4 | 5 | 6 |.

9. Use all the digits. Make the greatest possible sum.

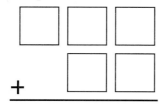

10. Use all the digits. Make the least possible sum.

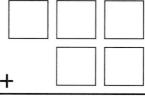

At Home Have your child use the exercises on this page to explain how subtraction is checked by addition.

Copyright © Houghton Mifflin Company. All rights reserved.

LESSON 10 Estimate Sums and Differences

Learn About It

Here is a way to **estimate** a sum or difference.

Review
Vocabulary

estimate

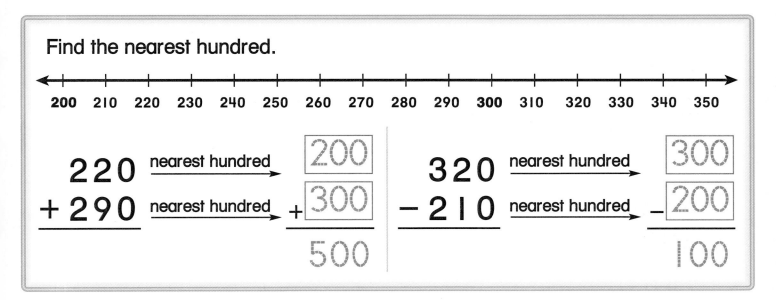

Find the nearest hundred.

| 200 | 210 | 220 | 230 | 240 | 250 | 260 | 270 | 280 | 290 | 300 | 310 | 320 | 330 | 340 | 350 |

$$\begin{array}{r} 220 \\ +290 \end{array}$$ nearest hundred → $\begin{array}{r} 200 \\ +300 \end{array}$ = 500

$$\begin{array}{r} 320 \\ -210 \end{array}$$ nearest hundred → $\begin{array}{r} 300 \\ -200 \end{array}$ = 100

Guided Practice

Find the nearest hundred.
Add or subtract.

1. $\begin{array}{r} 520 \\ +170 \end{array}$ → 500, + ☐, ☐

| 500 | 510 | 520 | 530 | 540 | 550 | 560 | 570 | 580 | 590 | 600 |
| 100 | 110 | 120 | 130 | 140 | 150 | 160 | 170 | 180 | 190 | 200 |

2. $\begin{array}{r} 610 \\ -280 \end{array}$ → ☐, − ☐, ☐

| 600 | 610 | 620 | 630 | 640 | 650 | 660 | 670 | 680 | 690 | 700 |
| 200 | 210 | 220 | 230 | 240 | 250 | 260 | 270 | 280 | 290 | 300 |

Explain Your Thinking How did you find the nearest hundred for each number in Exercises 1 and 2?

Independent Practice

Find the nearest hundred.
Add or subtract.

1.   520 ⟶ □

  +370 ⟶ + □
  ‾‾‾‾‾‾‾
      □

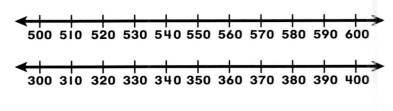
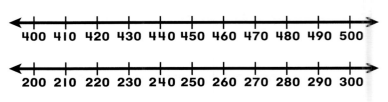

2.   490 ⟶ □

  −210 ⟶ − □
  ‾‾‾‾‾‾‾
      □

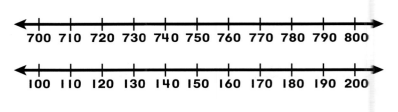

3.   740 ⟶ □

  −120 ⟶ − □
  ‾‾‾‾‾‾‾
      □

Problem Solving • Reasoning

4. **Estimate** On Sunday, 490 people visited Water Park. On Monday, 320 people visited the park. About how many fewer people visited Water Park on Monday?

about _____ fewer people

Draw or write to explain.

At Home Discuss with your child the times it would be helpful to estimate an amount rather than find an exact amount.

Copyright © Houghton Mifflin Company. All rights reserved.

Standards
NS 2.0, 2.2, 5.0, 5.2
AF 1.3

LESSON 11 Add and Subtract Money

Learn About It

Use a **dollar sign** and **decimal point** when you add and subtract money.

Sally has $4.75. She buys a 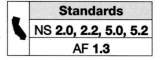 and . How much does she spend? How much does she have left?

$.65

$1.25

Add to find how much she spends.

```
    |
  $ 1.2 5
+    .6 5
  $ 1.9 0
```

Think:
```
  1 2 5
+   6 5
  1 9 0
```

Subtract to find how much money she has left.

```
   3 17
  $ 4.7 5
-   1.9 0
  $ 2.8 5
```

Think:
```
  4 7 5
- 1 9 0
  2 8 5
```

Guided Practice

Remember: Write **$** and **.** in your answer.

Add or subtract.

1.
```
    |
  $ 3.1 7
+   4.6 5
  $ 7.8 2
```

2.
```
  $ 7.6 5
-    .9 2
```

3.
```
  $ 2.6 2
+  3.2 8
```

4.
```
  $ 4.7 9
-  1.5 6
```

5.
```
  $ 5.9 5
+    .6 3
```

6.
```
  $ 3.2 9
-    .7 4
```

7.
```
  $ 6.5 1
+    .2 8
```

8.
```
  $ 6.0 0
-  4.2 0
```

Explain Your Thinking Does knowing how to find 575 − 268 help you find $5.75 − $2.68?

Independent Practice

Add or subtract.

> **Remember:** Write **$** and **.**
> in your answer.

7 12
1. $8.2̸2̸
    − 4.6 1
    ─────────
    $ 3.6 1

2. $4.3 8
    + 2.2 6

3. $3.5 4
    − 2.3 8

4. $6.7 2
    +   .8 1

5. $3.5 6
    + 4.3 5

6. $7.3 4
    − 4.4 2

7. $4.3 7
    + 1.4 8

8. $5.0 3
    +   .8 2

9. $6.5 2
    −   .4 8

10. $4.7 2
     − 2.8 1

11. $4.2 7
     + 4.9 1

12. $4.1 1
     − 2.0 7

13. $3.2 9
     + 2.6 4

14. $6.0 8
     − 2.9 3

15. $1.5 2
     + 3.7 6

16. $7.0 0
     − 5.6 0

Problem Solving • Reasoning

Using Data

Use the pictures to solve the problems.

pen
$2.75

key chain
$3.60

magnet
$1.50

17. Nan buys a pen and a key chain.
     How much does she spend? _____

18. If Nan had $6.50 to start with, how
     much change should she get? _____

> Draw or write to explain.

At Home Discuss with your child what bills and coins he or she would need to buy the items on this page.

Name_____

LESSON 12

Problem Solving: Guess and Check

Standards	
NS **2.0, 5.0, 5.2**	
AF **1.3**, MR **1.1, 2.2**	

You can use the Guess and Check strategy to solve a problem.

Joe spends exactly $5.40 for two tickets. Which tickets does he buy?

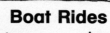

Boat Rides

One hour	$2.45
Two hours	$4.25
Child's ride	$1.15

Understand

What information would you use?

Joe spends $____._____ .

Joe buys _____ tickets.

Plan

Choose two different tickets. How can you check your guess?

add   subtract

Solve

Try the tickets for the one-hour and two-hour rides.

One-hour ride $2.45

Two-hour ride   + $4.25

Think: $6.70 is too much. Try again. $6.70

Two-hour ride $._____

Child's ride   ◯ $._____

Think: Do I have a sum of $5.40? $._____

Look Back

Did you find which two tickets Joe bought? How do you know?

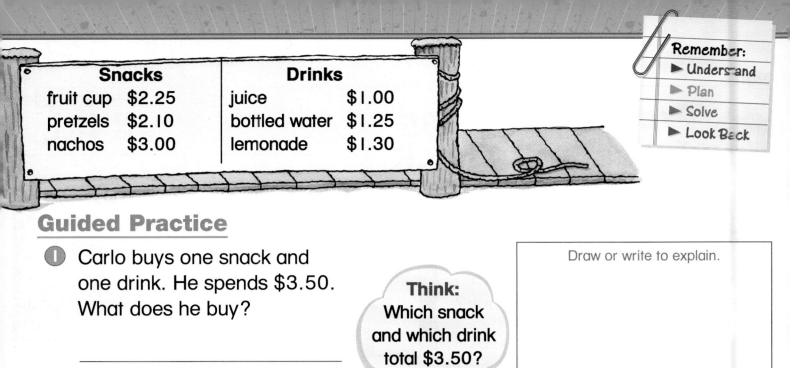

Snacks		Drinks	
fruit cup	$2.25	juice	$1.00
pretzels	$2.10	bottled water	$1.25
nachos	$3.00	lemonade	$1.30

Remember:
► Understand
► Plan
► Solve
► Look Back

Guided Practice

1 Carlo buys one snack and one drink. He spends $3.50. What does he buy?

Think: Which snack and which drink total $3.50?

_____

_____

Draw or write to explain.

2 Mrs. Jacob spends $3.90. She buys three of the same kind of drink. Which drink does she buy?

Think: Three of which drink totals $3.90?

_____

3 Martin had $4.50. He bought one snack. Now he has $1.50. Which snack did he buy?

Think: Will I add or subtract to solve the problem?

_____

4 Ella buys two of the same snack for her brothers. She spends $4.20. Which snack does she buy?

Think: Two of which snack totals $4.20?

_____

At Home Help your child figure out the prices of his or her two favorite foods, and then find how much it would cost to buy the two items.

Name_____

Choose a Strategy

Solve.

1 A ferry can take 20 cars across a river. If the ferry makes 4 trips, how many cars can it carry?

_____ cars

Draw or write to explain.

ferry

2 A subway ride costs $1.60. Jenny pays with a one-dollar bill and three quarters. What is Jenny's change?

_____ ¢

subway

3 It costs $2.25 to go one mile in a taxicab. If Chen spends $6.75, how many miles has he gone?

_____ miles

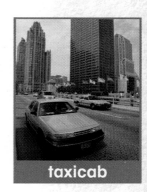

taxicab

4 An airplane leaves New York at 2:30. It lands 2 hours later. What time does it land?

_____ : _____

airplane

Name _____

Mixed Practice

Find each sum or difference.

1.	2.	3.	4.	5.
87 +12	36 +55	93 −64	38 − 5	96 −75

6.	7.	8.	9.
500 −300	375 −124	529 −346	830 −625

10.	11.	12.	13.
436 +217	128 +506	128 +325	257 +651

Multiply.  Memorize Your Facts

14.	15.	16.	17.	18.	19.
2 × 6	1 ×9	5 ×5	2 ×3	8 ×0	5 ×3

 Brain Teaser Missing Digits

Write the missing digits.

```
  3 □ 9          8 □ 5          □ 5 8
+ 1 8 □        − □ 4 7        + 4 □ 5
  □ 9 4          3 2 □          6 8 □
```

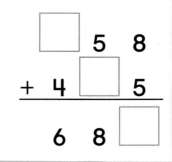

Internet Brain Teasers
Visit **www.eduplace.com/kids/mhm**
for more *Brain Teasers*.

Copyright © Houghton Mifflin Company. All rights reserved.

Name_____

Check Your Understanding of Lessons 8–12

Add or subtract.

1. 627 + 282

+ ⌐|⌐|⌐

2. 963 – 83

– ⌐|⌐|⌐

3. 253 + 609

+ ⌐|⌐|⌐

Subtract. Check by adding.

4. 8 2 3
  – 2 1 7
  _____   + _____

5. $6.08
  – 3.25
  _____   + _____

Find the nearest hundred. Add.

6. 4 7 0 ⟶ ☐
  + 2 2 0 ⟶ + ☐
  _____   ☐

```
   400 410 420 430 440 450 460 470 480 490 500

   200 210 220 230 240 250 260 270 280 290 300
```

7. Kyle spends $5.00 on popcorn. Which two bags does he buy?

Large	Medium	Small
$3.50	$2.50	$1.50

_____ and _____

Draw or write to explain.

Test Prep • Cumulative Review

Maintaining the Standards

Fill in the ○ for the correct answer. NH means Not Here.

1 Add.
$$471 + 258$$

213 229 729 NH
○   ○   ○   ○

2 Mark the number that comes between.

157		171

205 162 148 93
○   ○   ○   ○

3 Use your inch ruler to find how long the paper clip is. Mark how many inches long.

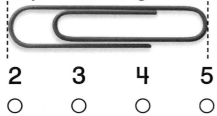

2   3   4   5
○   ○   ○   ○

4 Multiply.

$$10 \times 7 = \blacksquare$$

7   17   60   NH
○   ○   ○   ○

5 Subtract.
$$\$6.75 - 2.37$$

○ $3.10   ○ $8.02
○ $4.38   ○ NH

6 Mae saw 25 ants. Joe saw 30 ants. Mark the number sentence that shows how many ants they both saw.

○ $30 - 25 = 5$
○ $30 + 25 = 55$
○ $25 + 20 = 45$
○ $25 + 15 = 40$

7 Subtract.
$$378 - 149$$

Explain how you would use addition to check your subtraction.

_____

_____

Copyright © Houghton Mifflin Company. All rights reserved.

Safe Site

Internet Test Prep
Visit **www.eduplace.com/kids/mhm**
for more *Test Prep Practice*.

Chapter Review

Circle the correct word.

1. Did Max **regroup** ones or hundreds to subtract?

$$\begin{array}{r} {\small 2\ 15} \\ 3\,\cancel{5}\,4 \\ -\ 1\ 6\ 1 \\ \hline 1\ 9\ 3 \end{array}$$

ones

hundreds

2. Write the words for each red symbol.

$2.13

+ 1.78   _____

_____

dollar sign
decimal point

Add or subtract. Look for a pattern.

3.
$$\begin{array}{r} 5 \\ +2 \\ \hline \end{array} \quad \begin{array}{r} 50 \\ +20 \\ \hline \end{array} \quad \begin{array}{r} 500 \\ +200 \\ \hline \end{array}$$

4.
$$\begin{array}{r} 6 \\ -3 \\ \hline \end{array} \quad \begin{array}{r} 60 \\ -30 \\ \hline \end{array} \quad \begin{array}{r} 600 \\ -300 \\ \hline \end{array}$$

Add or subtract.

5.
$$\begin{array}{r} 578 \\ +113 \\ \hline \end{array}$$

6.
$$\begin{array}{r} 384 \\ +410 \\ \hline \end{array}$$

7.
$$\begin{array}{r} 792 \\ +\ \ 36 \\ \hline \end{array}$$

8.
$$\begin{array}{r} 228 \\ +257 \\ \hline \end{array}$$

9.
$$\begin{array}{r} 694 \\ -237 \\ \hline \end{array}$$

10.
$$\begin{array}{r} 605 \\ -274 \\ \hline \end{array}$$

11.
$$\begin{array}{r} 520 \\ -\ \ 16 \\ \hline \end{array}$$

12.
$$\begin{array}{r} 481 \\ -190 \\ \hline \end{array}$$

13.
$$\begin{array}{r} \$3.55 \\ +\ \ .26 \\ \hline \end{array}$$

14.
$$\begin{array}{r} 417 \\ +292 \\ \hline \end{array}$$

15.
$$\begin{array}{r} \$8.79 \\ -\ 5.28 \\ \hline \end{array}$$

16.
$$\begin{array}{r} 543 \\ -136 \\ \hline \end{array}$$

Rewrite the numbers. Add or subtract.

17. $254 + 694$

+ _____

18. $465 - 95$

− _____

19. $322 - 116$

− _____

Subtract. Check by adding.

20.
```
  9 1 7
− 7 9 2
```

+ _____

21.
```
  3 8 5
− 1 2 7
```
+ _____

Find the nearest hundred. Subtract.

22. $790 \longrightarrow$ ☐

700 710 720 730 740 750 760 770 780 790 800

$-310 \longrightarrow$ − ☐

300 310 320 330 340 350 360 370 380 390 400

☐

Use the table to solve each problem.

23. Jill buys two boats. She spends $3.55. Which two boats does she buy?

_____ and _____

Toy Boats	
Canoe	$2.70
Tugboat	$1.30
Sailboat	$2.25

24. Sam buys the canoe. He pays for it with $3.00. How much change will he get? Circle the number sentence you would use.

$3.00 + $2.70 = $5.70

$3.00 − $2.70 = $.30

Draw or write to explain.

Copyright © Houghton Mifflin Company. All rights reserved.

Name _____

Chapter Test

Add or subtract. Look for a pattern.

1.
```
   6       6 0      6 0 0
 + 2     + 2 0    + 2 0 0
```

2.
```
   7       7 0      7 0 0
 - 5     - 5 0    - 5 0 0
```

Add or subtract.

3.
```
  3 6 5
 + 2 1 9
```

4.
```
  5 4 3
 + 2 7 2
```

5.
```
  4 6 1
 + 3 1 9
```

6.
```
  8 7 2
 - 1 6 4
```

7.
```
  6 5 8
 - 3 7 5
```

8.
```
  4 1 5
 - 2 0 7
```

9.
```
  $7.5 5
 +   .8 4
```

10.
```
  $9.3 2
 -   4.7 1
```

11.
```
  $3.3 1
 +   1.2 5
```

Rewrite the numbers. Add or subtract.

12. 125 + 708

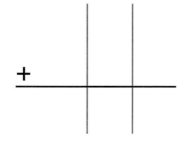

13. 548 − 273

14. 350 − 200

Subtract. Check by adding.

15.
```
   6 1 5
 - 2 3 2        +_____
```

16.
```
   2 9 3
 - 1 8 5        +_____
```

Find the nearest hundred.
Add or subtract.

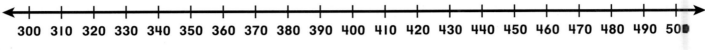

300 310 320 330 340 350 360 370 380 390 400 410 420 430 440 450 460 470 480 490 500

17.
```
  4 3 0  ———→  [  ]

 +3 1 0  ———→  +[  ]

             [  ]
```

18.
```
  4 9 0  ———→  [  ]

 -3 7 0  ———→  -[  ]

             [  ]
```

19. Marc buys two cars. He
spends $2.60. Which two
cars does he buy?

_____ and _____

Toy Cars	
red car	$1.35
blue car	$1.25
green car	$2.25

20. Mary buys the red car. She pays
for it with $2.00. How much
change will she get? Circle the
number sentence you would use.

$2.00 − $1.35 = $ .65

$2.00 + $1.35 = $3.35

Write About It

Lynn buys a toy boat for $1.40 and a toy
train for $2.70. She pays for them with $5.00.

How can she use addition and subtraction
to find how much change she will get?

_____

_____

Copyright © Houghton Mifflin Company. All rights reserved.

Add or Subtract to Win

Players 2–4

What You Need

- counters

- number cube labeled 1, 2, 3, 1, 2, 3

- pencil and paper for each player

How to Play

① Write 100 at the top of your paper. Put your counter on Start.

② Take turns tossing the number cube. Move that many spaces.

③ Follow the directions on that space. On each turn, add or subtract that number on your paper.

④ Continue until you reach the end. The player with the greatest final number wins.

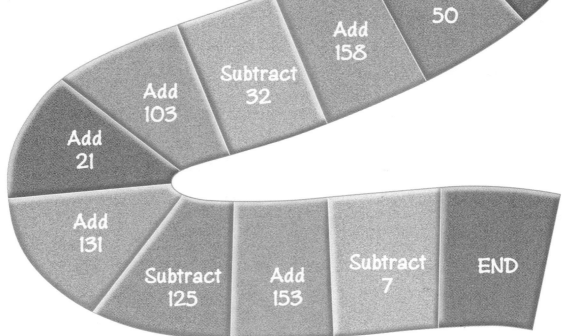

START with 100

Add 110

Add 206

Add 17

Subtract 50

Add 158

Subtract 32

Add 103

Add 21

Add 131

Subtract 125

Add 153

Subtract 7

END

Enrichment

Estimate to the Nearest Thousand

Find the nearest thousand on the number line.
Estimate the sum or difference.

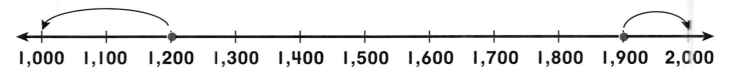

1,000 1,100 1,200 1,300 1,400 1,500 1,600 1,700 1,800 1,900 2,000

1. 1,2 0 0 nearest thousand → $\boxed{1,000}$

   +1,9 0 0 nearest thousand → + $\boxed{2,000}$

   $\boxed{3,000}$

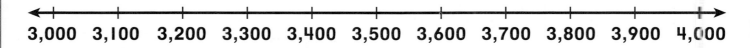

3,000 3,100 3,200 3,300 3,400 3,500 3,600 3,700 3,800 3,900 4,000

2. 3,2 0 0 → ☐

   +3,3 0 0 → + ☐

   ☐

3. 3,9 0 0 → ☐

   −3,1 0 0 → − ☐

   ☐

2,000 2,100 2,200 2,300 2,400 2,500 2,600 2,700 2,800 2,900 3,000

4. 2,6 0 0 → ☐

   +2,3 0 0 → + ☐

   ☐

5. 2,7 0 0 → ☐

   −2,2 0 0 → − ☐

   ☐

Copyright © Houghton Mifflin Company. All rights reserved.

Name _____

Picture Glossary

add

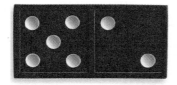

$$5 + 2 = 7$$

addend

$$5 + 6 = 11$$

addends

after

98, **99**

99 is after 98.

bar graph

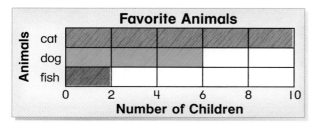

before

31, 32

31 is before 32.

between

81, **82**, 83

82 is between 81 and 83.

calendar

February						
S	M	T	W	T	F	S
1	2	3	4	5	6	7
8	9	10	11	12	13	14
15	16	17	18	19	20	21
22	23	24	25	26	27	28

cent sign

45¢

cent sign

centimeter (cm)

circle

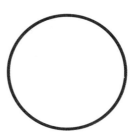

cone

congruent

same shape and size

cube

cup (c)

I cup

cylinder

data

Favorite Colors	
Color	Number of Children
red	IIII
blue	III

5 chose red.
3 chose blue.

decimal point

$1.00
↑
decimal point

difference

$$11 - 3 = 8$$

↑
difference

$$\begin{array}{r} 11 \\ -\ 3 \\ \hline 8 \end{array}$$

difference ⟶

digit

39
↑ ↑
digits

39 has two digits.

dime

 or

10¢ or 10 cents

Copyright © Houghton Mifflin Company. All rights reserved.

divide

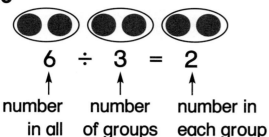

6 ÷ 3 = 2

↑   ↑   ↑

number   number   number in
in all   of groups   each group

division sentence

15 ÷ 5 = 3

15 divided by 5 equals 3.

dollar

 or

100¢ or $1.00

dollar sign

$2.00

↑

dollar sign

edge

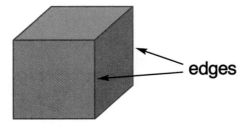

edges

An edge is where two faces meet.

equal

10¢   10¢

These amounts are equal.

equal groups

3 equal groups of 2.

estimate

$$
\begin{array}{r}
2\,8 \\
+\,2\,3 \\
\end{array}
\quad
\begin{array}{r}
\underline{\text{nearest ten}} \rightarrow \\
\underline{\text{nearest ten}} \rightarrow \\
\end{array}
\quad
\begin{array}{r}
3\,0 \\
+\,2\,0 \\
\hline
5\,0 \;\text{estimate} \\
\end{array}
$$

An estimate is an answer that
is close to an exact answer.

even number

8 is an even number.

A number where you make
pairs and have none left over.

face

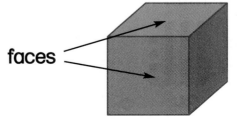

faces

fact family

Whole
16

Part	Part
9	7

$9 + 7 = 16$

$7 + 9 = 16$

$16 - 9 = 7$

$16 - 7 = 9$

half-dollar

or

50¢ or 50 cents

Fahrenheit (F)

50°F

half-hour

2:30

30 minutes = 1 half-hour.

foot (ft)

12 inches = 1 foot.

hour

2:00

60 minutes = 1 hour.

fraction

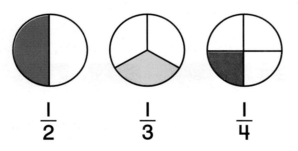

$\dfrac{1}{2}$ $\dfrac{1}{3}$ $\dfrac{1}{4}$

hundred

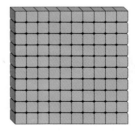

1 hundred
100

greater than

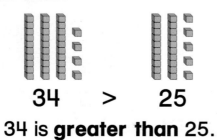

34   >   25

34 is **greater than** 25.

inch (in.)

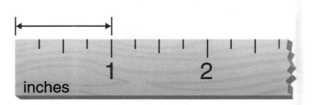

Copyright © Houghton Mifflin Company. All rights reserved.

kilogram (kg)

about 1 kilogram

less likely

The spinner is less likely to land on yellow.

less than

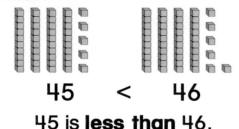

45   <   46

45 is **less than** 46.

line of symmetry

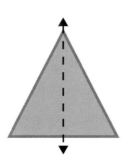

liter (L)

1 liter

meter (m)

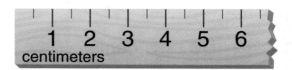

100 centimeters = 1 meter.

minute

60 seconds = 1 minute.

more likely

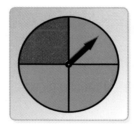

The spinner is more likely to land on blue.

multiplication sentence

2 × 5 = 10

2 times 5 equals 10.

multiply

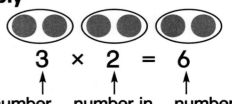

3   ×   2   =   6

number of groups   number in each group   number in all

nickel

5¢ or 5 cents

number line

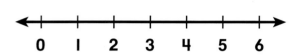

odd number

9 is an odd number.

A number where you make pairs and have one left over.

penny

 or

1¢ or 1 cent

perimeter

I in.

I in.   I in.

I in.

perimeter = 4 inches

pictograph

Each ▪ = 2 books.

pint (pt)

1 pint = 2 cups

pound (lb)

about 1 pound

product

$3 \times 2 = 6$

$$\begin{array}{r} 2 \\ \times 3 \\ \hline 6 \end{array}$$

product

pyramid

Copyright © Houghton Mifflin Company. All rights reserved.

quart (qt)

1 quart = 2 pints or 4 cups

quarter

or

25¢ or 25 cents

quarter-hour

1:15

15 minutes = 1 quarter-hour.

rectangle

rectangular prism

regroup

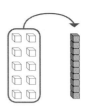

10 ones = 1 ten

related facts

$$9 + 4 = 13$$

$$13 - 4 = 9$$

remainder

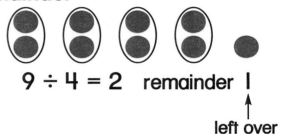

$9 \div 4 = 2$ remainder 1

↑
left over

round

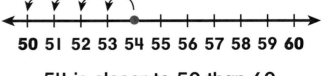

50 51 52 53 54 55 56 57 58 59 60

54 is closer to 50 than 60.
54 rounds to 50.

second

60 seconds = 1 minute.

side

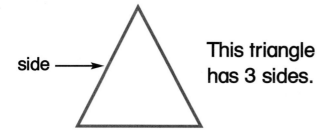

This triangle has 3 sides.

sphere

square

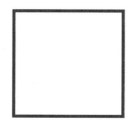

subtract

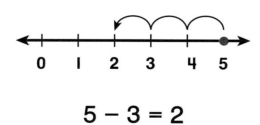

$$5 - 3 = 2$$

sum

$$4 + 3 = 7$$

$$\begin{array}{r} 4 \\ + 3 \\ \hline 7 \end{array}$$

sum ⟶ 7

tally marks

| stands for 1.

||||| stands for 5.

temperature

30°F

tens

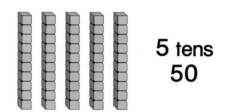

5 tens
50

triangle

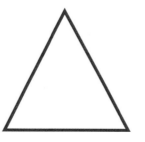

vertex, vertices

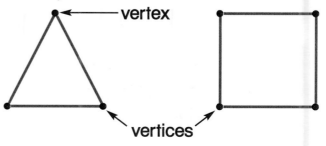

vertex

vertices

Copyright © Houghton Mifflin Company. All rights reserved.

Table of Measures

Length

| 12 inches = 1 foot | 100 centimeters = 1 meter |

| Inch | Foot | Centimeter | Meter |

Capacity

2 cups = 1 pint
4 cups = 1 quart
2 pints = 1 quart

| Cup | Pint | Quart | Liter |

Weight

Pound

Mass

Kilogram

Time

1 minute = 60 seconds	1 week = 7 days
1 hour = 60 minutes	1 year = 12 months
1 day = 24 hours	1 year = 365 days

1	2	3	4	5	6	7	8	9	10
11	12	13	14	15	16	17	18	19	20
21	22	23	24	25	26	27	28	29	30
31	32	33	34	35	36	37	38	39	40
41	42	43	44	45	46	47	48	49	50
51	52	53	54	55	56	57	58	59	60
61	62	63	64	65	66	67	68	69	70
71	72	73	74	75	76	77	78	79	80
81	82	83	84	85	86	87	88	89	90
91	92	93	94	95	96	97	98	99	100

Hundred Chart

Tens	Ones

Hundreds	Tens	Ones

Credits

Excerpts from MATHEMATICS CONTENT STANDARDS FOR CALIFORNIA PUBLIC SCHOOLS, Copyright © December 1997 are reprinted by permission of the California Department of Education.

PHOTOGRAPHY

All photographs by Houghton Mifflin Company (HMCo.) unless otherwise noted.

Cover: Mike Tesi for HMCo.

Coin photography by Mike Tesi for HMCo. Snap cube photgraphy by Carl Baker for HMco. vii: *b.* PhotoDisc, Inc. xxi: Parker/Boon Productions for HMCo. 9–10: Carl Baker for HMCo. 27–28: Carl Baker for HMCo. 33: Richard Hutchings/PhotoEdit. 35: *t.* Bob Daemmrich Photography; *m.t.* Tony Freeman/PhotoEdit; *m.b.* Lawrence Migdale/Pix; *b.* David Young-Wolff/PhotoEdit. 45: David Young/Picture Quest Network International/PNI. 47: *t.* Doug Armand/Tony Stone Images; *m.t.* Dan McCoy/Picture Quest Network International/PNI; *m.b.* Spencer Grant/PhotoEdit; *b.* Ron Dorsey/Stock Boston. 48: *l.* Seide Preis/PhotoDisc, Inc.; *m.* Jane Burton/Bruce Coleman Inc.; *r.* Jane Burton/Bruce Coleman Inc. 65: Richard Hutchings for HMCo. 73: Tony Scarpetta for HMCo. 75: *l.* John Warden/Tony Stone Images; *m.* Lawrence Migdale/Stock Boston; *r.* Tim Davis/Tony Stone Images. 77: *t.* Gunter Marx/Corbis; *m.t.* Kennan Ward/Corbis; *m.b.* Index Stock Imagery; *b.* Barb Gerlach/Dembinsky Photo Associates. 81: *t.* Carl Baker for HMCo. 85: Richard Hutchings for HMCo. 91: PhotoDisc, Inc. 93: *t.* Andrew Drake/Tony Stone Images; *m.t.* Barbara Stitzer/PhotoEdit; *m.b.* Brian Stablyk/Tony Stone Images; *b.* Keren Su/Tony Stone Images. 94: Cheryl Clegg for HMCo. 95: Carl Baker for HMCo. 101: Joel Benjamin for HMCo. 112: Mike Tesi for HMCo. 117: Richard Hutchings for HMCo. 119: Michael Gaffney for HMCo. 129: Andy Sacks/Tony Stone Images. 131: *t.* John P. Kelly/Getty Images; *m.t.* Ray Hendley/Index Stock Imagery; *m.b.* © Junebug Clark/Photo Researchers, Inc.; *b.* Mark Gibson/Index Stock Imagery. 171: *t.l.* Courtesy, United States Mint © 1999; *t.r.* Courtesy, United States Mint © 1999. 172: *b.l.* Courtesy, United States Mint © 1999. 174: *m.l.* Courtesy, United States Mint © 1999. 175: Bob Daemmrich Photography. 177: Michael Gaffney for HMCo. 198: *l.* © Aaron Haupt/Photo Researchers, Inc.; *r.* John Fennell/Bruce Coleman Inc. 212: Mike Tesi for HMCo. 219: *m.b.* Telegraph Colour Library/FPG International; *b.* Layne Kennedy/Corbis. 223: *b.m.* Richard Hutchings for HMCo. 229: Cheryl Clegg for HMCo. 233: *t.* Stan Osolinski/Dembinsky Photo Associates; *m.t.* © 1994 Dinamation International; *m.b.* Index Stock Imagery; *b.* Michael Grecco/Stock Boston. 235: *l.* John Fennell/Bruce Coleman Inc. 241: *b.* Joel Benjamin for HMCo. 263: Lawrence Migdale/Pix. 265: *t.* © Suzanne L. & Joseph T. Collins/Photo Researchers, Inc.; *m.t.* Getty Images; *m.b.* © Leonard Lee Rue III/Photo Researchers, Inc.; *b.* © Renee Lynn/Photo Researchers, Inc. 287: Kathi Lamm/Tony Stone Images. 289: *t.* Quarto, Inc./Artville Stock Images; *m.t.* CMCD/PhotoDisc, Inc.; *m.b.* Quarto, Inc./Artville Stock Images; *b.* Robert Dowling/Corbis. 309: Tony Scarpetta for HMCo. 312: *t.m.r.* Mike Tesi for HMCo.; *t.r.* PhotoDisc, Inc.; *m.t.l.* PhotoDisc, Inc.; *m.l.* PhotoDisc, Inc.; *m.m.r.* PhotoDisc, Inc.; *m.b.l.* PhotoDisc, Inc.; *m.b.r.* PhotoDisc, Inc.; *b.l.* PhotoDisc, Inc.; *b.m.l.* PhotoDisc, Inc.; *b.r.* PhotoDisc, Inc. 317: *m.* Tony Scarpetta for HMCo.; *r.* Tony Scarpetta for HMCo. 321: *t.* Michael P. Gadomski/Dembinsky Photo Associates; *m.t.* Michael Gaffney for HMCo.; *m.b.* Michael Gaffney for HMCo.; *b.* Michael Gaffney for HMCo. 322: Joel Benjamin for HMCo. 327: Tony Scarpetta HMCo. 337: Tony Scarpetta for HMCo. 339: *r.* Lawrence Migdale/Pix. 341: Michael Gaffney for HMCo. 347: *l.* PhotoDisc, Inc.; *m.l.* PhotoDisc, Inc.; *r.* PhotoDisc, Inc. 358: Larime Photographic/Dembinsky Photo Associates. 377: *b.l.* Joel Benjamin for HMCo. 379: Bob Daemmrich/Stock Boston/Picture Quest Network International/PNI. 381: *t.* Frank Krahmer/Bruce Coleman Inc.; *m.t.* Robert Ginn/PhotoEdit; *m.b.* Michael H. Black/Bruce Coleman Inc.; *b.* John Shaw/Bruce Coleman Inc. 385: Michael Gaffney for HMCo. 393: Jon Riley/Tony Stone Images. 412: *b.r.* Joel Benjamin for HMCo. 413: *m.t.* Mike Tesi for HMCo.; 416: *t.* Mike Tesi for HMCo.; *m.t.* Mike Tesi for HMCo.; *m.* Mike Tesi for HMCo.; *m.b.* Mike Tesi for HMCo. 417: *m.t.* Mike Tesi for HMCo.; *t.r.* Joel Benjamin for HMCo. ; *m.b.* Mike Tesi for HMCo.; *b.* Mike Tesi for HMCo. 419: *t.r* Joel Benjamin for HMCo.; *m.t.* John Brigham for HMCo. ; *m.b.* John Brigham for HMCo. . 426: Joel Benjamin for HMCo. 427: *m.l* Mike Tesi for HMCo. 429: *t.* to *b., l.* to *r.* Tony Scarpetta for HMCo.; HMCo.; Tony Scarpetta for HMCo.; HMCo.; Mike Tesi for HMCo.; Mike Tesi for HMCo.; HMCo.; PhotoDisc, Inc.; John Brigham for HMCo.; Mike Tesi for HMCo.; HMCo.; HMCo.; HMCo. 431: *t.l.* Tony Scarpetta for HMCo.; *t.r.* Tony Scarpetta for HMCo.; *l.m.* PhotoDisc, Inc.; *b.m.l.* PhotoDisc, Inc. 435: *t.l.* Tony Scarpetta for HMCo.; *t.m.* Tony Scarpetta for HMCo.; *t.r.* Tony Scarpetta for HMCo.; *m.r.b.* Mike Tesi for HMCo. 437: *t.* Mike Tesi for HMCo. 438: *t.r.* John Fennell/Bruce Coleman Inc. 439: *t.l.* © 1999 Mike Barlow/Dembinsky Photo Associates; *t.r.* © Richard Hutchings/Photo Researchers, Inc.; *b.l.* Bob Thomas/Tony Stone Images; *b.r.* © Fred Hirschmann. 443: *t.* Joel Benjamin for HMCo. 445: *t.* E.R. Degginger/Color-Pic, Inc.; *m.t.* Skip Moody/Dembinsky Photo Associates; *m.b.* Bob & Clara Calhoun/Bruce Coleman Inc.; *b.* K. Sandved/Bruce Coleman Inc. 446: John Brigham for HMCo. 448: Mike Tesi for HMCo. 451: *t.* PhotoDisc, Inc.; *b.l.* Mike Tesi for HMCo. 453: *t.* Mike Tesi for HMCo. 454: *t.* Mike Tesi for HMCo.; *m.t.* Mike Tesi for HMCo. 463: Cheryl Clegg for HMCo. 467: Richard Hutchings for HMCo. 473: M. Brodskaya/Bruce Coleman Inc. 475: Ulrike Welsch Photography. 477: *t.* Terry E. Eiler/Stock Boston/Picture Quest Network International/PNI; *m.t.* Index Stock Imagery; *m.b.* Bob Daemmrich Photography; *b.* Peter VanDerMark/Stock Boston. 479: *l.* David Young-Wolff/PhotoEdit/PictureQuest/Picture Quest Network International/PNI; *r.* David Young Wolff/PhotoEdit. 484: *t.l.* David Hiser/Tony Stone Images; *t.r.* Lonnie Duka/Tony Stone Images; *m.l.* Lawrence Migdale/Stock Boston/Picture Quest Network International/PNI; *m.r.* Rob Gage/FPG International/Picture Quest Network International/PNI; *b.l.* Joan Iaconetti/Bruce Coleman Inc.; *b.r.* Bob Daemmrich Photography. 487: *t.* Index Stock Imagery; *m.t.* Frank Fournier/Contact Press Images/Picture Quest Network International/PNI; *m.b.* Bill Bachmann/Stock Boston/Picture Quest Network International/PNI; *b.* Dick Luria/FPG International. 498: J. Messerschmidt/Bruce Coleman Inc. 499: Peter Menzel/Stock Boston. 500: Friends of Dinosaur Ridge. 501: Charlie Borland/Index Stock Imagery. 502: Adam Jones/Dembinsky Photo Associates. 503: C. McIntyre/PhotoLink/PhotoDisc, Inc. 513: Mike Tesi for HMCo. 514: Cheryl Clegg for HMCo. 517: Parker/Boon Productions for HMCo. 519: *t.* Janis Burger/Bruce Coleman Inc.; *m.t.* Daniel J. Cox/Tony Stone Images; *m.b.* Art Wolfe/Tony Stone Images; *b.* E&P Bauer/Bruce Coleman Inc. 529: Richard Hutchings for HMCo. 533: *r.* Bob Daemmrich Photography. 536: Michael Gaffney for HMCo. 538: *t.* Mike Tesi for HMCo. 543: Parker/Boon Productions for HMCo. 553: Joel Benjamin for HMCo. 561: Tony Scarpetta HMCo. 567: H. Armstrong Roberts, Inc. 569: *t.* Richard T. Nowitz/Corbis; *m.t.* Adam Woolfitt/Corbis; *m.b.* Roger Miller/H. Armstrong Roberts, Inc.; *b.* Kaiser/Index Stock Imagery. 581: Andre Jenny/Picture Quest Network International/PNI. 583: *t.* Deborah Davis/PhotoEdit; *m.t.* Cosmo Condina/Tony Stone Images; *m.b.* Hisham F. Ibrahim/PhotoDisc, Inc.; *b.* Erik Simonsen/Getty Images. 593: Carl Baker for HMCo. 595: Courtesy, United States Mint © 1999.

ILLUSTRATIONS

viii–x: Chuck Primeau. 1–8, 12–14, 16–17, 22, 27, 30, 32, 34, 40, 43: Deborah Melmon. 57–64, 73–74, 76, 83–84, 86, 89–90: Sheila Bailey. 103–112, 114, 116, 123–128, 137: Susan Swan. 141–151, 153–154, 156–157, 160, 165–166, 168–170, 173: Shari Warren. 185: Nathan Young Jarvis. 187–198, 201, 209–211, 213–214, 220, 224–226, 237: Gary Johnson. 243–250, 252–254, 259–261, 264, 269, 271, 273: Jackie Urbanovic. 274: Karen Lee Schmidt. 280, 284: Jackie Urbanovic. 287: Karen Lee Schmidt. 290, 293, 296: Jackie Urbanovic. 299–306: Megan Halsey. 311–312: Patrick Gnan. 318: Deborah Drummond. 320: Megan Halsey. 323–324: Patrick Gnan. 331: Megan Halsey. 334, 336: Deborah Drummond. 338: Megan Halsey. 344–346: Deborah Drummond. 347: Patrick Gnan. 348:

Deborah Drummond. 351–362: Nathan Young Jarvis. 364: Bryan Ballinger. 365–367, 369–372, 376, 378–380, 386, 388, 393: Nathan Young Jarvis. 399: *t.* Gary Johnson; *b.* Nathan Young Jarvis. 401, 403: Nathan Young Jarvis. 405–412, 414–415. Lyn Martin. 417: Ken Batelman. 418: Lyn Martin. 419: Ken Batelman. 420–422, 430, 432: Lyn Martin. 433–434: Bryan Ballinger. 436: Lyn Martin. 437: *t.* Lyn Martin; *b.* Bryan Ballinger. 438: Lyn Martin. 439: Russell Benfanti. 440: *t.* Russell Benfanti; *b.* Lyn Martin.441: *t.l.* Ken Batelman; *t.m.* Bryan Ballinger; *t.m.* Lyn Martin; *t.r.* Russell Benfanti; *b.* Lyn Martin. 442: *t.* Lyn Martin; *b.l.* Ken Batelman; *b.m.* Lyn Martin; *b.m.* Russell Benfanti; *b.r.* Bryan Ballinger. 446: Bryan Ballinger. 447: *t.* Russell Benfanti; *b.l.* Russell Benfanti; b.*m.* Ken Batelman; *b.r.* Lyn Martin. 448: Ken Batelman. 449: Lyn Martin. 450: *t.* Lyn Martin; *m.* Bryan ballinger; *b.* Russell Benfanti. 451: *t.* Lyn Martin; *b.* Bryan Ballinger. 452: *l.* Russell Benfanti; *r.* Lyn Martin. 453: *t.* Ken Batelman; *b.* Lyn Martin. 454: *t.* Lyn Martin; *b.* Ken Batelman. 455–465, 471, 474, 476, 478, 481–482, 485–487, 495: Greg Scheetz. 497–505, 507, 511–512, 516, 519: Sharon Hawkins Vargo. 526: *t.* Sharon Hawkins Vargo; *b.* Gary Antonetti. 529–533: Sharon Hawkins Vargo. 545–553, 557, 562, 564–565, 570, 573–574, 578, 581–582, 585: Tuko Fujisaki. 591: Nathan Young Jarvis. 593: Ken Batelman. 594: *t.* Patrick Gnan; *m.* Patrick Gnan; *b.m.* Bryan Ballinger; *b.* Patrick Gnan. 595: Nathan Young Jarvis. 596: *t.* Russell Benfanti; *m.* Ken Batelman; *b.* Ken Batelman. 597: *t.* Ken Batelman; *b.* Bryan Ballinger. 598: *t.* Bryan Ballinger; *b.* Patrick Gnan. 599: *t.* Bryan Ballinger *b.* Patrick Gnan. 600: *l.* Patrick Gnan; *r.* Ken Batelman.

Copyright © Houghton Mifflin Company. All rights reserved.